EASTERN EUROPE

IN THE AFTERMATH OF SOLIDARITY

ADAM BROMKE

EAST EUROPEAN MONOGRAPHS, BOULDER
DISTRIBUTED BY COLUMBIA UNIVERSITY PRESS
NEW YORK

1985

Burgess

DJK

50

KWA8O6TIW

1985

c.1

Printed in the United States of America

To my students in Political Science 3M6, 3FF6 and History 3FF3
who have helped me to clarify my thoughts about
Eastern Europe's past and future

CONTENTS

INTRODUCTION

The upheaval in Poland in 1980-81 was the latest and—as the Communists themselves admit—the most profound in a series of crises which have taken place in Eastern Europe in the post-war period. Many books (some good and some not so admirable) have already been written about the rise and fall of "Solidarity". It is time now to look at the Polish crisis from a perspective of time, and place it within a broader context of developments in the region as a whole as well as that of East-West relations.

This modest volume attempts to do precisely this. A large portion of it is devoted to Poland (which happens also to be the country which I know the best), but it deals with Eastern Europe as a whole. Its unifying theme is the historical relationship in the region between geopolitics and ideology. Against this background the post war political, economic and social developments are traced, with special attention being given to the role of religion. The changes in relationship between the USSR, which remains the dominant power in the area, and the individual Eastern European countries are described. Finally, the impact of the Sino-Soviet split and the rise of Eurocommunism in Western Europe are evaluated; and the Western, and particularly the American, policies towards Eastern Europe are analyzed.

The three appendices refer exclusively to the Polish experiences, but they clearly have broader ramifications. The first is the official report issued in the fall of 1983 by the Polish Communist party presenting its own version of the sources of recurrent crises in that country. The second is the analysis of the situation in Poland written in the spring of 1984 by a renowned sociologist, Professor Jan Szczepanski. And the third is the programmatic essay written by a young historian, Aleksander Hall, and issued clandestinely in the fall of 1982, evaluating Poland's future prospects.

The massive workers' upheaval in Poland, of course, is important not only as a historical event, but because at one time or another it may erupt anew in that country, or for that matter, somewhere else in Eastern Europe. In the present global context, the Western influence over the developments in the region is restricted, but it is certainly within the West's power to assist the various Eastern European countries in their legitimate aspirations to expand their freedom. This, however, must be based on a realistic assessment of the situation throughout the area and should lead to the adoption by the West of imaginative and dynamic policies there. Some suggestions along these lines are presented in the last chapter.

The author would like to thank Professor Szczepanski for permission to include his essay in this volume. He is also much obliged to Mr. Lawrence Miller for his valuable editorial assistance, both in preparing his own text and in the translation of the appendices from Polish into English.

A. B.
Dundas, Ontario
August 1984

I.

GEOPOLITICS VS. IDEOLOGY

Eastern Europe is a small part of the world. In area it is not much bigger than Quebec. Even if Finland and Greece are included, its inhabitants number only some 150 million which is approximately the same as Indonesia—representing about 3 per cent of the world population. And the region is not endowed with any natural resources which cannot be obtained elsewhere.

Yet, Eastern Europe has often played a significant part in world affairs. It occupies a crucial geographic position. Its central part ties Atlantic Europe to Russia, and then, across the vast Siberian plain, to the shores of the Pacific. And its southern portion, through Turkey and the Eastern Mediterranean, links Western Europe to the Middle East. As such the region has traditionally bridged different races and empires.

The geographical importance of Eastern Europe has been reflected in its stormy history. In the 4th century B.C. Alexander the Great of Macedonia conquered the Middle East all the way to India. And it was through this region that during the great migrations in the First Millenium the various waves of Asian conquerors came to destroy the Roman Empire and to give rise to the modern European nations. The Bohemians and the Magyars at one time built great kingdoms of their own. In the 16th century Poland, united with Lithuania and Ukraine, was a great European power; in 1683 in the battle of Vienna the Poles dealt a crushing blow to the Turks, stopping their further advance into Europe.

In more recent history both world wars started in Eastern Europe. And with the spread of Communism there at the end of World War II the area has become one of contention in East-West relations. It was over political developments in Eastern Europe, more than anything else, that the Cold War started; and periodic crises there have poisoned the atmosphere between the Soviet Union and the United States.

Due to its transitional location, moreover, Eastern Europe fits not only between the East and the West, but also between the North and the South. In terms of modernization it stands somewhere between the developed and the developing nations. The industrial regions

[1]

of Saxony, Bohemia or Silesia are not much different from the Ruhr, the Midlands and Pennsylvania; yet, in the countryside in some parts of Romania, the Turkish districts in Bulgaria, or Kosovo in Yugoslavia, primitive farming still is dominant. As such Eastern Europe is an indispensable laboratory for studying social change in the world.

And the region has also given birth to rich and diverse cultures. It is from there that Plato and Immanuel Kant, Martin Luther and Karol Wojtyla, Euclides and Copernicus, Karel Capek and Ferenc Molnar, as well as Frederick Chopin and Antonin Dvorak, have come. The Charles University in Prague and the Jagiellonian University in Cracow, founded in 1348 and 1370 respectively, are among the oldest and most prominent centres of learning in Europe.

For almost a century now Eastern Europe has been an object of systematic study in the West. Especially with the spread of modern nationalism in the area in the late stages of the 19th century, the French, German and British scholars, linguists as well as historians, developed interests in the area. These endeavours were accelerated by the emergence of many new independent states in the inter-war period with their perilous impact upon European politics, which ultimately erupted into another world conflict. In the post-war years, when Eastern Europe became the centre of East-West confrontation, western interest further intensified. Moreover, since indigenous scholarship has had to conform to the strictures of the dominant Communist ideology, many of the most influential studies of the region—particularly by historians and social scientists—have appeared in Western Europe and North America.[1]

In a celebrated study of Eastern Europe in the immediate post-war period, a British historian, Hugh Seton-Watson, presented a three-stage model of the Communist seizure of power in Eastern Europe: successively, a genuine coalition government, a bogus coalition dominated by the Communists, and Communist one-party rule.[2] The author admitted that his model was an oversimplification for it did not neatly fit all the countries, but nevertheless it helped the students of the region's politics to think about the events there in a systematic fashion. His paradigm has provided valuable insights into the overall Communist strategy and, accordingly, has served as a foundation for many later studies of political developments in the area.[3]

In a paper written almost thirty years later George Schöpflin expanded upon Seton-Watson's model.[4] He argued that World War II, which destroyed the pre-war ruling elites, paved the way for the Communists' takeovers in various Eastern European countries and, therefore, should be regarded as an additional preliminary phase.

There is no doubt that Adolf Hitler was as much an architect of the post-war political order in Eastern Europe as was Joseph Stalin; and as were, although passively, the British and American leaders, who resigned themselves to Soviet domination of the region.[*] World War II was a profoundly traumatic experience for Eastern Europe—much more so than for the western part of the continent—and was bound to lead to a radical break with the past.

Yet, one wonders whether Eastern Europe after the war was really such a *tabula rasa* as Schöpflin would have us believe. The subsequent developments in the area suggest that, in fact, the old traditions have survived to a remarkable degree. During the revolution in Hungary in 1956 there was a conscious effort to revert to the genuine coalition stage of 1945-47, and some politicians from that period even staged a temporary comeback. In Czechoslovakia in 1968 Masaryk's democratic traditions from prior to 1948 were explicitly revived. And in Yugoslavia in the 1970s the historical animosity between the Croats and the Serbs reappeared.

Even in Poland, which—as Schöpflin rightly observes—suffered the most during the war,[†] the old political culture was not altogether extinguished. If nothing else was left, there was still the Catholic church as custodian of the historical values. Its influence in the post-war period, culminating in the election of the Polish Pope in 1978, can hardly be exaggerated. But the continuity of the old intelligentsia, with its roots in ancient *szlachta*, was also largely preserved. In 1970 Jan Szczepanski observed that the traditional national values: "individualism, sense of honor, pride in national military glory, a cult of national heroes and patriotism in the sense of dedication to national

---

[*] "Poland's fate was essentially decided in a bilateral conversation between Churchill, Eden and Stalin [in Teheran on November 28, 1943] The British plan—to move Poland westward, compensating for Soviet gains by ceding German lands to Poland—was illustrated by Churchill with the aid of three matchsticks. He observed that the idea 'pleased Stalin'. Roosevelt later assured Stalin that he too supported the Soviet annexation of the eastern half of Poland, although, given the strength of the Polish-American voting bloc, he preferred not to participate in any decision on Polish boundaries until after the 1944 presidential election." Joseph L. Nogee and Robert H. Donaldson, *Soviet Foreign Policy Since World War II* (Pergamon: New York, 1981. p. 48)

[†] In terms of lives lost the two Eastern European countries suffered particularly heavily during the war. There were 220 Poles and 108 Yugoslavs killed out of every 1,000 of these countries' populations respectively (the intensity of killings, however, was roughly equal for the German occupation in Poland lasted 6 years and in Yugoslavia only 3 years). Corresponding figures were 15 for France, 8 for the United Kingdom and 1.4 for the United States. *Straty wojenne Polski w latach 1939-1945* (Wydawnictwo Zachodnie, Warsaw, 1960, p. 41).

interests", were still dominant among the Poles. "Thus the self-image of the Polish society remains almost the same as it was in interwar society."[5] And during the "Solidarity" period, political debates among the younger generation were often reminiscent of the old divisions among the socialists, the populists, the Pilsudskiites and the national democrats.[6]

Schöpflin himself admits that World War II alone does not represent a sufficient break with the past to explain the rise of Communism. He by no means deprecates the critical nature of the Soviet involvement—as in Romania in 1945 or in Hungary in 1947—in establishing the Communist rule in specific countries. Even more significantly, he also partially attributes the defeats of the old political elites to their inherent weakness, stemming from the lack of democratic traditions, as well as the sharp class and ethnic divisions, in the different Eastern European societies. This is undoubtedly true. But, if so, are we not faced here with still another preliminary phase, prior to World War II? And, furthermore, is it not legitimate to ask what were the reasons, rooted even deeper in history, for the existence of this situation itself in the interwar years? Are we not back to the classical question about what is new and what is old at each historical stage?

*   *   *

There are basically two different approaches to the study of the post-war developments in Eastern Europe. The first, which is popular among scholars prone to geopolitical thinking, tends to view the region as a "transitional" or "shatter" zone of the European continent which has often been subject to foreign domination. Due to the relative weakness of the Eastern European nations, as compared to the outside powers, the politics of the area have been governed by the principle of *Primat der Aussenpolitik*—paramountcy of foreign over domestic political developments. In modern history most of them only rarely have been allowed to have their independent states.

In the nineteenth century the position of the Eastern Europeans resembled that of colonial peoples in Asia and Africa, except that the former were dominated by the land, and the latter by the maritime, powers. At the time of the Congress of Vienna (except for the Montenegrins who held against the Turks in their mountain redoubts), not a single Eastern European nation was independent. The entire region was divided among the Ottoman, Austrian and Russian Empires and the Kingdom of Prussia. With the decline of the Ottoman Empire the South-Eastern Europeans gradually freed themselves from the Turkish rule, and, after World War I, with the collapse of the Habsburg Empire, the defeat of Germany and the revolution in Russia, the Central and North-Eastern Europeans attained independence. In 1918 a whole belt of new states emerged stretching from Yugoslavia to Finland.

The independence of the Eastern European states, however, did not last long. During World War II they were all occupied by the Germans, and in 1944-45, in turn, most of them were conquered by the victorious Soviet armies. The USSR used this opportunity to consolidate its western boundaries, incorporating the Baltic states and seizing considerable territories from Finland, Germany, Poland, Czechoslovakia (to which Hungary also made claims), and Romania. With the establishment of the Soviet occupational zone in East Germany, moreover, the USSR's military presence in Eastern Europe was perpetuated. The whole area was transformed into a Soviet zone of influence and Communist governments were introduced everywhere. The only two countries which escaped this fate were Greece in the south, which was protected initially by Britain and then by the United States and ultimately joined NATO, and Finland in the north* which, while preserving freedom in domestic affairs, has adopted friendly neutrality towards the Soviet Union.

The adherents of the geopolitical approach, then, see Communism as basically a new phase of outside intervention in Eastern Europe. To them the countries in the area are independent only in name, while being Soviet satellites in fact. Marxism-Leninism merely serves as an ideological façade—as were Orthodoxy or Panslavism in the past—for the traditional Russian imperialism.[7] The rise and perpetuation of the Communist regimes in Eastern Europe is attributed primarily to the preponderance of Soviet power in the region.

This approach also does much to explain the relative backwardness of Eastern European societies as compared with those of Western Europe. The foreign Empires have shown little concern about economic progress in their peripheries (Bohemia, locked in the midst of the German lands, being an exception). And the lack of native political institutions has not facilitated the growth of democracy, although the nations under the German rule, in contrast to those in the despotic Tsarist or Ottoman Empires, at least profited from the concept of the *Rechtsstaat*.

---

* Adam Ulam makes the interesting observation that Finland's salvaging of its internal independence was helped by American "unwitting containment". The wave of anti-Soviet indignation which swept the United States following the Soviet attack upon "little Finland" in 1939 made Stalin proceed with caution with that country after World War II. *Dangerous Relations* (Oxford, 1983, pp. 18-19).

Some of the Eastern Europeans' historical experiences which still shape their reality today go back even beyond the nineteenth partitions (should they perhaps be regarded as a sixth, preliminary stage?). For instance, the ancient cleavage between the Catholic north and the Orthodox south—which somewhat resembles the division in Western Europe between the northern more advanced Protestant lands, and the southern less developed Catholic countries—continues to accentuate differences among different nationalities in the area, and even occasionally cuts within them (as in Yugoslavia between Croatia and Serbia). Other divisions—especially ethnic and linguistic—reach into the period of great migrations in the first millenium, and even into the Roman days. In terms of its historical traditions Eastern Europe is at least as heterogeneous as the Western part of the continent.

Not only a historical, but also a geographical definition of Eastern Europe is elusive. Prague is located west of Vienna, and Poznan is at approximately the same lattitude as Stockholm. The GDR is a member of the Warsaw Pact, but it is also a part of the German nation which, of course, has always been considered Western European; while eastern Galicia and Carpathian Ruthenia, which until 1914 belonged to the Habsburg Empire, are now a part of the USSR. So are the Baltic states, despite their close past ties with Poland, Germany and Scandinavia. "Eastern Europe", thus, as the term is being used currently, is primarily a political concept. It denotes those states which are Communist-ruled—even Finland and Greece, because they have democratic governments, are excluded.

The other approach to the study of Eastern Europe, which is more popular among the scholars who tend to look at history in ideological context, accepts the emergence of Communism as a starting point. It views the events in the area basically as an extension of those in the USSR—in the sense that the Communist revolutions in Eastern Europe were a continuation of, and were also facilitated by, the Bolshevik revolution in Russia. In its search for historical roots this approach focuses upon the influence of Marxism, and subsequently of Leninism, as leading to the rise of Communist movements in the various Eastern European countries in the inter-war period.[8]

The ideological or Communism model is a legitimate type of analysis, for it does provide a coherent, albeit one-sided, framework for the study of events in Eastern Europe. It does offer, moreover, a tool for evaluating political changes in the region. The deviations from the Soviet system, fitting more the local needs along the lines of polycentrism, are duly noted and accounted for.[*] In a way it is similar to the study of political evolution of the various countries in the British Commonwealth which accepts as a point of departure the Westminster model that, at one time or another, was introduced into all of them, but was subsequently modified, or even altogether abandoned, in accordance with the local conditions.

Yet, the "Communism-polycentrism" model—like its British Commonwealth counterpart—is profoundly ahistorical, for it tends to regard the countries under study as *tabula rasa* in respect of their previous experiences. This could indeed be considered true in the case of those Brititsh Dominions which were populated by British settlers and whose political traditions were derived from the home country—although even in the cases of Canada and South Africa the presence of the French and the Dutch immigrants, respectively, has made an important difference. But it is certainly not true with regard to most of the Asian and African countries in the Commonwealth, where socio-economic backwardness and a lack of democratic traditions have re-asserted themselves with a vengeance, leading to the collapse of the Westminster model and its replacement by one-party or army dictatorships. The mistake of the British law-givers in the 1940s and the 1950s was that they adhered to the optimistic belief, widely shared at that time by western historians and political scientists, that democracy would be appropriate for all societies regardless of their stage of development.[9]

The "Communism-polycentrism" model likewise does not provide an entirely satisfactory intellectual framework for the study of political evolution in Eastern Europe. In a way its adherents admit this. For the very concept of polycentrism implies recognition, even though through the back door, of continuing historical forces, which, after having been temporarily suppressed, re-surface. In Eastern Europe, however, the impact of old political forces has generally been in the opposite direction to that in the British Commonwealth. For if the Eastern European nations, in terms of their socio-economic development and democratic traditions, have historically lagged behind the West, they have been generally ahead of Russia. The optimism of the Communist-polycentrism model, then, proves to be more warranted in studying Eastern Europe than that of the Westminster model is in studying the British Commonwealth. Yet, conversely, the democratic

---

[*] For a brilliant application of this approach see: Zbigniew K. Brzezinski, *The Soviet Bloc, Unity and Conflict* (Cambridge: Harvard 1960). Brzezinski, however, rather than using the term "polycentrism", labeled the adjustment of Soviet Communism to the local needs in various Eastern European countries as "domesticism".

political system in Britain was one of the important reasons which prompted the peaceful relinquishing of its colonial empire; while in the case of the autocratic Soviet Union the urge to perpetuate its dominance over Eastern Europe has been considerably stronger.

Thus, both geopolitical and ideological approaches—although in different ways—contribute to our better understanding of the changes in Eastern Europe.[*] In terms of the prospect of the Eastern European countries' achieving freedom from the Soviet domination, each model is both pessimistic and optimistic. The geopolitical model is pessimistic in the sense that it assumes that as long as the USSR remains a great power adjacent to Eastern Europe—and there are no signs that this situation will change soon—it will continue to exert dominant influence in the region; and it is optimistic in reminding us that in the past the Eastern European peoples have survived long periods of foreign domination without abandoning either their own traditions or their aspirations for independence. As such it promises more radical changes, but only in an undetermined, distant future. In contrast, the concept of polycentrism is more optimistic in allowing for the revival of some national traditions sooner; but it is also more pessimistic because by definition it posits that the changes will stay within the confines of a Soviet, or at least Soviet-derived, Communist political system.

*   *   *

The Communist model—especially in its pure version, devoid of polycentrism—is derived from the official Soviet ideology. To the Marxist theoreticians the Communist revolutions and the adoption throughout Eastern Europe of political systems patterned after the USSR's by no means represent the traditional Russian imperialism, but rather embody the progressive unfolding of historical materialism. The Soviet role in the Communist takeovers in the region, as well as the subsequent Soviet military interventions there (facts which are openly acknowledged), are explained as natural manifestations of proletarian internationalism. This doctrinal position is derived from Karl Marx, who in the *Communist Manifesto* asserted that: "The working men have no country."[10]

---

[*] In a recent study Andrzej Korbonski, although using a different conceptual framework, takes a similar position; he characterizes Soviet-Eastern European relations as a synthesis between the traditional imperialism and the hierarchical regional system. "Eastern Europe" in Robert F. Byrnes (ed.), *After Brezhnev, Sources of Soviet Conduct in the 1980s* (Indiana: Bloomington, 1983, pp. 292-293).

In accordance with Marxism-Leninism thus, the workers every-where—once they attain revolutionary consciousness—cannot be anti-Communist or anti-Soviet. They genuinely support Communism as the system best serving their needs. Their true aspirations are articu-lated by their vanguard: the Communist party. The workers, more-over, are linked by firm bonds of proletarian solidarity transcending national differences. Since the USSR was the country which blazed the revolutionary road and is the most advanced on that road towards full-fledged Communism, the workers all over the world naturally look to it for guidance. The periodic upheavals in Eastern Europe, then, have been dismissed by Moscow as the doings of residual nation-alist, bourgeois, and occasionally religious elements, supported, and often instigated, by the western imperialists.

Yet, since the days of Lenin the Bolsheviks have also been keen practitioners of power politics. The geopolitical model, thus, is not far beneath the surface; in fact, it is often openly used to supplement the ideological one. The Soviet leaders have revealed themselves per-fectly capable of defending their interests in Eastern Europe with geo-political arguments. They point, for instance, to the historical role which the area has played as a springboard for invasions of Russia. Conversely, since the Soviet armies freed the region, at considerable cost, from Germany at the end of World War II, they tend to regard the area as their rightful sphere of influence. And the overt rationale for the Warsaw Pact is to protect the Eastern European nations from a revived German danger (although the Soviet troops stationed in the northern tier are also conveniently placed to guard their allies' ideo-logical purity).

The way the Soviet Union has imposed its domination over Eastern Europe is, in fact, not altogether different from the way Britain ruled colonial India. The direct annexation of the eastern periphery of the region into the USSR makes it resemble those parts of the Indian subcontinent which were run directly from London; while the main-tenance of the façade of sovereignty and a degree of actual autonomy in the remaining countries of Eastern Europe comes close to the Brit-ish doctrine of paramountcy in the various semi-independent Indian states. By linking the interests of the ruling elites—be it the maharajas or the leaders of the Communist parties—to the imperial power, the centre's basic objectives are distanced from unrest among the local populations.

Marxist-Leninist ideology plays an important role here. It has been transformed into an effective instrument of power in the area. Since the ruling elites in the various Eastern European countries all adhere to it—either from conviction or expediency—they are obliged to follow the same course as the USSR does. And for straying away from the common Communist line, as interpreted by Moscow, the local rulers may be removed from power (as were Nagy, Dubcek and Ulbricht). The same fate moreover, may await those local rulers who fail to control their populace effectively (as was the case with Rakosi, Novotny, Gomulka and Gierek).

To the Kremlin leaders there is no contradiction in their simultaneously resorting to ideological and geopolitical reasoning, for both fit into their *Weltanschauung*. They apparently tend to look at Eastern Europe through the prism of the USSR's own experiences. After several generations of political indoctrination a good part of the Soviet populace has become genuinely committed to Communism; for all intents and purposes Marxism-Leninism has been absorbed into the mainstream of the Russian national tradition. The Soviet workers take great pride, bordering on xenophobia, in the international accomplishements of their state.

The Russians have been reared under autocracy—from Orthodoxy and the Tartars' rule they moved into the Tsarist despotism and the Bolshevik dictatorship—and democratic values are largely alien to them.[11] (This is less true, however, in the Western peripheries of the USSR historically more exposed to the West's influence, notably in the Baltic countries and the Ukraine[12]). The democratic dissidents' movement in Russia has been pitifully small.[*] Indeed, it often fits more into the Russian than the Western tradition. The dissidents' great readiness to make personal sacrifices resembles that displayed by the revolutionaries against the Tsarist autocracy; and their occasional moral strictures on the West echo the nineteenth century Slavophiles. If democracy is ultimately to prevail in the Soviet Union, thus, it will still take a uniquely Russian form—but so far such an eventuality is nowhere in sight.

The USSR is faced at present with an urgent need to decentralize the rigid economic system which has become an impediment to its continued growth. This may necessitate—if only to offer greater scope to individual initiative—a measure of political reform too. During his brief reign Andropov recognized this, and initiated at least some policies aimed at eliminating sloth and corruption in the Soviet economy, and at expanding the scope of decision-making of individual factory managers; and upon coming to power Chernenko expressed his intention to continue these policies. Yet, these economic steps, if only to enable the requisite individual initiative, may necessitate at least some political reforms too.

---

[*] Yet, ironically, the Soviet dissident movement had a considerable impact in the 1970s in Poland, where the democratic opposition welcomed it as a harbinger of major political changes in the Soviet Union.

Unless some such changes are introduced soon, the declining standard of living may lead to discontent among the Soviet workers. Hence the Kremlin leaders' great concern about "Solidarity", which not only struck a particularly sensitve aspect of Marxism-Leninism by refuting the claim of the Communist party to be the sole representative of the working class, but, adding insult to injury, also appealed to the workers in other Eastern European countries and in the USSR itself to follow in its footsteps by forming trade unions of their own. The Soviet workers, incidentally, reacted to this proposal with indignation—which was at least partially genuine—smacking of the old-fashioned Russian contempt for the Poles.

*   *   *

The Kremlin leaders hope that eventually the East Europeans will become like the Russians in genuinely succumbing to Communism. Since the establishment of their influence in the region they have never ceased trying—although with varying zeal at different times—to mould the Eastern Europeans in their own image. This has been evident both in the conduct of their power politics in the region and in the attitudes which they have adopted towards its ideological evolution.

During the initial Communization of Eastern Europe, corresponding roughly to Seton-Watson's first two stages, the Soviet leaders proceeded cautiously. Stalin, it seems, was not then certain whether the Soviet influence in the area was there to stay, and he did not want to unduly alarm the western powers by revealing prematurely his real objectives.*

The independence of the individual Eastern European countries was emphasized and their internal transformations, although being such as to move them closer to socialism, were depicted as being basically different from those in the USSR. To buttress this position an obscure statement of Lenin's that ". . . all nations will reach socialism—this is inevitable—but not all will reach it completely the same way", was dug up and elevated into a major doctrinal pronouncement. One of the first Soviet theoreticians to address himself to this topic was E. S. Varga, who even argued, in 1946, that the new type democracies in Eastern Europe represented a final form of capitalism—"state capitalism," as he put it—rather than an embryonic socialist system.[13]

---

* Stalin's tactics were best depicted by Djilas. The Soviet leader did not conceal from his Yugoslav comrades that the Communization of the areas under his military control was his ultimate goal, but at the same time he urged them not to reveal this plan to the West. In the spring of 1944 he even scolded the Yugoslav partisans for wearing the red star on their hats. "The form is not important but what is gained", he exclaimed angrily. Milovan Djilas, *Conversations with Stalin*, (Harcourt, Brace and World: New York, 1962, p. 73).

By 1947, corresponding to the completion of Seton-Watson's third stage of the Communist monopoly of power, the concept of different roads was played down. Varga was taken to task for his static formulation and he soon abandoned it in favour of a dynamic one—the Eastern European countries, he admitted, ". . . can, while preserving the present state form, gradually transfer to socialism."[14] With the establishment of the Cominform in the fall of 1947 and the Communist coup in Czechoslovakia early in 1948, the new ideological approach became clearer, and after the Soviet-Yugoslav break in the same year, it crystalized.[15] The progressive evolution of the political systems in the Eastern European states—the people's democracies, as they had become known—towards the Soviet model became mandatory. Early in 1949 a Hungarian Marxist theoretician, Jozef Revai, put it bluntly: "We must liquidate the notion that a people's democracy is some quite specific kind of state which differs from the Soviet state not only in form but also in its essence."[16] From then on there was only one road, i.e., the Soviet one, for the Eastern European Communist states to follow.

Immediately after Communizing the area, thus, Stalin moved into the next stage—supplementing Seton-Watson's three-stage pattern—of sovietization. In line with the then prevailing political practice in the USSR, it was enforced quite ruthlessly. Close integration of the Eastern European countries with the USSR was rapidly advanced and their domestic as well as socio-economic and cultural institutions were gradually made more like their Soviet counterparts. New constitutions patterned after the Soviet one were adopted by all the people's democracies.[17] Some historians even believe that this was in preparation for another stage supplementary to Seton-Watson's model: Eastern Europe's ultimate absorption within the USSR—and had Stalin lived longer he would have carried this process to its logical conclusion.[18]

Under Khrushchev, and especially in the wake of Soviet-Yugoslav rapprochement, de-Stalinization and the dissolution of the Cominform in 1956, the concept of different roads was resurrected. The joint declaration of the Soviet and Yugoslav parties issued on June 20 stressed that ". . . the path of socialist development differs in various countries [and] that their cooperation shall be based on complete equality."[19] Moreover, a declaration issued by the Soviet government on October 30, 1956 explicitly admitted that in its policies toward the Eastern European countries there had been committed ". . . violations and errors which demeaned the principle of equality in relations among the socialist states".[20] And, elaborating on this theme, an article in the Polish Communist party theoretical journal, *Nowe Drogi*, written by the young sociologist Jerzy Wiatr, underlined that the former practice of ". . . glorifying every act of the USSR leadership must be abandoned."[21]

There were reasons to believe, then, as Palmiro Togliatti did in June 1956, that the polycentric concept of Communism virtually became a reality. "The Soviet model should no longer be obligatory," the Italian Communist leader argued. "The complex of the system is becoming polycentric, and in the Communist movement itself one can no longer speak of a single guide".[22] The USSR experience, he added, remains the first example of ". . . conquest of power by the working class, and of utilization of this power in the most energetic and effective manner in order to succeed. . . in constructing a new economy and society. . . . But this experience cannot include either the ready-made solution of all problems which today present themselves in those countries which are already ruled by the Communist parties. . .". There has been established a "polycentric system: corresponding to . . . new types of relations among the Communist parties themselves."[23]

With the suppression of the Hungarian revolution and new friction between the Soviet Union and Yugoslavia, the concept of different roads was not abandoned, but it was drastically circumscribed.[24] As early as on November 6, 1956, a speech by Mikhail Suslov emphasized that certain features of the Russian revolution had universal significance and should be adopted by all socialist countries.[25] This notion was elaborated by several other Soviet theoreticians. A. P. Butenko argued that while the path to socialism in each country includes two components, the common as well as the different characteristics, the former represent the "basic contents of building socialism", and the latter merely arise "from methods and modes of utilizing common laws."[26] The precedence of the universal over national principles, thus, was clearly established. For, as the Soviet theoretician concluded, ". . . although there are national forms of application of universal laws . . . there are no specific national laws of socialism."[27]

The universal principles, derived from the Soviet experience, were clearly elaborated. They consisted of: i) the existence of a Marxist-Leninist party; ii) establishment of the dictatorship of the proletariat; iii) nationalization of the means of production and adoption of economic planning on a national scale; iv) conduct of international relations in accordance with proletarian internationalism. The national characteristics were given less attention. Indeed, it appears as if the main difference between the USSR and the Eastern European countries was that the former initially built socialism alone, while the latter were assisted by the very presence of the Soviet Union—leading again, in a roundabout way, to the significance of the Soviet experience.

An excessive emphasis on the national road, according to the Soviet theoreticians, which ignores the primacy of the universal Soviet experience, leads to a deviation from Marxism-Leninism. It is deliberately encouraged by the imperialist propaganda promoting the concept of so-called "national Communism". But since Communism by definition is international, the very term "national Communism" is a contradiction. It is ". . . nothing else but a new, subtle form of nationalism adapted to deceive the masses".[28] Nevertheless the Yugoslav and some Polish Communists fell into this trap.* By accepting the existence of a cleavage between the USSR and other Communist countries, they played right into the hands of the enemies of socialism.

The Soviet theoreticians' ambiguity between the universal and specific principles, it seems, was deliberate. The inconclusiveness called for an arbiter, who could interpret their true meaning. This task, of course, was reserved for the foremost party of the Communist movement: the Communist Party of the Soviet Union. Starting with the world conference of Communist leaders in Moscow in 1957, at which the Soviets played a dominant role, the ideological bonds among the Communist parties were tightened. Despite all of the theoretical trappings the concept of different roads once more became what the USSR's policy required it to be. A familiar union between ideology and power, thus, was restored.

In the late years of Khrushchev's rule, and subsequently under Brezhnev, the more traditional methods of integrating Eastern Europe with the Soviet Union also proceeded apace. Cooperation within the multilateral framework of the Council of Mutual Economic Assistance (CMEA) and the Warsaw Pact Organization (WTO) was expanded.[29] In 1962 Khrushchev propounded the idea of an international division of labur within the CMEA, and in 1968 Brezhnev used the WTO as a vehicle to invade Czechoslovakia. In 1969 the structure of the Warsaw Pact was streamlined with its Political Consultative Committee (composed of the first party secretaries, prime ministers as well as foreign

---

*While the Yugoslav leaders themselves were accused of succumbing to the erroneous concept of national roads the Polish leaders were merely chided for ". . . tolerating thoughtless treatment of ideological problems" in the party ranks. S. I. Mikhailov and E. A. Komarov, "Starye pagubki na novyi lad", *Voprosy Filosofii*, June 1957. p. 112.

and defence ministers) emerging as the main forum of regular consultations within the alliance. In 1971 the Comprehensive Programme of Socialist Integration was adopted, providing for closer cooperation of economic plans by the CMEA countries.

In 1960 another Communist world conference was held in Moscow. In 1972 regular annual consultations between the Soviet Union and the various Eastern European leaders in the Crimea were initiated. In 1973 the first session of the Communist party secretaries responsible for ideological ties was convened in Moscow. Indeed, the nature of relations between the Communist states was at times depicted by the Soviet theoreticians as if they were exactly like relations among nationalities within the USSR.[30] Also during the 1960s the constitutions in most of the Eastern European countries were once again amended—reflecting the next phase beyond people's democracies and moving into so-called "mature socialism"—to bring them still closer to the Soviet prototype.

In Poland the constitutional amendment of 1976 led to open apprehension that this step would ultimately lead to the country's incorporation into the Soviet Union. Even though in response to widespread protests the most drastic proposals were modified (notably in the retention of the name "People's Poland", instead of the proposed "Socialist Poland"), the Gierek government's amendment had farreaching political repercussions. It paved the way for the intellectuals' closing ranks with the restive workers, contributing to the popular explosion and the rise of "Solidarity" in 1980.[31]

The USSR's attitude towards the Polish revolt followed the familiar ideological lines. "Solidarity" was depicted by the Soviet media as a counter-revolutionary organization composed of workers who were manipulated by renegade intellectuals and stupefied by western anti-Communist propaganda. A Soviet commentator asserted in 1983 that the events in Poland had been ". . . a carefully hatched conspiracy of the reactionary forces. . . conducted in full compliance with the imperialist strategy and tactics"; it was this way that "a part of the young people , who had enthusiastically welcomed the trade movement. . . was diverted to a false path of adventurism and counterrevolution."[32]

It is precisely for these reasons, the Soviet writer added, that ". . . the elimination of the crisis and its consequences on Polish soil and the consolidation of socialist gains in Poland are of exceptional importance for the successful development of the entire socialist community. "The crisis," he ominously noted, ". . . is not over yet [and the] Polish Communists and Marxist scholars are faced with the difficult tasks of drawing the corresponding scientific, theoretical and paractical conclusions."[33]

NOTES

1. For history and the current state of Eastern European studies in the West see: Arnold Nucholtz (ed.), *Soviet and East European Studies in the International Framework* Transnational: Cobbs Ferry, N.Y., 1982), and Roland H. Linden, *East European Studies: Towards a Map of the Field and its Needs* (Pittsburgh: Carl Beck Papers in Russian and East European Studies).

2. Hugh Seton-Watson, *The East European Revolution* (Methuen: London 1956), pp. 167-171.

3. For a later penetrating study of the Communist seizure of power in Eastern Europe see: Thomas Hammond (ed.), *The Anatomy of Communist Takeovers* (Yale: New Haven, 1975).

4. George Schöpflin, "Communist Takeovers in Eastern Europe: Three Stages or Four? An Essay in Historical Reinterpretation", Paper presented to the Conference "History and Historians in Central and South-Eastern Europe", 11-14 July 1983, School of Slavonic and East European Studies, London. (Mimeographed).

5. Jan Szczepanski, *Polish Society* (Random House: New York, 1970), p. 199.

6. See Adam Bromke, "The Revival of Political Idealism in Poland", *Canadian Slavonic Papers*, (Vol. XXIV, No. 4, December 1983).

7. For an early view of Communism as merely a new façade for the traditional Russian imperialism, see: Jan Kucharzewski, *The Origins of Modern Russia* (The Polish Institute of Arts and Sciences in America; New York: 1948). The book is an abbreviation of a large (seven volumes) study in Polish published in 1923-1935, which had much impact upon the Poles' thinking about Russia in the inter-war years. Yet, not all Poles shared this view; for its opposite, that it is primarily Communism which leads to Soviet expansion, see: Jozef Mackiewicz, *Zwyciestwo prowokacji* (München, 1962). Mackiewicz's view has been shared by some Russian emigré historians, notably Michael Karpovich, "Russian Imperialism or Communist Aggression? ", *The New Leader*, (June 4 & 11, 1951); and more recently by Alexandr Solzhenitzyn, "Misconceptions About Russia Are a Threat to America", *Foreign Affairs*, (No. 4, Vol. 58, Spring 1980).

8. An example of this approach is the section by F. R. Leslie in *History of Poland Since 1863* (Cambridge, 1980) where, in covering the events from 1863 to 1914, he deliberately, it seems, focuses on the then marginal role of the Marxist movement in Poland, in order to trace the roots of the post-war developments. For my critique of this approach see *Canadian Slavonic Papers* (Vol. XXIII, No. 1, December 1981, pp. 496-7).

9. See, for instance, Sydney D. Bailey (ed.), *Parliamentary Government in the Commonwealth* (Hansard Society: London, 1951); Sir W. Ivor Jennings, *The Approach to Self-Government* (Cambridge, London, 1956); and his *Problems of the New Commonwealth* (Cambridge, London, 1958); and Nicholas Mansergh *et al.*, *Commonwealth Perspectives* (Cambridge, London, 1956). For an early penetrating critique of this approach see: Keith B. Callard, *Political Force in Pakistan, 1947-1959* (Institute of Pacific Relations: New York, 1959).

10. Karl Marx, *Communist Manifesto* (Gateway: Chicago, 1954), p. 33.

11. For a celebrated discussion of the three motives in Soviet foreign policy: national interests, the Communist ideology and totalitarian government, see Samuel L. Sharp, R. N. Carew Hunt and Richard Lowenthal in Alexander Dallin (ed.) *Soviet Conduct in World Affairs* (Columbia: New York, 1960).

12. For the influence of the Czechoslovak developments in 1968 in the Ukraine see: G. Hodnett and P.J. Potichnyj, *The Ukraine and the Czechoslovak Crisis* (AUN: Canberra, 1970); and for an influence of the Polish events in 1980-81 upon the Baltic countries see: V. Stanley Vardys, "Polish Echoes in the Baltic", *Problems of Communism* (Vol. XXXII, No. 4, July-August 1983).

13. E. S. Varga, *Iamenia v ekonomike kapitalizma w itoge vtoroi mirovoi voiny* (Moscow, 1946), p. 291.

14. E. S. Varga "Democratia novovo tipa", *Mirovoe khoiziastvo i mirovaia politika*, No. 3, 1947. p. 7.

15. For the original Soviet-Yugoslav split see Adam B. Ulam, *Titoism and the Cominform* (Harvard: Cambridge, 1952).

16. J. Revai, *Tarosdalmi Szemle*, March-April 1949. For the early evolution of the concept of different roads see: A. Bromke and A.N. Pol, "The Concept of People's Democracy in the Post-Stalinist Era", *Revue de l'Université d'Ottowa*, Octobre-Décembre 1959. pp. 473-498.

17. For the constitutional evolution in Eastern Europe in the late 1940s and the early 1950s see: Samuel L. Sharp, *New Constitutions in the Soviet Sphere* (Foundation for Foreign Affairs, Washington, 1950).

18. Zbigniew K. Brzezinski, *The Soviet Bloc, Unity and Conflict* (Harvard: Cambridge, 1960), p. 144.

19. In Paul E. Zinner (ed.), *National Communism and Popular Revolt in Eastern Europe* (Columbia: New York, 1956), p. 13.

20. *Ibid.*, p. 496.

21. J. Wiatr, "Krzyzs internacjonalizmu" *Nowe Drogi*, Nos. 11-12, November-December 1956. pp. 109.

22. *L'Unità*, June 17, 1956. In Walter Laqueur and Leopold Labedz (eds.), *Polycentrism, The New Factor in International Communism* (Praeger: New York, 1962), p. 127.

23. *L'Unità*, June 26, 1956. in the Russian Institute, Columbia University, *The Anti-Stalin Campaign and International Communism* (Columbia: New York, 1956), pp. 214-5.

24. For the second Soviet-Yugoslav dispute see: Robert Bass and Elisabeth Marbury (eds.), *The Soviet Yugoslav Controversy, 1948-1958* (Prospect: New York, 1959); and Vaclav L. Benes and others (eds.), *The Second Soviet-Yugoslav Dispute* (Indiana: Bloomington, 1959).

25. *Izviestia*, November 7, 1956.

26. A. P. Butenko, "Natzionalnyy komunism-ideologichcheske oruzhe bur-zhuasii", *Voprosy Filosofii*, June 1958. p. 9.

27. *Ibid.*, p. 4.

28. *Ibid.*

29. For the progress and difficulties in integrating the Communist bloc see: Kazimierz Grzybowski, *The Socialist Commonwealth* (Yale: New Haven, 1964); Robin Alison Remington, *The Warsaw Pact, Case Studies in Communist Conflict Resolution* (MIT, Cambridge, 1971); and Robert W. Clawson and Lawrence C. Kaplan (eds.), *The Warsaw Pact, Political Purpose and Military Means* (Scholarly Resources, Wilmington, 1982).

30. Teresa Rakowska-Harmstone, "Socialist Internationalism and Eastern Europe—A New Stage", *Survey*, No. 1 Vol. 22, Winter 1976.

31. Adam Bromke, *Poland, The Protracted Conflict* (Mosaic, Oakville, 1983), pp. 75-6.

32. A. Gorshkov, "Imperialist Conspiracy Against Poland", *International Affairs* (Moscow), October 1983, pp. 143-144.

33. *Ibid.*, 143-145.

II.

NATIONALISM VS. COMMUNISM

Pressure for independence from the USSR among the different Eastern European peoples stems in the first place from their nationalistic impulses, measured by the intensity of their animosity towards the USSR.* No nation, of course, likes to be dominated by another, but since the Eastern Europeans, and especially those in the northern part of the region, consider themselves more advanced than the Russians this sentiment on their part tends to be even stronger. They are all the more embittered by watching the various developing Asian and African peoples obtaining independence, while being themselves, as Europeans, denied the right to self-determination.

The intensity of enmity towards Russia, however, differs considerably from country to country throughout the region. The only people who have consistently maintained pro-Russian feelings, dating back to the Tsarist support of their struggle against the Turks, have been the Bulgarians. Panslavic sentiments, directed against the Germans, were also present among the Serbs, Croats and the Czechs, but they diminished considerably after the Soviet threats to Yugoslavia in 1948-49 and the Soviet-led Warsaw Pact invasion of Czechoslovakia in 1968.

Conversely, strong anti-Russian feelings have historically existed among the Poles, and particularly those from the eastern territories, who for over a century were sugjugated to the Tsarist Empire. Similar sentiments prevail among the Romanians, the Hungarians and the Germans, who, at one time or another, have all been exposed to Russian invasions. In the case of these four nations the traditional animosity towards Russia was aggravated by their territorial losses to

---

* H. Gordon Skilling, although his conclusions are generally similar to those of Brzezinski, Korbonski and this author, characterizes the aspirations of the Eastern Europeans towards greater independence from the USSR as a conflict between national and international Communism. See his: "The crisis in Eastern European Communism: national and international", *International Journal*, (No. 2. Vol. XXXIX, Spring 1984). pp. 429-455.

the USSR at the end of World War II.[*] It was further intensified by the Soviet crushing of the popular upheavals in East Germany in 1953, and Hungary in 1956, and, most recently, by Moscow's role in the suppression of "Solidarity" in Poland in 1981.

Historically the strength of the Communist parties in the region has varied inversely with the intensity of anti-Russian sentiment among the local populace. In the inter-war period the parties were weak in Poland and Romania (with the national minority groups playing disproportionately large roles in them[1]), and, conversely, relatively strong in Czechoslovakia, Yugoslavia and Bulgaria. In Yugoslavia, and with its assistance in Albania, the Communists came to power largely on their own at the end of World War II (although later on this contributed to both countries' resisting Soviet meddling in their internal affairs), and the same was true of Czechoslovakia in 1948 (though the broad popular appeal which the Czechoslovak party enjoyed in 1968 did not help it then).

The pressure for democratic reforms has been stronger in the predominantly Catholic and former Austrian and German northern part of the region than in the south, which was long exposed to Byzantine and Turkish despotic rule. (In the case of Albania the pressure has been virtually nil.) Democratic aspirations have also been more tangible in those lands—again located in the north—where Marxism came originally from Germany, than in those where it came through Russia, already with a strong admixture of peculiarly Russian 19th century revolutionary tradition, itself tainted by autocracy.

The fact that in the inter-war period the Czechoslovak Communist Party was at times depicted as "the best social democratic party in Europe", no doubt facilitated the revival of that tradition in 1968. And the cleavage between those people who came from the ranks of the Polish Workers' Party (a successor of the Social Democracy of

---

[*] Yutoka Akino makes an interesting linkage between Soviet territorial annexations and the spread of Communism in Eastern Europe. In his opinion the shift of the USSR's borders westward, in effect, predetermined the path of Communism for Poland and Romania: "The annexations of the Polish and Romanian territories turned out to have doomed the two countries to be within the Soviet zone of exclusive influence. For the seizure caused such an appalling anti-Soviet feeling among the populaces as to ensure that any government established there through free elections would be unfriendly to the Soviet Union." "Soviet Policy in Eastern Europe, 1943-1948, A Geopolitical Analysis", *East European Quarterly* (Vol. XVII, No. 3, September 1983). In the case of Finland, however, despite its loss of territory to the USSR during World War II, the subsequent emergence of a government friendly to the Soviet Union proved feasible.

the Kingdom of Poland and Lithuania, which before 1914 maintained close bonds with the Russian revolutionaries), and those who entered from the Polish Socialist Party (which prior to World War I had a strong base in Austrian-ruled Galicia), persisted after the two parties merged into the Polish United Workers' Party in 1949, and surfaced again in 1956. *

As to modernization, George Schöpflin is right in asserting that in the wake of World War II Eastern Europe was ripe for major social changes and that the weakening of the pre-war ruling elites was a significant factor. But this does not mean that the only road to advancement open to the Eastern Europeans was signposted by Communism.- As Adam Ulam reminded us recently the United States and Britain had it within their power—at some greater cost in their war against Germany, but probably without starting one against the USSR—to prevent such a development.[2] Only in Yugoslavia and Albania were there genuine Communist revolutions, and even in those instances, had the western allies decided to invade Europe through the Balkans rather than France, the outcome could have been different.

In all other countries the Communists probably would have been at best partners in true coalition governments. In other words the political developments would not have gone beyond Seton-Watson's first stage, and, as in Finland, the Communists might eventually have been eliminated from the coalition. East Germany would have been a part of the democratic FRG, and Czechoslovakia would have preserved its parliamentary government.[†] In Poland, Hungary, Romania

---

* Yet, some of the turncoat socialists such as Grotewohl in Germany or Cyrankiewicz in Poland (he actually came from Galicia), have proved to be no less loyal to Moscow than the life-long Communists.

[†] It is interesting to speculate what would have happened had the Polish government-in-exile in London during the war (under Sikorski, had he not perished in Gibraltar in 1943, or any of his successors) joined the Czechoslovaks under Benes in trying to cooperate with the USSR in order to preserve their domestic autonomy. Most Polish historians claim that this would have changed little since Stalin was bent on achieving his goals in Eastern Europe, and a Polish coalition government would have been overthrown in the same fashion as the one in Czechoslovakia in 1948. Yet one wonders: in such a situation in Poland the transitional period before the stages of Communization and Sovietization would probably have been prolonged, with the result that the changes in that country in 1956 would have been more profound; such a development could also have been of a considerable help to the Czechoslovaks in their withstanding Soviet pressure until the West ultimately changed its stand towards the Soviet Union in the late 1940s.

and Bulgaria, initially, the peasant parties, possibly in cooperation with the socialist ones, would probably have emerged as dominant. In due time the right of centre parties, within the democratic processes, could have been returned to power; although temporary relapses into authoritarian right-wing regimes or even military dictatorships, as in Greece, would have been possible. Under such circumstances modernization, naturally, would have also advanced, but in a different socio-economic framework, resembling more—depending on the starting point in the different countries—that of Austria or Portugal. Economic progress could have been greatly assisted by the inclusion of Eastern Europe into the Marshall Plan.

Under Communism, modernization was hindered by the exclusion of the region from the European Recovery Program, and, at least in the early post-war years, by its exploitation by the Soviet Union.[*] Yet, the picture is not altogether one-sided. In a way it was easier for the Communists, unrestrained by democratic niceties, to force rapid industrialization. As in the USSR this was accomplished at great human cost and many mistakes were made in the process: there was severe imbalance between heavy and light industries, agriculture was generally neglected (although the Bulgarians somehow have managed to maintain its viability), and the entire system became over-centralized and rigid. Nevertheless the threshhold of modernity was crossed, transforming basically agricultural societies into industrialized ones, with a substantial working class coming into existence everywhere. Urbanization has been advanced, educational strides have been made, and life in general has improved. Even in still largely primitive Albania some progress has been made: the old tribal system has been undermined and the first steps towards industrialization taken. The standard of living throughout the area has remained considerably lower than in the West but it is doubtful, regardless of the path they travelled, whether the Eastern Europeans could have quickly caught up with the Western Europeans who were both more prosperous before the war and less ruined by it.

*   *   *

---

[*] Paul Maurer has pointed out that in this way Eastern Europe was doubly penalized, for the amount of Soviet economic exploitation of the region amounted roughly to what it would have received from the United States under the Marshall Plan. "The Political Economy of Soviet Relations with Eastern Europe: 1945 to the Present", a paper presented at the Annual Meeting of the International Studies Association, New York, March 1973. (Mimeographed). pp. 15-16.

The success of advancing modernization has enabled the Communist regimes in Eastern Europe to win the support of at least some segments of their societies. A new class of political and economic bureaucrats has arisen. It is predominantly composed of former workers and peasants who took advantage of the new opportunities to advance on the social ladder. Since they owe their careers to the transformations under Communism, they have acquired a vested interest in perpetuating the existing system. The new intelligentsia is quite substantial. In Poland in the first thirty-five years after the war—with the population approximately the same: 35 million in both 1939 and 1980—the number of persons with higher education increased tenfold: from 110,000 to over a million[3]. Among the political and industrial elite, of course, a disproportionately large number are party members, providing a restricted, but nevertheless genuine, popular base[4].

In East Germany, Czechoslovakia, Poland and Bulgaria, in order to expand the size of the new class, a surrogate democracy has even been preserved. The existence of political parties other than the Communist one is tolerated—populists, liberals and even Christian democrats. And they are provided with a small representation in the parliaments and the governments. Their members, thus, are given an opportunity to participate in the Communist political system without formally subscribing to Marxism-Leninism. Yet, of course, these are not genuine, but rather what Seton-Watson characterized as bogus, coalitions. The smaller parties all subscribe to the principle of Communist leadership, and they are carefully integrated into an overall political framework through the national fronts in which the dominant role is played by the Communist party.

The new class has been crucial to the Communist governments in controlling their societies and, since the positions of its members have been dependent upon the good graces of the political leadership,, it has fulfilled its function dutifully. Yet, its political role has not been all one-sided. The middle-rank functionaries have also served as a conveyor of popular sentiments from the communities from which they originated (and particularly from the rural population) and with which they have often retained close personal links. This has helped to moderate at least some Communist policies. The abandonment of collectivization of agriculture in Yugoslavia in 1953 and in Poland in 1956, and the greater tolerance shown towards religion—especially deeply entrenched in the countryside—seem to have been assisted this way.

Since the commitment of the new class to the political system has been primarily motivated by their attaining power and privilege, the role of the Communist ideology has been diluted. Marxism-Leninism has become largely ritualistic, consisting of lip service to the slogans about social progress, egalitarianism and, of course, faithful friendship to the Soviet Union; but in reality it has been increasingly ignored. The situation was well summed up by an anonymous Hungarian intellectual who declared: "We tell the Russians we love them. But then, we also tell them we are all Communists."[5]

To buttress the declining Marxism-Leninism another ideology has been evolved—a new type of nationalism. In order to distinguish it from the old-fashioned "bourgeois" nationalism, it has been labelled "patriotism".[*] The new nationalism has naturally persisted in espousing close ties to the USSR, but these no longer are advocated merely in the name of proletarian internationalism, but as serving the national interests too. Even the progress of modernization has often been presented less in doctrinal terms, than as a vehicle to enhance the position of the different Eastern European countries in the world.

In order to make patriotism more credible at least some of the old national traditions have been rehabilitated. In Poland after 1956 the wartime exploits of the non-Communist forces (even those serving under the British command) were praised, and the Polish army was given uniforms resembling those from the past. Romanian history was re-written in the 1960s in a more nationalistic vein, and various past figures not known for their sympathies towards Communism were commended (such as the foreign minister from the mid-1930s, Nicolae Titulescu). And in East Germany Frederick the Great, Bismarck and, most recently, Martin Luther, were acclaimed as national heroes. The traditional Polish and Czech animosities towards Germany (although directed exclusively at the FRG and not the GDR), have been cultivated. Indeed, even some territorial disputes with other Eastern European nations have been exploited to arouse "patriotic" sentiments. In 1983, to the discomfort of the Yugoslavs, the Bulgarians celebrated the anniversary of the Illiden Macedonian uprising of 1903; and in the same year the Romanians commemorated their annexation of Transylvania from Hungary in 1918.

With the passage of time, however, the new social structure has ossified. A new class—as Milovan Djilas shrewdly observed already in 1957[6]—has become mainly interested in perpetuating, and even expanding, its own privileges. To retain the loyalties of the political

---

[*] The distinction between nationalism and patriotism has been particularly artificial in Poland, where, after the territorial shift at the end of the war, the primary allegiance of the populace clearly has not been to the patrimony, but to the nation.

and economic bureaucracies the Communist governments have responded favourably to their demands. The income differential—particularly in Poland under the Gierek regime—has been sharply accentuated. In addition the new class has been given some other benefits: better housing, inexpensive cars, subsidized vacations (often abroad) and special health services. The children from this social stratum have had easier access to the universities and, subsequently, to the select jobs in the state administration. The revolutionary élan of the early post-war years has largely evaporated and new social cleavages have emerged.

In the immediate post-war years the political opposition was still led by the former upper classes. In 1956 in Hungary some political figures from the pre-Communist period re-emerged, with Jozef Cardinal Mindszenty becoming a symbolic leader of the abortive revolution.[7] Gradually, however, the old intelligentsia was replaced in opposition by a new one. In the mid-1960s in Poland disillusioned Marxists: Leszek Kolakowski, Jacek Kuron and others, turned against the Communist system. The intellectual ferment in 1968 was joined by the students—some of them, such as Adam Michnik, coming from prominent Communist families.[8] And in Czechoslovakia the vanguard of the Prague Spring was predominantly the new intelligentsia.[9]

The programmes espoused in the 1970s by the Praxis group in Yugoslavia, the New Left in Hungary, the Committee for the Defence of the Workers (KOR) in Poland and the Chartist 77 movement in Czechoslovakia were not opposed to Communism per se. Indeed, they subscribed to its original goal of social justice but wanted this to be implemented in practice and supplemented by expansion of political liberties. They were especially interested in respect for human rights and freedom of cultural expression.[10] Needless to add, such a platform, coming so close to the western concept of social democracy, was totally incompatible with the Soviet version of Marxism-Leninism, which was binding in most of the Eastern European states. But abstract ideals of justice and freedom had little appeal among the workers either.

The rising working class, at first, represented neither a cohesive nor a potent political force. It was largely composed of the first generation of former peasants for whom their new station in life was already a significant social advancement, and among whom the most ambitious individuals could still move on into white collar jobs. The workers were primarily concerned with economic issues and showed little interest in the ideas of cultural and political freedom that absorbed the intellectuals. In Czechoslovakia the Novotny regime de-liberately exploited the gap between the workers and the intelligent-sia, and the two groups really closed ranks only after the Soviet inva-sion in August 1968. In Poland, after the rebellion in Poznan in June 1956 the workers joined the intellectuals in pressing for reforms, but after the "Polish October" the two once again parted ways. The fer-ment among the intellectuals and the students in 1968 received no support from the workers, and the intelligentsia had no part in the workers' revolt in the coastal cities in December 1970.[11]

With the coming of age of the new generation of workers, who had already been brought up in an urban environment, were largely con-centrated in the big industrial enterprises and were better educated, the situation began to change. At the same time the ossification of social structures—bringing growing inequality of income and reduced opportunities for upward social mobility—contributed to the emer-gence of a separate working-class consciousness. The more active in-dividuals, seeing the avenues for moving on into the white collar jobs closed to them, emerged as its natural leaders.[12] Paradoxically, the official Communist ideology—with its egalitarian pretenses and its stress on the leading role of the working class in a socialist society—accelerated this process. The readily apparent gap between promise and reality aggravated the labourers' frustrations and awoke their political aspirations.[13]

The impact of the surrogate nationalisms also pushed the Eastern European societies in the direction of greater political activism. The partial rehabilitation of national traditions aroused curiosity, espec-ially among the younger people, about the complete historical truth. And what they found often stimulated anti-Russian sentiments—never far below the surface among the Eastern Europeans. In the countries which had freed themselves from Moscow's suzerainty, Yugoslavia and Albania, this posed no problem; if anything, the animosity to-wards the USSR contributed to their national unity and strengthened the Communist governments there. The Romanian Communist re-gime also exploited the popular anti-Soviet feelings to consolidate its political position. In a subtle but unmistakeable fashion, it even used the residual resentment over the Soviet annexation of Bessarabia to the same effect.

In the countries which remained closely tied to the USSR, how-ever, the revival of nationalism posed serious problems. It put into question the essential tenet of the Communist doctrine, namely, prole-tarian internationalism. The opposition, frustrated in its efforts to reform the Communist system from within, increasingly attributed its shortcomings to the outside Soviet influence, and began to press, if not for complete self-determination, at least for a more assertive interpretation of the concept of different roads. In the 1960s in Poland the partisans' faction in the ranks of the Communist party—in a fashion similar to the Romanian Communists'—disavowed any democratic aspirations, but played up traditional nationalism to the point where it actually acquired some anti-Soviet overtones. And a decade later some of the democratic opposition groups, notably the Confederation of Independent Poland (KPN) openly embraced a programme of restoring the country's sovereignty from the USSR.* Significantly, the Confederation's followers consisted mostly of young people.

*   *   *

In the first half of the 1970s social conflicts were mitigated by the relative economic prosperity. In the six WTO states the average annual growth of national income was a respectable 7.3 per cent.[14] The Communist governments, then, followed a policy of what Khrushchev once called during a visit to Hungary a "goulash Communism"—an attempt to enhance the standard of living of the entire population. Both the political and industrial elites and the working class received their due. The former got more than the latter, but the position of the labourers was also improving. Their wages were increasing, without the requiring of any great strain on their part. In the conditions of full employment they could always find a job where not much was demanded of them.

Historically, Eastern Europe enjoyed a period of prosperity unprecedented in modern times. Even in Czechoslovakia the memories of the invasion of 1968 were eased by material comforts. Whenever there was a shortage of monies, moreover, additional funds could be borrowed from the West. In the conditions of détente, and with a recession in the West and a surplus of petrodollars, the western bankers were only too happy to invest in the region.† In 1970-75 the aggregate

---

* The political evolution of the group's leader, Leszek Moczulski, is instructive. He was accused by some of his political opponents of sympathizing with the partisans in the 1960s; in 1977 he emerged as a leader of the Movement for the Defence of Human and Civil Rights; and then he split from it and formed his own openly nationalistic, although committed to democracy, Confederation of Independent Poland.

† The western bankers, evidently considered Eastern Europe a solid investment. After all, there were no real trade unions, and no strikes which would interrupt the flow of production, and the bankers dealt with the Communist governments which were expected to squeeze hard upon the workers to repay their loans. The rise of "Solidarity" in Poland in 1980, and the ensuing economic chaos in that country, no doubt came as a rude awakening to the western financiers.

hard-currency debt of the six Eastern European countries went up
from $6.0 to $21.2 billion—Poland being the main debtor.[15]
In the second half of the 1970s, however, the economic situation
gradually deteriorated. In 1975-80 the annual growth of national income went down to 4 per cent, and at the same time the total hard-
currency debt increased to $56 billion.[16] Various international as
well as domestic developments contributed to this trend. Continued
recession in the West reduced demand for Eastern European exports,
especially since they were usually of inferior quality compared to
the western manufactures. The new industries developed with the
help of western technology, moreover, were often dependent on the
continued imports of western parts and materials, aggravating an unfavourable balance of trade. As a result more and more of the export
income was used merely to cope with the mounting hard currency
debts. To make matters worse, after 1975 the prices of Soviet oil,
which hitherto had been available to the Eastern European countries
on highly favourable terms, were sharply increased.

The domestic problems endemic in the Communist type of economy
were also there. The rigid, over-centralized system became an impediment to continued economic growth. There was a tendency towards
overinvestment in heavy industry, at times bordering—particularly in
Poland and Romania—on gigantomania; while agriculture was ignored,
making it extremely vulnerable to climatic fluctuations. Various
branches of industry, moreover, were not properly coordinated and,
largely because of poor labour efficiency, the quality of goods which
they turned out was low. Price structures were obsolete, with many essential consumer goods, and especially food, being heavily subsidized
by the government.

As a result the standard of living also began to fall. Prices rose, inflation was accelerated and there were repeated shortages of consumer goods. Popular dissatisfaction with this state of affairs was only
aggravated by the aroused consumer expectations from the early
1970s, which were even further exaggerated by the Communist propaganda. By the late 1970s the economic situation became quite dramatic with an aggregate hard currency debt among the six WTO states
rising to $56 billion.[17] There was an urgent need to bring the indebt-
edness to the West under control. As in the USSR—and even more
because of Eastern Europe's greater dependence on international
trade—there was a necessity of a major economic reform: a shift
from intensive to extensive economic growth.

Yet, economic reform was generally ignored by the Communist governments in Eastern Europe. In 1966-68 Czechoslovakia tried to introduce "market socialism", but this experiment was aborted by the WTO invasion. Only in Hungary was a serious effort to move in this direction made. In 1968 the New Economic Mechanism was introduced, providing for the reduction of central planning, adoption of economic incentives rewarding efficiency on the part of the managers and labourers alike, the encouragement of technological improvements, greater respect for market forces, especially by introducing more realistic prices, and support for agriculture and small-scale private enterprises. By 1974 NEM temporarily ran into difficulties, but subsequently its progress was resumed and handsomely paid off. The Hungarian economy managed to weather the storm with a declining, but still relatively high standard of living, averting in this way any widespread popular discontent.

In contrast, the Polish Communist regime ignored the need for economic reform, and in trying to prevent the decline in the standard of living continued to rely on heavy borrowing from the West. The government commission appointed after the workers' rebellion in 1970 failed to recommend any major structural changes. In 1976 an attempt was made to increase food prices, which had been kept artificially low by the government subsidies, but with new workers' strikes it was promptly abandoned. Subsequently the Gierek regime tried to patch up the situation by instituting the so-called New Economic Manoeuvre—reducing the level of investments and allocating greater resources to consumer industries—but it was a half-hearted measure which failed to reverse the downward trend. Despite many alarming signs (by 1980 the Polish debt to the West stood at $20 billion), and repeated warnings about the impending catastrophe, coming both from outside and inside the Communist ranks (including Gierek's own advisors), the Communist government adamantly refused to change its course. At the party Congress early in 1980 the prime minister changed, but the policy stayed the same.[18]

The deteriorating economic conditions provided a fertile ground for activities of the political opposition. The strikes in 1976 offered the intellectuals, already irked by the constitutional amendment earlier in the same year, an opportunity to close the gap between themselves and the workers. In September the Committee for the Defence of the Workers—composed predominantly of the pre-war social democrats and the young leaders of the students' rebellion from 1968—was established. It rushed to the defence of workers who had been born and raised in People's Poland. In many respects the Polish outburst fitted into the classic Marxist vision where the obsolete mode of managing the economy had become fetters for the productive forces and had to be burst asunder. Yet, since the economic system in Poland had been basically patterned after the Soviet one, the aspirations of the workers quickly acquired anti-Russian overtones and merged with the traditional Polish strivings for democracy and national independence.

In trying to defuse tensions in the country the Jaruzelski regime, despite its introducing martial law in 1981, has promised to carry out substantial domestic changes—similar to those in Hungary. Early in 1982 the parliament adopted a package of economic reforms patterned largely after the NEM. Replicating the Hungarian model in Poland, however, may prove to be difficult. In contrast to Hungary in the late 1960s, Poland's present economic situation is desperate: it has no reserves to carry it through a period of economic experimentation. It is projected that the country will restore its national income level from 1979, only in 1990.[21]

No less important is the fact that after a euphoric period of "Solidarity", the Poles, unlike the Hungarians after several years of severe repressions, are not in a compromising mood and may not be satisfied with moderate changes confined within the limits of the Communist system.[22] An underground "Solidarity", despite all the government's efforts to suppress it—by persecutions as well as by offers of amnesty—continues to operate. It poses no immediate threat to the Jaruzelski regime, supported by the army, but another dramatic deterioration of the economic conditions may provide it with an opportunity to gain broad popular support. In the local government elections in June 1984 a boycott advocated by "Solidarity" was not heeded, but at the same time the government admitted that less than 75 per cent of the people voted (in some districts it was even less than 50 per cent, so a second round of elections had to be held). A stalemate, thus, exists in Poland, threatening to erupt with a new popular upheaval, possibly even more serious than that in 1980.[23]

Conditions similar to those in Poland exist in some other Eastern European countries. The aggregate national income for the WTO states is expected to increase in 1981-85 only by 1.4 per cent annually. The Romanian economy is in sorry shape. Like Poland's, it is plagued by inefficiency and burdened by a heavy western debt. In 1983 Yugoslavia had a $19 billion hard currency debt (although it has been assisted in coping with it by the West), and it is suffering from rampant inflation. Czechoslovakia, although it did not borrow that heavily, persecuted by the Communist authorities for their involvement in the strikes, and generally addressed itself to articulating the labourers' grievances. The rise of KOR, in turn, led to the emergence of other opposition groups, among them the Movement for the Defence of Human and Civil Rights, and, later on, the Confederation of Independent Poland, as well as the Movement of Young Poland. The government's attitude towards the opposition groups was relatively lenient: they were submitted to all sorts of chicaneries, but were not suppressed outright. The Gierek regime was evidently reluctant to transform the economic crisis into a political one.

In the summer of 1980, when once more the food price increases were introduced, a popular explosion ensued. Workers' strikes spread throughout the country culminating in the establishment in August 1980 of the free trade unions called "Solidarity". The ferment quickly acquired a political character—with "Solidarity" pressing for virtual replacement of Communism with democracy. The Poles demanded not only the existence of free trade unions, but also participation of the workers in management of the enterprises, the abolishment of censorship, independence of the courts, the removal of the police from Communist control and free elections. They stopped short of insisting upon Poland's withdrawal from the WTO, but advocated cutting defence expenditures. And at its first Congress in September 1981 "Solidarity" issued an appeal to the workers in the other Eastern European countries, and, indeed, in the Soviet Union itself, to follow in its footsteps and form free trade unions of their own.

So in 1981 a revolutionary situation developed in Poland. It was non-violent and gradual—incremental in its demands—but it was a revolution nevertheless. It aimed to change radically Poland's position vis-à-vis the USSR.[19] Meanwhile, the economic situation—with the centralized government controls collapsing and strikes taking place all over the country—continued to deteriorate. In 1980 total production, in comparison with that in 1979, declined by 25 per cent.[20] With the ruling Communist party losing almost all authority conditions became quite chaotic. On December 13, 1981 the popular rebellion was brought to an end by the army's stepping in—an unprecedented move in a Communist state, testifying to the gravity of the situation.

A new situation, thus, emerged in Eastern Europe. If the other rebellions could have been explained as having been led by the pre-war bourgeoisie (Hungary 1956), or by the Communist intellectuals of the social democratic ilk (Czechoslovakia 1968), "Solidarity" was par excellence a proletarian movement—composed mostly of workers is not doing much better—it finds it increasingly difficult to maintain its relatively high standards of living and its industrial plant is badly in need of modernization. In Bulgaria, where generally the economic situation has been better, there have also been complaints about poor quality of goods and a lack of labour discipline. Even Hungary has recently been exposed to recession: it has been able to cope with an unfavourable balance of trade only at the expense of reduced economic growth and the retrenchment of living conditions. The Kadar regime, however, has not retreated from its economic reforms; on the contrary in 1983 the NEM was further expanded as the only course to effectively deal with the economic problems.

Generally, thus, Eastern Europe is exposed to severe recession: rates of growth are declining, investments are decreasing, there are serious energy shortages and foreign trade problems are aggravated by high hard currency indebtedness. As a result inflation has accelerated and the standard of living has declined. The period of "goulash Communism" of the 1970s—when various Eastern European governments strove to win a measure of popular support by satisfying consumer needs—is over. The only way out of this situation is to move along the lines similar to those being explored by the Kadar government in Hungary. Just muddling through—the way the Gierek regime did in the late 1970s—will lead to further economic deterioration, mounting popular dissatisfaction, and possibly another workers' outburst, similar to "Solidarity", somewhere else.

Yet, the road of economic reforms will not be easy either—it will require, at least temporarily, severe austerity measures. Decentralization of the economy, moreover, by releasing individual initiative, may pave the way for demands for political freedom. Yugoslavia was the first country to recognize this and, starting with the workers' councils experiments in the 1950s, has proceeded with de-centralization of its federal system and a general relaxation of political controls in the country. In the 1970s Hungary also took some cautious steps along this road. The trade unions' authority was expanded and more meaningful consultations with the workers over socio-economic issues have been introduced; at the same time the new electoral process, offering a somewhat broader choice of candidates, has been adopted. These innovations, however, have been carefully kept within the limits of a Soviet-derived Communist system, and they in no way have challenged the authority of the ruling Communist party.[24]

As in Poland, towards the end of the 1970s and in the early 1980s political opposition has continued, although on a more modest scale, in several Eastern European countries. In Romania in 1977 a small but vocal dissidents' movement appeared, led by a well-known writer, Paul Goma, and in the same year miners' strikes took place in the Jui Valley. The dissidents were suppressed (with Goma being exiled to the West), and the miners' unrest was quelled by the Ceausescu regime, but in 1979 there were reports of clandestine free trade unions being formed in that country. In Czechoslovakia the Charter 77 movement, despite severe repressions by the Husak regime, has persisted in its activities, and the *samizdat* publications issued by the Padlock House flourish. In Hungary the confrontation between the dissidents and the Communist government has also sharpened, with the authorities in 1983 closing down Laszlo Rajk's boutique of *samizdat* editions.[*] In the same year in East Germany the peace movement came into existence—opposed to the acceleration of the arms race by both the West and the East, composed predominantly of young people, and enjoying tacit support from the Evangelical church. And in Yugoslavia in April 1984 28 dissidents (one of whom was Milovan Djilas), who met to discuss the programme of reforms, were arrested and maltreated by the police.

The seeds of a new ferment in Eastern Europe, then, are there. With the passage of time, moreover, the new opposition, led by younger people, is gaining in experience. Their errors often serve as lessons for improving their methods of opposing the Communist regimes. Combined with growing dissatisfaction over economic and social issues this may result, in one country or another, in a new popular explosion, Certainly the pressures towards the transformation of the region towards greater polycentrism will continue; and if these are resisted by the USSR, the revolts may be transformed—as in Poland in 1980-81—into struggles for external independence along the lines of the geopolitical-optimistic scenario.

*   *   *

The Polish upheaval of 1980-81 was not only important *per se*, but regardless of its outcome, is bound to have repercussions throughout all of Eastern Europe. Poland is the most populous nation in the region

---

[*] Modern technology greatly facilitates the activities of the democratic opposition. Western television is now being widely watched in East Germany, and in the western borderlands of Bohemia and Hungary (as well as in Estonia). Simpler and cheaper reproduction techniques have contributed to the widespread issuance of the *samizdat* publications, and the advances in electronics have even made it possible for the underground "Solidarity" to broadcast its messages to the Polish population. Short of resorting to wholesale terror, these practices cannot be extinguished by the Communist governments.

and an important trading partner. The country is a middle power which on various occasions in the recent past has played a crucial role in international politics: in 1920 the Poles stopped the advance of the Red Army into Central Europe; in 1939 they were the first to oppose Nazi Germany with arms; and at the end of World War II it was over the future of Poland that the first skirmishes of the Cold War were fought between the Soviet Union and the West. Furthermore, the country is located at the crucial border of the USSR; it is through Poland that the Soviet lines of communication to East Germany and Czechoslovakia run, so control over the Polish territory is essential to Moscow's continued influence in Eastern Europe. Yet, precisely because of Poland's historical proximity to Russia, and the resulting rivalry btween these two nations, the anti-Russian sentiments among the Poles have an exceptionally keen edge.

No less important has been the fact that the developments in that country, more than anywhere else, reflect the new social trends, and the new tensions, in Eastern Europe. The Gierek regime in the 1970s, with its ineptitude, corruption and conceit, served almost as a classic example of a Communist system in decay. The rise of "Solidarity", in turn, heralded the rise of a new generation of Eastern Europeans brought up in a more snug atmosphere and, therefore, more prone to to be assertive in their political demands (and, as such, also more susceptible to the impulse to revert to their forefathers' traditions of uncompromising struggle for independence). Even with the imposition of martial law these Polish aspirations have not been extinguished, although their full impact has been deferred. The way the Jaruzelski regime handles the continued crisis in Poland, thus, could be highly instructive to the future of Eastern Europe as a whole.

Significantly, with the introduction of martial law the debates about the nature of the Polish crisis, and finding the way out of it, have not ended. Paradoxically, the freedom of the press has been greater under the military government than under the Gierek regime (although, of course, considerably less than during the "Solidarity" period). An intense soul-searching has taken place among the Communists themselves. On the pages of the traditionally reformist weekly *Polityka* (whose former editor-in-chief, Mieczyslaw Rakowski, in 1981 became a deputy premier in the Jaruzelski government), and in the newly-founded weekly *Tu i teraz* (Here and Now), as well as some other party papers, various writers have probed deeply into the problems facing contemporary Poland. Towards the end of 1983, in fact, a selection of their writings appeared as a book.[25]

In *Tu i teraz* Professor Janusz Reykowski acknowledged "Solidarity's" broad appeal and called for a thorough examination of the reasons for it. "What was it that made the Movement so popular?" he asked. "Why did it arouse so much hope and enthusiasm? What were the sources of its moral strength?" The answers to these questions, asserted the author, can be found in the very nature of the Gierek regime itself: ". . . the declining standard of life, the ineptness of public and state institutions, corruption, nepotism and lawlessness." What was worse, he added, was the fact that all of these negative phenomena were affirmed not ". . . only by Gierek himself, but by the party as a whole. It was proclaimed in the name of the party that we were going from success to success." "Solidarity's" popular appeal, concluded Reykowski, stemmed from turning against all of those abuses. "The Movement must have had some rational basis, it must have represented some values, which could not be denied by its adversaries—the reactionary tendencies of some of its segments notwithstanding."[26]

Writing in *Polityka* a well-known publicist, Krzysztof Teodor Toeplitz, praised "Solidarity" for imbuing the trade union movement with the values of "self-government and authenticity", which went beyond "purely cosmetic changes" and aimed at introducing a genuine ". . . pluralistic system of values within the socialist democracy." The revival of the Polish economy, he observed, will not be feasible unless ". . . it will be supported by the authentic workers' self-government." In this respect, Toeplitz underlined, ". . . as there can be no retreat from socialism in Poland, there can be no return to the situation which existed before August 1980."[27] And Reykowski carried this argument to its logical conclusion. It is obvious, he wrote, "that it is not possible to achieve the effective functioning of the economic system unless the broad masses of the society become interested in utilizing all the resources and the opportunities inherent in it. Economic progress requires initiative, inventiveness and an organizational ability of hundreds of thousands, and perhaps even millions of people. . . . And in order to get people involved [in the working of the system], they have to believe that they have a say in it."[28]

By far the most important document emanating from the Communist ranks was the report prepared by a special party commission which was assigned the task of inquiring into the causes of recurrent social conflicts in Poland. The commission was appointed by the Extraordinary Congress of the party in July 1981, and it was headed by a Politbureau member, and a well-known sociologist, Professor

Heronim Kubiak. Among its 35 members there were other Politbureau members and party secretaries, as well as several cabinet ministers, including Deputy Premier Rakowski; and about half of its members were prominent scholars. In May 1982 the Commission arranged for a special conference at the University of Poznan at which ten papers examining Poland's post-war history were presented. One of them was given by a Commission member and the newly appointed director of the Institute of Marxism-Leninism, Professor Jerzy Wiatr.[29]

The Polish Marxist theoretician underlined that it is only the enemies of socialism who see ". . . the history of postwar Poland as an unbroken sequence of failures, errors, or even crimes. In fact, the political course followed by the Polish Left gave the country. . . a lasting independent statehood, stabilized boundaries and internal peace." Furthermore, the post-war Polish crises have been less intense than those in the inter-war years, and if they are submitted to severe criticism, it is only because of the more acute social consciousness. But, he added, ". . . the cause of socialism should be defended. . . by means of the full, unadulterated truth."[30]

The roots of the present Polish difficulties go back, argued Wiatr, to World War II. The establishment of the Communist system in Poland ". . . did not arise as a result of a classic proletarian revolution, as in Russia. . . but emerged. . . mainly from the international political situation which determined the results of the struggle for power."[31] The Polish people at that time were sharply divided between the Left, which enjoyed the support of the USSR, and the London camp, ". . . which was supported by the majority of Poles."[32] The majority is not always right, explained the speaker, but he did not conceal that ". . . the Poles' anti-Soviet feelings.. had been intensified by ". . . the entry of the Soviet army into the territory of what was the Polish state. . . and the fact that the part of the Polish population which in September 1939 passed under the Soviet administration often shared the tragic consequences of Stalin's 'personality cult'."[33] The sharp division among the Poles resulted in a ". . . conflict bloody enough to be called a limited civil war and scar the minds of the next generation."[34]

By 1947 the Polish Left, Wiatr continued, ultimately prevailed. An effort was made at that time to evolve the concept of Poland's own road to socialism. "The advocates of the 'Polish Road' were convinced that the new People's Poland, allied with the Soviet Union, could and should carry out revolutionary changes in its own way, one consorting with the specific conditions of the country." These included a greater role of the parliament, repudiation of collectivization of agriculture, acceptance of the private sector in the economy, and a sympathetic attitude towards the Catholic church, along the lines of what later the Italian Communists labelled "the historical compromise." Yet, "the Polish road. . . has never become a fully developed theory."[35] In 1948-49 it was checked by both the dogmatic wing in the ranks of the Polish Communist party, and the "pressure of Stalinism."[36] The events of that period ". . . weighed heavily on the whole of Poland's subsequent evolution. They resulted in a policy of groundless repressions. . . adoption of an economic model which was a mechanical copy of the Soviet system. . . estrangement of the rural population through efforts to forcibly collectivize agriculture. . . exacerbation of Church-State relations. . . and irregularities in Polish-Soviet relations."[37]

The changes in 1956 ". . . brought about at least a temporary revival of the political belief that Poland should find a road which would accord with its cultural and political tradition. But, ". . . in later years the idea was again forgotten or deformed. . . the struggle to give a proper shape to the construction of socialism in Poland was not completed." The new social conflicts in 1968, 1970, 1976 and 1980 followed. And defining the "Polish road", asserted Wiatr, remains now ". . . a crucial theoretical problem: its solution is indispensable to steering the further evolution of the Polish political system in the right direction and the patterning of socio-economic change."[38]

The experience of the past, observed the Polish Marxist theoretician, ". . . leads us to conclude that the most important prerequisite for solving the present crisis and avoiding any future one is a thorough reform of the economy and the state, a reform which should be based on a careful analysis of the experience of other socialist countries and which should take into account both the universal ideological premises of socialism and the particular circumstances of the Polish historical process." The introduction of martial law, he concluded, ". . . scotched the bid of anti-socialist forces to seize power. . . . The turn in the political situation which took place on 13 December 1981 did not, however, eliminate the need for economic and political reforms."[39]

*   *   *

The Party Commission did not conceal that its assignment to examine the difficulties encountered in the process of socialist construction in Poland was not an easy one. The first draft report was submitted to the Politbureau in August 1982; it apparently underwent several revisions before it was finally published in a special issue of the party theoretical monthly *Nowe Drogi* towards the end of 1983.[40]

The final report addressed itself not only to the crisis of 1980-81 — which it admitted was the most serious one—but also examined the two previous, the first starting in 1948 and culminating in 1956, and the second from the late 1960s climaxing in the workers' revolt of 1970. The roots of the last upheaval were also traced to the developments in the several preceding years, and particularly to the workers' strikes in 1976. Without saying so explicitly, thus, the Commission conceded that almost half of Poland's post-war history has been characterized by socio-political instability. After describing the three crises in some detail,[41] the last part of the report addressed itself to general observations about the reasons for the repeated turmoils.

Among negative historical legacies the Commission singled out the backwardness of the country resulting from over a century of foreign rule, and the persistence of the ancient *szlachta* mentality, with its libertarian, and even anarchistic, features. As a result post-war Poland lacked the ethos of modern industrial society, and, above all, a developed work and political culture. The Commission, of course, unequivocally rejected the view that the reasons for recurrent crises were inherent in the nature of the Communist system itself; on the contrary, it argued that the progress in modernizing the country was made precisely because of the existence of Communism. And after each upheaval, the report stressed, the party mended its ways and proceeded with new achievements.

The main reason for the endemic social conflicts, continued the report, was the ". . . poor functioning of the state's institutions and the leading organs of the party, and in particular the errors committed by some of its leaders."[42] In the political domain there was incompetence on the part of the rulers, aggravated by their demeaning of the experts' advice. They repeatedly tended to drift towards autocratic centralism. Principles of socialist democracy were violated, the authority of the government, and particularly of its elected bodies, was circumscribed, and the party itself was strictly subordinated to the will of its central organs. Bureaucracy grew and became increasingly concerned with merely protecting its own interests. At times there was also lawlessness and, especially in the late 1940s and the early 1950s, there were even gross violations of personal liberties. The leading role of the working class was ignored and the position of the trade unions declined.

In the economic sphere grave errors were made. Unrealistic goals, divorced from economic theory, were advanced. An over-centralized system, with tendencies for excessive investments, particularly in heavy industry, was adopted. At the same time the development of agriculture was neglected, and the policies towards small-scale private enterprises were subject to frequent change. The price mechanism was unsatisfactory and necessary adjustments of the food subsidies were postponed too long. In the 1970s, with the growing differentiation in income, the gap between the quality of work and its reward widened; while at the same time social services, and especially health care and education, deteriorated. As a result awareness of social injustice spread.

Each time conditions in the country became acute, the working class stepped out and compelled the leadership to correct its erroneous policies. The older workers who had dominated the post-war scene were deeply committed to socialism, but in the 1960s, and especially in the 1970s, this situation changed. Among the younger generation of labourers "... many elements which made their fathers sincerely adhere to socialism were missing."[43] The young people took the existing system for granted and expected more from the state. This is precisely what made the crisis in 1980-81 so profound.

The recurrent crises provided fertile ground for the emergence of anti-socialist opposition. The economic decline in the mid-1970s, combined with the mishandling of the workers' strikes in 1976, "... created favorable conditions for organized anti-socialist activities (especially by the KOR and the KPN). These aggravated the nature of the crisis in 1980-81, leading to a systematic counter-revolutionary onslaught—after first gaining control of Solidarity's leadership—against the party and the socialist state." The opposition received encouragement and support from the western centres of political subversion, "... the effectiveness of their penetration rising with the growing intensity of tensions and internal conflicts in the process of socialist construction."[44] Significantly, however, the report stopped short of putting all the blame for the country's difficulties on the western subversion. "It would be a mistake," the document emphasized, "to regard the international situation and its unfavorable changes as the main reason for the critical situation arising in People's Poland."[45]

The report, naturally, affirmed Poland's firm commitment to alliance with the USSR, and praised Soviet economic assistance as helpful to advancing modernization in the country. At the same time, however, it pointed to Stalin's negative role in the abuses which took place in the late 1940s and the early 1950s. Even more importantly, it suggested that one of the reasons for the past mistakes was insufficient elaboration of the Polish road to socialism. "The prevention of crisis situations," it concluded, "not only requires respect for the universal characteristics of socialism, but also the observance of the Leninist principle that they should be implemented in accordance with the concrete conditions existing in each country.[46]

The report laboriously listed all the steps which were taken to correct the old errors under the Jaruzelski regime. It pointed out that during martial law, which was finally lifted in July 1983, the parliament remained quite active in both reviewing the government policies and enacting new legislation. Notably, the Minister of Internal Affairs regularly reported to it. Economic reforms were introduced and a special body, the Economic and Social Council—composed of workers, farmers and some prominent experts—was appointed to advise the parliament in this sphere. The Council of Ministers, moreover, established a special centre for sounding out public opinion. Along with "Solidarity" the old, compromised trade unions were disbanded, and new ones established. The principle of private ownership in agriculture was consolidated. The differences in income were substantially reduced, and the family allowances and pensions increased.

Major changes have also been carried out in the personnel composition of the government. Among its 448 top posts, consisting of the ministers, deputy ministers and the department directors, 323 have new incumbents. And the former Premier, Piotr Jaroszewicz, and one of his deputies, were brought before a State Tribunal to answer charges of abusing their authority. The old Front of National Unity was replaced by a new political coalition: the Patriotic Movement of National Revival, composed of, in addition to the Communist party, the peasants' and democratic parties as well as the three Catholic lay political groups. And more posts in the government were given to members of the aligned parties and to non-party people.

Important changes were carried out in the Communist party itself. Before the Congress in mid-1981, 48 of 49 provincial party secretaries were changed. Furthermore, 894 members of the party—including its former First Secretary, Edward Gierek, and the two former Premiers, Piotr Jaroszewicz and Edward Babiuch, as well as six former Politbureau members—were expelled from its ranks. Since 1981 a new Central Committee has been composed predominantly of workers and farmers. A deliberate policy to increase the workers' components in the party has been adopted.

The Jaruzelski regime, then, seems to be deliberately following in the footsteps of the Kadar government in Hungary. Writing in *Polityka* in early 1982, Jerzy Robert Nowak explicitly compared the situation in Poland in the early 1980s to that in Hungary after 1956, when ". . . the nation was deeply divided and the country was in a very difficult economic situation." The author praised Kadar for, on the one hand, firmness in dealing with the anti-Communist opposition, and, on the other hand, flexibility in winning the people to his side. The Hungarian leader's refusal to bow to the conservative elements in the party—who wanted to exploit the suppression of the revolution to return to the sterile methods of the Rakosi regime and to extinguish all the reforms—was singled out by Nowak as Kadar's special accomplishment."[47]

In 1982 a special session devoted to the review of Hungary's experiences in overcoming the 1956 crisis, and their relevance to contemporary Poland (chaired by the Institute's director, Professor Wiatr) was held at the Institute of Marxism-Leninism in Warsaw. The participants in the meeting commended Kadar's resolve in simultaneously conducting the struggle on two fronts: against the supporters of both Nagy and Rakosi, which helped to achieve the ". . . national reconciliation and understanding." It was underlined that as part of this policy ". . . non-party people were placed in responsible posts in the state administration. . . and a significant role was assigned to the trade unions."[48] The new economic policy effectively promoted the cause of national consolidation, since it was aimed to improve the standard of living of the population and, as such, served the specific Hungarian needs. A strong sentiment at the meeting in Warsaw was evidently that the best way for Poland to cope with its present problems was to follow Hungary's example. The Polish Communists, thus, while decisively rejecting the geopolitical-optimistic scenario, have remained committed to the polycentric model.

NOTES

1. See: R. V. Burks, *The Dynamics of Communism in Eastern Europe* (Princeton: 1961), *Passim*.

2. Adam B. Ulam, *Dangerous Relations, The Soviet Union in World Politics, 1970-1982* (Oxford: 1983). Ch. 1.

3. For the educational changes in post-war Poland, see: Joseph R. Fiszman, *Revolution and Tradition in People's Poland, Education and Socialization* (Princeton, 1972).

4. The process of socio-economic transformation in the region is dealt with at length in: Charles Gati (ed.), *The Politics of Modernization in Eastern Europe, Testing the Soviet Model* (Praeger: New York, 1974); and Alexander Matejko, *Social Change and Stratification in Europe. An Interpretative Analysis of Poland and Her Neighbors* (Praeger: New York, 1974).

5. Frantisek Silnitsky, Larisa Silnitsky and Karl Reyman (eds.), *Communism and Eastern Europe* (Karz: New York, 1979), p.v. See also: Stephen Fischer-Galati, *Eastern Europe in the 1980s* (Westview: Boulder, 1982), p. 2.

6. Milovan Djilas, *The New Class* (Praeger: New York, 1957).

7. For accounts of the Hungarian revolution see: General Assembly of the United Nations, *Report of the Special Committee on the Problem of Hungary* (United Nations: New York, 1957); Ferenc A. Vali, *Rift and Revolt in Hungary, Nationalism versus Communism* (Harvard: Cambridge, 1961); Paul Kecksementi, *The Unexpected Revolution: Social Forces in the Hungarian Uprising* (Stanford, 1961); Paul E. Zinner, *Revolution in Hungary* (Columbia: New York, 1962).

8. For accounts of March 1968 events in Poland see: *Wydarzenia Marcowe 1968* (Instytut Literacki: Paryz, 1969); Lucjan Perzanowski and Antoni Kuczmierczyk (eds.), *New Ma chleba bez wolnosci, Reportaz dokucentalny* (Polonia: Londyn, 1971); Marek Tarniewski, *Krotkie spiecie (marzec 1968)* (Instytut Literacki: Paryz, 1977); Peter Raina, *Political Opposition in Poland 1954-1977* (Poets' and Painters' Press: London, 1978), Ch. 5; and Adam Bromke, *Poland, the Protracted Conflict* (Mosaic: Oakville, 1983), Ch. II.

9. For accounts of the Prague Spring see: Robin Alison Remington (ed.), *Winter in Prague: Documents of Czechoslovak Communism in Crisis* (MIT: Cambridge, 1969); Philip Windsor and Adam Roberts, *Czechoslovakia, 1968* (Columbia: New York, 1969); Radoslav Selucky, *Czechoslovakia, The Plan That Failed* (Nelson: London, 1970); Galia Golan, *Reform Rule in Czechoslovakia: The Dubcek Era 1968-1969* (Cambridge, 1973); and H. Gordon Skilling, *Czechoslovakia's Interrupted Revolution* (Princeton, 1976).

10. For the activities of the opposition in Eastern Europe in the 1970s see: Silnitsky, *op. cit.*; Rudolf L. Tokes (ed.), *Opposition in Eastern Europe* (Johns Hopkins: Baltimore 1979); and Walter D. Connor, "Dissent in Eastern Europe", *Problems of Communism* (No. 1, Vol. XXIX, January-February 1980); H. Gordon Skilling, *Charter 77 and Human Rights in Czechoslovakia* (Allen and Unwin: London, 1981); Jane Leftwich Curry (ed.), *Dissent in Eastern Europe* (Praeger: New York, 1983).

11. For December 1970 events in Poland see: Paul Barton, *Misère et révolte de l'ouvrier polonais* (Confédération Force Ouvrière: Paris, 1971); Ewa Wacowska (ed.), *Rewolta szczecinska i jej znaczenie,* (Instytut Literacki: Paryz, 1971); and Bromke, *op. cit.*, Chs. III, IV.

12. For the changing nature of the working class in an industrialized socialist society see: Jerzy J. Wiatr, "Mobilization of Non-Participants During the Polish Crisis, 1980-81," a paper presented at the XII Congress of the International Political Science Association, Rio de Janeiro, August 1982. (Mimeographed).

13. For the growing class conflict in Eastern Europe see: Walter D. Connor, "Social Change and Stability in Eastern Europe", *Problems of Communism* (No. 4, Vol. XXXI, July-August 1982). p. 1.

14. Jan Vanous, "East European Economic Slowdown", *Problems of Communism* (No. 4, Vol. XXI, July-August 1982). p. 1.

15. *Ibid.*, p. 3.

16. *Ibid.*, pp. 1, 3.

17. *Ibid.*, p. 3.

18. For the policies of the Gierek regime in the late 1970s see: George Blazynski, *Flashpoint Poland* (Pergamon: New York, 1979); Maurice D. Simon and Roger E. Kanet (eds.), *Background to Crisis: Policy and Politics in Gierek's Poland*, (Westview: Boulder, 1981); Adam Bromke, *Poland, The Last Decade* (Mosaic: Oakville, 1981); Jean Woodall (ed.), *Policy and Politics in Contemporary Poland, Reform, Failure and Crisis* (Pinter: London, 1982); and Abraham Brumberg (ed.), *Poland, Genesis of a Revolution* (Vintage: New York, 1983).

19. Bromke, "Protracted Conflict", *op. cit.*, Chs. XIV, XVII, XXI-XXIII.

20. Krzysztof, , Teodor Toeplitz, "Co bylo, co jest, co byc moze", *Polityka*, February 20, 1982.

21. Vanous, *op. cit.*, p. 11.

22. Zespol redakcyjny konserwatorium "Doswiadczenie i Przyszlosc", *Polska wobec stanu wojennego, Raport czwarty* (Typed. Warsaw, April 7, 1982). p. 41.

23. For an evaluation of martial law see: Bromke, "Protracted Conflict", *op. cit.*, Chs. XVIII, XXII-XXIII.

24. For political changes in Eastern Europe in the 1970s see: George W. Simmonds (ed.), *Nationalism in the USSR and Eastern Europe* (Detroit, 1977); Teresa Rakowska-Harmstone and Andrew Gyorgy (eds.), *Communism in Eastern Europe* (Indiana: Bloomington, 1979); and Stephen Fischer-Galati (ed.), *The Communist Parties in Eastern Europe* (Columbia: New York, 1979).

25. Jerzy Adamski (ed.), *Gwalt i perswazja, Antologia publicystyki z lat 1981-1983* (Pnstwowy Instytut Wydawniczy: Warszawa, 1983).

26. Janusz Reykowski, "Podstawowy dylemat", *Tu i teraz*, June 30, 1982. For a collection of Professor Reykowski's writings see: *Logika walki, Szkice z psychologii konfliktu spolecznego w Polsce* (Ksiazka i Wiedza: Warszawa, 1984).

27. Toeplitz, *op. cit.*

28. Reykowski, *op. cit.*

29. Jerzy Wiatr, "The Sources of Crises", *Polish Perspectives*, No. 4, Vol. XXV, Autumn, 1982.

30. *Ibid.*, p. 9.

31. *Ibid.*, p. 10.

32. *Ibid.*, p. 12.

33. *Ibid.*, p. 11.

34. *Ibid.*, p. 13.

35. *Ibid.*, p. 14.

36. *Ibid.*, p. 15.

37. *Ibid.*, p. 16.

38. *Ibid.*, p. 17.

39. *Ibid.*, p. 21.

40. "Sprawozdanie z prac Komisji KC PZPR powolanej dla wyjasnienia przyczyn i przebiegu konfliktow spolecznych w dziejach Polski Ludowej", *Nowe Drogi*, October 1983.

41. See Appendix I.

42. "Sprawozdanie...", *op. cit.*, p. 72.

43. *Ibid.*, p. 64.

44. *Ibid.*, p. 71.

45. *Ibid.*, p. 61.

46. *Ibid.*, p. 72.

47. Jerzy, Robert Nowak, "Jak Wegry wychodzily z kryzysu", *Polityka*, April 24, 1982.

48. Andrzej Kupich, "Doswiadczenia wgierskie - kryzys i konsolidacja", *Problemy marksizmu-leninizmu* (No. 1, 1983). Pp. 162-7.

III

THE RISE OF POLYCENTRISM

The prospects for most of the Eastern European nations' attaining the goals prescribed by the geopolitical-optimistic model, i.e., complete independence, are bleak. Moscow continues to regard its domination of the area, as it has ever since the end of World War II, as of primordial significance. Communization of Eastern Europe has provided a *cordon sanitaire* isolating the USSR from the West, and in strategic terms the region has performed the role of a buffer zone—useful both for defensive and, possibly, for offensive purposes—separating the Societ Union from Western Europe. The USSR's growing involvement in some other parts of the world has not changed this situation. The existence of the Communist regimes in Eastern Europe encourages various revolutionary forces in the Third World to follow their example; and the close alignment of most states in the region to the USSR is considered essential to its retaining its position as one of the two global superpowers.

The northern tier of Eastern European states is particularly important to the Soviet Union. Control over the GDR provides Moscow with a key role in the determination of the German problem, which, in turn, remains crucial to the future of Europe; while the Soviet lines of communication to East Germany run through Poland and Czechoslovakia, with Hungary protecting their southern flank. The USSR's commitment to the defence of the northern tier, thus, comes next only to protecting its own homeland and, in all probability, it would not permit itself to be dislodged from this area short of war. Significantly, Soviet military garrisons are maintained in all of these four countries.

The southern tier apparently is of lesser strategic significance to Moscow, hence its somewhat greater tolerance of independence of the Communist states there. Yugoslavia's refusal to submit to sovietization in the late 1940s and its independent course, both in domestic and foreign policy, has been assisted by its peripheral geographic position bordering three non-Communist countries. Albania in the early 1960s was able to assert its independence, and even to close the

Soviet naval base on its territory, because, paradoxically, it was separated from the Communist bloc by its traditional adversary: Yugoslavia. When, after the invasion of Czechoslovakia in 1968, relations between Tirana and Belgrade temporarily improved, Albania formally left the WTO.

Romania shrewdly exploited the withdrawal of the Soviet troops from its territory in 1958. It successfully opposed the primarily agricultural role within the CMEA assigned to it by Khrushchev in 1962. Ever since, its participation in the Warsaw Pact also has been less extensive than that of any other member-country.[1] Due to its less favourable geographical position, however, Romania's scope of political manoeuvre remains more restricted than that of Yugoslavia or Albania. It is surrounded by Communist states, one—both to the east and the north—being the USSR. To the south, moreover, Romania is flanked by Bulgaria which is both a loyal WTO member and a country faithfullly following the Soviet type of Communism, an external threat to which could be treated by the USSR as seriously as one to any state in the northern region.

The USSR has repeatedly demonstrated that it is not prepared to accept the abandonment of Communism by any Eastern European country where it was introduced at the end of World War II. Moscow, apparently, is concerned that adoption of democracy in one state could produce a chain reaction undermining Communism all over the area (and could perhaps even spill over, via the Soviet western republics most vulnerable to such an influence, into the USSR itself). Consent to the restoration of democracy in Eastern Europe, moreover, would amount to an admission by the Soviets that Communism is a political system like any other, devoid of its special claim as being an inevitable outcome of history. As such, that would deal a major blow to Marxism-Leninism and dangerously undermine the *Weltanschauung* to which the Kremlin leaders adhere.

Indeed, the internal preservation of the Communist system appears to be as important to Moscow as the external alignment of any Eastern European state to the USSR. Hence, another reason for the Soviet tolerant attitude towards Yugoslavia, Albania and Romania—for they, while straying from Moscow's line in their foreign policies, have all retained Communism at home (although Yugoslavia moved in the direction of expanding internal freedom, while Albania preserved a crude, oppressive domestic system). There is an important symbolic element involved here. This was well depicted by a Polish writer in 1980. As long as the deviant country stays Communist, he observed,

"... it never fully and completely falls out of the Soviet orbit. ... in spite of all 'errors', it is still a member of the community; the prodigal son does not cease to belong to the family."[2]

In contrast, the Soviet Union moved decisively to suppress the rebellions in East Germany,[3] Hungary and Czechoslovakia, which aimed at restoring not only independence, but democracy as well. Moscow's insistence on the maintenance of Communism in Eastern Europe was especially strongly underlined after the suppression by the Warsaw Pact of the "Prague Spring" in 1968—what was dubbed in the West "the Brezhnev doctrine". At that time *Pravda* bluntly declared that: "The sovereignty of individual socialist countries cannot be counterposed to the interests of world socialism and the world revolutionary movement."[4] The suggestions made both in 1956 and in 1981 that Poland should assume a stance similar to Finland's, i.e., aligned to the USSR in foreign policy, but maintaining democracy at home, were also decisively dismissed.[5] And Moscow was firmly behind the Jaruzelski regime in its suppression of "Solidarity" in December of 1981.

*   *   *

Yet, after almost forty years of dominating the region, and repeated popular upheavals there, the Kremlin leaders must realize that the sovietization of Eastern Europe is an elusive goal. The ideological *Gleichschaltung* is nowhere in sight; on the contrary Communism is still seen by most of the Eastern Europeans as a foreign system imposed upon them by force. Thus, as true Leninists—firmly wedded to their own ideology, but willing to adjust it to fit the existing reality—the Soviet leaders have *de facto* accepted the Communism-polycentrism model. At least to a degree, the distinctiveness of each Eastern European country has been recognized.

The USSR's tolerance of independence of three out of four Communist states in the southern tier—although with the proviso that they must retain Communism at home, and in the case of Romania must continue as a WTO member—best illustrates its grudging acceptance of polycentrism. But the same trend has been evident, although more in the domestic sphere than in the external, in the northern tier. In the 1960s Hungary was permitted to adopt economic reforms and to expand personal liberties at home, In 1956 in Poland collectiviztion of agriculture was discontinued and the persecution of the Catholic church terminated.[6] In the 1970s the country's contacts with the West, especially in the economic sphere, were greatly intensified and in the later part of the decade the activities of the democratic opposition were largely tolerated. And in 1979 no Warsaw Pact forces, other than the Soviet ones—in view of popular resentment which this could create in Eastern Europe—were used to support the Communist regime in Afghanistan.

The suppression of "Solidarity" has not reversed the polycentric trends in the northern region of Eastern Europe. Since that time Hungary has consolidated its economic reforms and it has considerably expanded its contacts with the West. And the GDR, despite the sharp decline of East-West détente, has been permitted to cultivate its special ties (even after the replacement of the Social Democrats by the Christian Democrats as the government in Bonn), with the FRG. Even the Soviet line towards Poland has not been entirely consistent. While continuing to issue sharp attacks against "Solidarity", Moscow has occasionally acknowledged the need for moderate domestic reforms as espoused by the Jaruzelski government.

There are several reasons why acceptance of polycentrism in Eastern Europe could be advantageous to the USSR. First of all, adjustment of the Soviet type of Communism better to fit local conditions makes it less foreign, and, therefore, less objectionable in the eyes of the Eastern Europeans. And the more the Communist regimes are legitimized, the less is the danger of popular explosions.[*] Polycentrism, furthermore, could serve as a safety valve for Moscow in that the unrest in any country would not necessarily acquire anti-Soviet overtones. Coping with it would be the responsibility of the local Communist government. This was probably one of the major reasons why "Solidarity" was suppressed by using the Polish rather than Soviet, troops.[†]

An evident tension also exists between Moscow's ideological and security objectives in Eastern Europe. Rigid application of the Soviet

---

[*] Although, as the rise of a new class has demonstrated, the broader popular support works both ways: it helps the Communist regimes to consolidate their position, but it also absorbs them into the local traditions. Some observers, thus, believe that from Moscow's point of view small, ruling elites, even somewhat alienated from their own societies, are easier to control. See Peter Summersdale, *The Eastern European Predicament* (St. Martins: New York, 1982, p. 29).

[†] Soviet reluctance to intervene militarily in Poland in 1981 (as in 1956) may have also been influenced by the fact that the Poles have a long tradition as fierce fighters in resisting foreign invasions. The same, of course, was true of Yugoslavia in 1949. In contrast, the lack of such tradition among the Czechs may have facilitated their being overrun by the WTO in 1968. Indeed, at that time some Yugoslav observers speculated that had the Czechoslovaks made it clear that they were going to resist the invasion with arms, it would not have taken place.

type of Communism there, insofar as it aggravates popular discontent and even leads to periodic rebellions against the Communist regimes, internally weakens the Warsaw Pact. The Polish troops which since 1981 have been watching their own compatriots cannot be effectively used for any other military tasks. And the Soviet military strategists have to allow that, in the event of a conflict in Europe, substantial Soviet forces would have to be deployed to protect their rear from attacks by the disgruntled populace in the eastern part of the continent.

Last but not least, popular uprisings in the region—as was demonstrated during the crises in 1956, 1968, and again in 1980-81—are detrimental to the Soviet efforts in pursuit of East-West détente. And, conversely, stable Eastern European governments, as in Poland in the early 1970s, and in more recent years in Hungary or the GDR, by cultivating their own diplomatic channels to the West, could be of assistance to the USSR in promoting this goal. And Yugoslavia's non-aligned policy could be useful to the Soviet Union as a bridge to the Third World—if only by making Communism in those areas more credible.

In contrast to the early post-war years, moreover, Eastern Europe is increasingly less of an asset, and has become more of an economic liability, to the USSR.[7] The Soviet Union has been exporting raw materials and energy to the various countries in the region at favourable prices, thus foregoing more profitable opportunities for trading with the West. Even when after 1974, following the dramatic world oil price increases, the Soviet Union raised the price of its oil exports to Eastern Europe, they still stayed below world levels. In 1980 the aggregate Soviet subsidies to the six WTO countries amounted to $17.5 billion.[8] These are partially offset by the low prices of some of the Eastern Europeans' exports to the USSR, but since their manufactures are often of a poor quality which would not be acceptable in the western markets, the transactions are still profitable to them.*

The USSR has apparently been willing to pay this economic price to protect its military and political position in Eastern Europe. It probably regards the subsidies as a substitute for additional defence costs, especially since the WTO states naturally contribute to the alliance's military expenditures too. Soviet economic aid, moreover, by mitigating their economic hardships, enhances the political stability

---

* This situation was well illustrated by a Polish economist: in 1981 Poland spent some $50 million on the purchase of western equipment for the ships exported to the USSR, and it also sold coal to the Soviet Union at prices lower than those which would have been received from the West, its loss amounting to approximately $250 million; in the same year, however, Poland paid $1.2 billion for Soviet oil, while similar purchases from the West would have cost it $2.2 billion—Poland's net gain being some $700 million. Aleksander Bochenski, *Gwalt i perswazja* (Panstwowy Instytut Wydawniczy: Warsaw 1983), pp. 203-4.

of the various Communist states in the region. Significantly, at the time of the acute political crises there—such as the one in Czechoslovakia in 1968, or in Poland in 1976 and again in 1980—Soviet aid was stepped up to bail out the local Communist regimes. And, conversely, the USSR's economic assistance has been used to reward the most pliable Eastern European states, and to penalize the least reliable ones—with Bulgaria having been the chief per capita recipient of Soviet aid, while Romania has received virtually nil.[9]

Soviet assistance is further offset by the participation of some Eastern European countries (Romania being a conspicuous exception) in the joint projects run under the aegis of the CMEA, which require them to make considerable investments in the USSR. The states from the region also contribute substantial aid to the Third World countries aligned to the Communist bloc, such as Cuba, Vietnam, Ethiopia or Angola. Gearing the Eastern European economies to the Soviet Union has an additional major disadvantage to them in that it tends to perpetuate their inefficiency. The structural reforms which in the short-run could be painful, but in the long-run would be the only viable way out of their present economic impasse—and would also open them more to the world economy—are impeded.

Should the USSR undertake decentralization of its own economic system, it would become easier for the Eastern European countries to proceed with their own economic experimentation.[*] Short of systemic changes, however, the WTO member states have little choice but to continue to rely on Soviet aid. Without it they could be thrown into deep economic recession. The Polish economic catastrophe—which, moreover, complicated the implementation of some CMEA plans as a whole—could be replicated in some other countries. Recently, in view of their heavy indebtedness to the West, not only Romania, but even Yugoslavia, have been turning more to the USSR in their foreign trade. And during the visit of General Jaruzelski to Moscow in May 1984 Polish-Soviet economic ties were visibly tightened.

In the 1970s the burden of the USSR's aid to Eastern Europe was eased by its relative prosperity, assisted by favourable world prices for its exports, especially gold and oil; but in the 1980s the Soviet economy has been under greater strain. Moscow evidently is still willing to pay the economic price for perpetuating its political influence in the region, but it would undoubtedly like to keep the subsidies as

---

[*] And, in turn, as both Brezhnev and Andropov observed, economic experiments in Eastern Europe could be useful to the USSR as test cases for its own economic directions.

low as possible. The problem may become more acute if the economic conditions in the USSR continue to deteriorate. Polycentrism, then, may be helpful to the Soviet Union in reducing the costs of its economic aid to Eastern Europe. The more independent countries, as the case of Romania illustrates, may try to rely more on their own resources or to turn for assistance to the West.

*   *   *

Yet, if permitted to grow unchecked, polycentrism may also pose dangers to Moscow's dominant position in the region. At one time or another it may merge with local nationalisms or/and democratic traditions, in challenging Soviet political influence in the various Eastern European countries or/and the Soviet type of Communism—even to the point of striving for restoration of complete independence and democracy along the lines of the geopolitical-optimistic scenario. It is through a series of such confrontations, by leaps and bounds rather than through some systematic arrangements, that the limits of polycentrism in the area have been determined.

At each confrontation the loyalties of the new class have been tested. These have oscillated between two opposing sentiments. On the one hand apprehension about losing their privileges has led many Communists, even if it meant siding with the Soviet Union against their own compatriots, to uphold the status quo; on the other hand their surrogate nationalism tends to become transformed into a real one, pushing some of them, even when it has been prejudicial to their special social status, into joining the struggle for national emancipation. In such circumstances the behaviour of the satellite political parties has been particularly symptomatic—with some segments of them defending the surrogate democracy, and others trying to transform the bogus coalitions into more genuine ones.

In Yugoslavia, Poland in 1956, Albania and Romania, the new class dilemma has been eased by the fact that Communism was there to stay anyway, and, therefore, greater independence from Moscow did not threaten its privileged position. This has contributed to greater internal unity, and has helped these nations to attain their national goals. In contrast, in Hungary and Czechoslovakia and Poland in 1981, where the pressures for external independence merged with aspirations for internal democratization, the cleavages within the new class have been sharper, weakening the internal cohesion of these nations and making the attainment of their external objectives more difficult.

At the times of crisis, of course, a crucial political role has been played by the Communist rulers. They have had to stay at the helm by reconciling the conflicting Soviet and local interests. Straddling the line between the two, however, has not always been easy, and leaning too far, either in one direction or the other, has often been fatal. Identifying too closely with popular demands led to the defeats of Imre Nagy and Alexander Dubcek; but opposing them to the point of provoking a major outburst led to the fall of Matyas Rakosi, Antonin Novotny, Wladyslaw Gomulka in 1970, and Edward Gierek. And conversely, the subtle counterposing of external and internal pressures: curbing the domestic opposition by exploiting its fear of the Soviet intervention, and at the same time expanding the scope of freedom from Moscow by threatening the USSR with the spectre of massive resistance, has enhanced the local rulers' authority. Playing such a political game has been difficult but Josip Tito, Enver Hoxha, Gomulka in 1956, and Gheorghe Gheorghiu-Dej all have played it with consumate skill and won.[*]

The settlement of each confrontation, thus, could be either retrogressive or progressive. In Czechoslovakia under the Husak regime political conditions in the country have deteriorated beyond what they were during the late years of Novotny's rule. Yugoslavia, however, managed to consolidate both its external and internal freedom and has maintained them even beyond Tito's death in 1980; while the Hoxha regime in Albania has retained its independence in foreign policy and a free, although distinctly heavy, hand at home. Romania has preserved its autonomy in external affairs, but in recent years its domestic tensions have been mounting.

Any specific settlement, moreover, need not be permanent. Janos Kadar, who initially was regarded as a traitor of the revolution in 1956 and relied heavily on repression, has gained substantial popular support in Hungary since introducing popular reforms in the 1960s. And, conversely, Gomulka, who after winning considerable internal autonomy for Poland in 1956 became virtually a national hero, went down in disgrace after adopting retrogressive policies which culminated in the workers' rebellion in 1970. Gierek, who at first tried to avoid his predecessor's autocratic style, eventually fell into the same trap and was overthrown by another workers' upheaval in 1980.[10]

---

[*] Using the background of the local Communist leaders as an indication of how they are going to behave at a critical moment, however, may be misleading. Tito, Nagy and Dubcek, who had strong personal ties with the Soviet Union, all turned against it; while Gomulka, Kadar and Husak, whose political careers had been in the Communist ranks at home, eventually all turned out to be strong Moscow supporters.

The lessons from Eastern European history were not heeded by "Solidarity". The cardinal error of the Polish opposition in 1981 (in contrast to 1956) was their alienation of both the Communist leadership and most of the new class. Gierek's successor, Stanislaw Kania, at first tried to steer a middle course, but soon lost control over the course of events. In the spring of 1981 there emerged a considerable ferment in the Communist ranks and the new leadership elected (in a truly democratic fashion) at the party congress in July emphasized its commitment to "socialist renewal".[11] By pressing for changes going beyond the Communist system, especially at its own congress early in the fall, however, "Solidarity" alienated its potential allies among the new class. Feeling threatened in its position, the party apparat firmly turned against "Solidarity's" radical programme. Kania was replaced as the party leader by General Wojciech Jaruzelski and the army stayed loyal to its commander.* In December martial law was introduced and "Solidarity" was suppressed.[12]

In 1980-81 there was a genuine possibility of a compromise in Poland—similar, although expanded, to that of 1956. It could have involved, in addition to acceptance of private farming and a strong position for the Catholic church, the existence of genuinely free (although strictly confined to the socio-economic sphere) trade unions, greater respect for human rights and intellectual freedoms, and an enhanced role for the local government and the parliament.[13] The opportunity to attain those liberties, however, was forfeited by "Solidarity's going too far and too fast.

*   *   *

---

* Jaruzelski's personal background is unusual for a Communist leader. On the one hand he joined the Polish army in the USSR during the war and took part in its campaigns on the eastern front, and, then, as a young officer he participated in the suppression of the anti-Communist partisans and in 1947 became a Communist party member. He rose through the ranks during the Stalinist years, attaining the rank of General at 33. In the various military posts which he subsequently occupied: the head of the political administration of the armed forces; chief of staff; deputy, and, finally, minister of defence, he must have maintained close ties with the Soviet military establishment, and, presumably, enjoyed its confidence. On the other hand, however, he comes from a family of minor gentry with strong patriotic traditions and before the war attended an exclusive Catholic boarding school; moreover, he found himself in the Soviet Union not by his choice, but after being deported there. His personal demeanor, significantly remains that of a member of the pre-war intelligentsia.[12] For a profile of Jaruzelski see: Andrzej Korbonski, "The Dilemmas of Civil-Military Relations in Poland: 1945-1981", *Armed Forces and Society* (No. 1, Vol. 8, Fall 1981. p. 7); and Adam Bromke, *Poland, The Protracted Crisis*, (Mosaic: Oakville, 1983, pp. 217-8).

Polycentrism, then, reflects in each Eastern European country a subtle equilibrium between the Soviet and national objectives—with the Communist rulers, and to some extent the new class, acting as power brokers. The political situation in the region, within limits is imposed by the geopolitical realities, has been fluid. The changes have been taking place, at times even simultaneously, in opposite directions: towards greater freedom of individual countries from Moscow and vice versa. Observing the trend in the past forty years, however, some generalizations could be attempted.

Expanding upon Seton-Watson's model by including Eastern Europe's experiences prior to 1945 (as Schöpflin suggests) as well as those after 1949, and further adding two preliminary and two supplementary stages, the options before the different countries have historically been as follows:

Preliminary stages		old fashioned despotism
		right wing dictatorship
	0	democracy without Communist participation
	1	a genuine coalition with the Communists' participation
Seton-Watson's model	2	a bogus coalition led by the Communists
	3	Communist monopoly of power
Supplementary stages		sovietization
		annexation into the USSR

In this continuum at present only Finland and Greece have democratic governments, although Greece in the 1970s was ruled by the military. In contrast the Baltic countries have been incorporated into the USSR, while Bulgaria comes closest to sovietization (although had the attempted military coup in that country in 1965 succeeded, the situation could have been different). In the mid-1970s rumours even circulated that Bulgaria was considering becoming a Soviet republic.[14] It is doubtful, however, if there was much substance to these reports. Incorporating Eastern Europe into the USSR would have transformed the international disputes between the various peoples in the region and Moscow into domestic concerns—thus changing completely the nature of Soviet internal politics. If anything the USSR has been careful to shelter itself from Eastern European political and cultural influence; in fact, it controls its contacts with the different peoples in the area almost as carefully as it controls those with the West.

East Germany and Czechoslovakia, with the satellite non-Communist parties tolerated, fit neatly into the bogus coalition situation. Hungary, with its fairly broad participation of non-party people in the administration, and Poland, with its acceptance of the small Catholic opposition since 1956, both are a little closer towards the genuine coalition.[15] Combinations of Communism and old political traditions, however, has also produced some strange hybrids. The Communist system in Romania has absorbed some features of right wing dictatorship;[*] and the one in Albania, behind its militant revolutionary rhetoric, is basically an old fashioned despotism.

Yugoslavia is the most difficult country to classify in these categories. It has evolved a novel political system, largely *sui generis*, genuinely Communist and at the same time relatively free. It was theoretically elaborated in 1978 by Edvard Kardelj, who rejected both multiparty democracy and a tight communist one-party rule. He believed that in Yugoslavia the party's monopoly of power should continue to be effectively tempered by the workers' self-management system.[16] As such the Yugoslav model has a lot to offer for the other Eastern European Communist states on the road of polycentrism. The idea of workers' participation in the management of the economy, which was picked up by the Polish labourers in 1956,[17] and again during the "Solidarity" period, is one of them.

In recent years, however, internal problems have been mounting in Yugoslavia. No new leader has emerged to replace Tito, (Kardelj, who would have been Tito's natural successor, having died even before him). The economic situation has been aggravated by a highly decentralized federal system and the nationalism displayed by the various republics. In 1981 unemployment was 15 to 20 per cent; but, while in Slovenia it was only 2 per cent in Kosovo it was as high as 40 per cent. And in the spring of that year strife flared up between the Albanians and the Serbs in Kosovo. The workers' self-government has been largely stifled by political bureaucracy.[18] To cope with these problems, towards the end of 1983 a Communist party veteran, Mijalko Todorovic, called for the democratization of political life in the country. He advocated transforming the Socialist Alliance into a genuine democratic

---

[*] Yugoslav observers have also compared the period of martial law in Poland (pointing to Jaruzelski's atypical social origin) to Marshal Pilsudski's inter-war dictatorship. (*Start*, Zagreb, September 25, 1982).

mass movement and the activization of the trade unions as an organization truly representing the workers' interests.[19]

Yugoslavia, then, finds itself at a crossroads. It can follow the path of democratic reforms which would bring it closer—but without requiring the abandonment of its non-aligned course in foreign policy—to Western Europe. Or it can let the tensions build up, which may ultimately lead to a takeover by the army (with its officer corps largely dominated by the Serbs and the Montenegrins). The latter course—as in Poland—may also lead to a revival of the Communist party orthodoxy, and may even offer an opportunity for the USSR to try to meddle once again in Yugoslav internal affairs.

In Albania, Hoxha, who has ruled the country with an iron hand since World War II, is aged and reportedly ill. The mysterious death of his top lieutenant Mehmed Shehu in January 1982, and the purges in the party and the government which followed this event, suggest that the struggle for Hoxha's mantle has already begun. At present his most likely successor seems to be a Politbureau member in charge of ideology, Ramiz Alia. He has strongly emphasized his commitment to continuing a militantly Communist line at home and an isolationist course in foreign policy. Albania's attitude towards the two superpowers, he asserted in 1982, "... has been and remains clear-cut, unwavering and consistent. We do not have, nor will we ever maintain any relations of whatever kind of nature with them."[20] Yet, once Hoxha is actually gone the situation may change. In view of the Albanians' fierce nationalism and the country's favourable geographical position, the chances that it will return to the Soviet bloc are remote. If it is to abandon its present isolationist stance, then, more likely the country will move closer to the West, this being coupled with at least somewhat greater moderation in its domestic policies.

In Romania mounting economic and social problems may culminate in popular unrest. Paradoxically, worker rebellion against Ceausescu's stern rule might be welcomed by the Soviets, who clearly cherish no warm feelings towards the Romanian leader. They may hope that the internal difficulties will bring Romania back into closer association with the Communist bloc. Even in Hungary the economic and political problems might bring about internal instability. Kadar, now in his seventies, may not be around for long, and the defeatist memories of the abortive revolution in 1956, and the ensuing terror, are no longer there among the younger generation. This may result—as in Poland—in a more assertive stand by the Hungarian workers. The problem of succession in the top party posts will also arise before the end of the 1980s in Bulgaria, East Germany and Czechoslovakia, since Todor Zhivkov, Erich Honecker and Gustav Husak are all in their seventies too.

In Poland military rule was fairly lenient. Terror was used discriminately and there were relatively few casualties. In mid-1983, although the Communist government retained broad emergency powers, martial law was finally lifted. Most of the political prisoners, except a handful of the KPN, the KOR and the most radical "Solidarity" leaders, as well as those who continued in the underground and were caught, have been released. The church has retained its privileged position and in the spring of 1983 John Paul II visited the country. The government does not conceal from the people the grave economic situation the country is in. Even the economic reforms which were adopted in 1982 have been slowed down, due to the need to cope with immediate problems. General Jaruzelski, however, has repeatedly stressed that they will ultimately be implemented and that socialist democracy will be expanded as well. In his speech to the party conference on March 18, 1984, he once again underlined his commitment to "socialist renewal" and emphasized that the party will not abandon this course.[21] The Polish leader, thus, seems to be genuinely trying to follow in the footsteps of Kadar rather than Husak.

In some respects Jaruzelski is in a better political position than Kadar was in 1956. Kadar was installed in power in Budapest by the Soviets, and, at least at first, he was clearly regarded as their puppet; while Jaruzelski assumed the positions of both Premier and First Secretary of the Communist party in a legitimate fashion (indeed, at the party congress in July he received the highest number of votes in what were quite genuine elections to the Politbureau). Even more importantly, by suppressing "Solidarity" on his own, paradoxically, he has retained some scope of manoeuvre vis-à-vis Moscow.* And also, because repressions in Poland in 1981-83 were not as severe as in Hungary in the late 1950s, an eventual national reconciliation should be easier to bring about in the Polish case.

An important step in that direction was the declaration in July 1984—on the fortieth anniversary of People's Poland—of a general amnesty for all the political prisoners. Altogether 652 persons, including the KOR and the KPN leaders as well as several top "Solidarity" activists who had been in detention since 1981, and the rest being

---

*This situation was highlighted in a report prepared in the spring of 1982 by a highly respected group of Polish intellectuals: "the fact," it observed, "that in the last instance the USSR did not let itself be drawn into a direct intervention in Poland indicates that some possibilities for the future still exist." Zespol redakcyjny Komitetu "Doswiadczenie i przyszlosc", *Polska wobec stanu wojennego*, Raport czwarty (Typed, Warsaw, April 7, 1982, p. 32).

people who had been apprehended for participation in the underground, were unconditionally released. At the same time a new chance was given to those underground members who would like to step forward and resume normal life. They were all, however, sternly warned that should they resume political activities they would be re-arrested. Yet, there is little doubt that the general amnesty, by cleaning the slate, has contributed to easing tensions in the country. Thus, it must not be ruled out that the upheaval in Poland will ultimately have the same delayed effects as in Hungary, and that some time in the next few years a broad domestic relaxation in the country will take place.

Yet, there are also serious obstacles ahead for Jaruzelski in trying to emulate Kadar. Many Poles in their anger at his suppression of "Solidarity" profoundly hate the Polish Communist leader. In their eyes the fact that General Jaruzelski acted on his own (although at the same time, and not with much consistency, they recognize that he was pushed in this direction by the Russians), makes him an even worse traitor than Kadar was. They adamantly refuse, therefore, to cooperate with him. At the same time Jaruzelski has been prodded to follow "normalization" in the country along the Czechoslovak, rather than Hungarian, lines by the conservatives in the Polish Communist party, and, last but not least by the Soviet ideologues.

*   *   *

The Soviets have once again resorted to the ideological weapon to indicate their displeasure with the continued (even though greatly moderated in comparison with the "Solidarity" period), reformist trends in Poland, and to pressure General Jaruzelski to contain them. In May 1983 in *Novoye Vremia* Andrei Ryzhov carried out a major attack under an ominous title: "When Bearings Are Lost," against *Polityka*.[22] He selected 13 articles, all of which appeared in the Polish weekly after the introduction of martial law, to present its systematic deviation from what the Soviet author views as the true Marxism-Leninism. The paper, he wrote, though carrying on its front page the slogan " 'Workers of All Lands Unite!' considers it quite normal to propound views alien to proletarian, Communist ideology".[23]

Among the writers whom Ryzhov denounced by name were Professor Jerzy Wiatr, as well as his predecessor as director of the Institute of Marxism-Leninism, Andrzej Werblan, and Krzysztof Teodor Toeplitz. The former editor-in-chief of *Polityka*, and subsequently Deputy Premier in the Jaruzelski government, Mieczyslaw Rakowski, was not named, but his involvement was made clear by an allusion to an interview which he granted in 1982 to Oriana Fallaci. "Solidarity lost," wrote the Soviet author. "But the idea 'pluralism instead of socialism' did not go underground with the extremists from 'Solidarity'." In late 1982 Krzysztof Toeplitz even argued that "Poland must be proclaimed for all time a country of ideological and political pluralism. This was not a slip of the tongue in the heat of polemics. It was an ideological and political position."[24] As an illustration of what *Polityka* means by pluralism, Ryzhov pointed to an article by Professor Wiatr in which he said that the views published in the underground "Solidarity" press should be taken into account in the political debates in Poland. Wiatr's position, asserted his Soviet accuser, grants "... the counter-revolutionary elements in hiding in the underground... the right to participate in the debates over the meaning of People's Poland."[25]

Special Ryzhov wrath was directed at the authors who attributed the difficulties in implementing the Polish model of socialism to Soviet influence. A well-known economist, Michal Dobroczynski, was singled out for sharp criticism for observing that the roots of the Polish economic difficulties could be traced to the imitating of the Soviet system in 1948. And the deputy editor-in-chief of *Polityka*, Daniel Passent, was scolded for claiming that Poland's "... geopolitical position compels [the country] to follow some sort of socialist path of development and that every revolt against this status quo is doomed to defeat. The only way out of the given situation is submission to fate, to the system, while at the same time seeking to improve it, to work for reform in general". Indeed, Passent was accused by Ryzhov of hoping that the Yalta system, like the Versailles system in the interwar period, will ultimately disintegrate, offering Poland greater scope of manoeuvre in the international sphere.[26]

"Socialism cannot be built," conceded the Soviet author, "without scrupulously taking into account the national specific features. That is an axiom. However, many *Polityka* articles press on the reader the magic formula of 'true', 'Polish', 'unprecedented' socialism. The underlying idea is that the projected 'land of ideological and political pluralism' is destined to be primarily a 'bridge', a 'mediator' between East and West." And in concluding Ryzhov resorted to the 19th century Russian derogatory phrase about the Poles as traitors to the idea of Panslavism: "Latins among the Slavs and Slavs among the Latins. This is the notion which the Western political scientists invariably operate with", he exclaimed.[27]

Ryzhov's article was followed in the December 1983 issue of *Voprosy Filosofii* by a brutal personal attack against Professor Wiatr by another Soviet theoretician, A. V. Kuznetzov.[28] The director of the Polish Institute of Marxism-Leninism was denounced for his shallow grasp of Communist ideology and outright sympathizing with "Solidarity". His "nihilistic criticism" of various aspects of the situation in Poland ". . . could not help aggravating the tensions in the country."[29]

There are two theories, observed Kuznetzov, explaining the reasons for the Polish crisis in 1980-81. The first points to the errors of political leadership, ". . . its departing from the scientific Marxism-Leninism approach to solving the problems of socialist construction. . . neglecting ideological work [and] tolerating anti-socialist attitudes even among members of the party."[30] The other theory claims that the ". . . causes of the crisis are inherent in the very nature of socialism. . . which allegedly does not allow the manifestations of national traditions."[31] Wiatr, according to Kuznetzov, subscribes to the latter view. The Polish Marxist theoretician attributed the crisis of 1980-81 to the ". . . abandonment of the Polish model of socialism at the end of the 1940s", rather than seeing its roots correctly ". . . in the exploiting of the party and state leadership errors by the counterrevolution."[32] Indeed, in suggesting that it was the imposition of an outside, i.e. the Soviet, model of socialism upon Poland, Wiatr shifted the blame for the Polish crisis to the USSR.

The Polish model of socialism which Wiatr advocated would take into account such traditional Polish values as respect for the rule of law, democratic freedoms, and the fact that the overwhelming majority of the Poles are Catholics. According to Kuznetzov, however, Wiatr did not distinguish between the values adhered to by the "fighters for the liquidation of capitalism", and those espoused by the "leaders of the reactionary regimes."[33] As a result the Polish scholar ignored the leading political role of the Communist party and even proposed that it should share power with the Catholic church and "Solidarity."

Kuznetzov decisively rejected Wiatr's account of Polish post-war history. In 1948, the Soviet theoretician argued, when the Communist and socialist parties merged, a great step forward was taken by Poland, paving the way for its many future accomplishments: "Modern industry was developed, unemployment was liquidated and the surplus of population was removed from the villages. Millions of people were given well-paid jobs. In 36 years the living conditions steadily improved in both the cities and the villages. Towns grew and the level of culture was enhanced. Broad masses participated in the socio-political life of the country. A new generation of well trained specialists emerged. The country assumed a respected position in the world."[34] *"The true history of socialism in Poland"*, asserted Kuznetzov, *"is altogether different from that presented by Wiatr.* It is not the history of a passing from one crisis into another, but *a history of general advance and gradual development of the Polish society on the road of socialist construction."*[35] Thus, the true reasons for the crisis in 1980-81 must not be attributed to this course of events. While it is correct to observe that the initial causes for it were the errors of the Polish Communist leadership, "... *the main responsibility and blame for transforming this situation into a sharp and prolonged conflict and its spread throughout the entire country, rests with the counter-revolutionary forces."*[36]

At the roots of the Polish mistakes, continued Kuznetzov, was the erroneous understanding of the concept of different roads. While formulating this idea Lenin emphasized the common characteristics of the transition to socialism binding upon all countries. There "cannot exist the general without the specific, nor the specific without the general, yet with *the dominance, in appropriate proportions, of the general over the specific."* Thus, concluded the Soviet theoretician, Wiatr, under the façade of defending the Polish road to socialism, in effect neglected "... *the basic, common features of development which are binding upon all countries building socialism."*[37]

Ryzhov's attack was ignored by the Polish Communists.* Indeed, *Polityka* responded to it in a sarcastic fashion by pointing out his numerous distortions of the quotations used against the writers in that weekly.[38] Kuznetzov's article, however, was more serious. It contained an implicit warning to General Jaruzelski to abstain from carrying out any major reforms in Poland. Even though the *Voprosy Filosofii* did not resort to any over criticism of the Polish leader, and in fact quoted him approvingly several times, nevertheless it clearly implied a lack of a proper vigilance on his part. After all, Professor Wiatr assumed the directorship of the Institute of Marxism-Leninism parallel to Jaruzelski's ascendancy to the leadership of the Polish Communist party. Kuznetzov made the implications of this fact clear by quoting in a pharisaic fashion Jaruzelski himself: "As Comrade Jaruzelski pointed out... great is the responsibility of those who have been entrusted with elaborating the theory, strategy and practice of the party."[39]

---

* The weekly *Tu i teraz* was not singled out, like *Polityka*, for direct criticism; instead, the Soviets have registered their displeasure by denying this Polish paper distribution rights in the USSR.

The invoking of the perennial doctrine of different roads and, once again, giving it a narrow interpretation, clearly indicated Moscow's continued anxiety over the developments in Poland. It also testified that while *de facto* the Soviet leaders have accepted the existence of polycentrism in Eastern Europe, they still want to circumscribe its scope as much as possible. In this respect the Kremlin's attitude has not changed much from Stalin to Chernenko. Neither, however, have the attitudes of the Poles undergone any major transformation. The merger of the Warsaw Institute of Marxism-Leninism with the Higher Party School of Social Sciences towards the end of 1983 provided a convenient excuse for the removal of Professor Wiatr from his post. But he has not revised his views. In an article in the government paper *Rzeczpospolita* early in 1984, in which he expressed sorrow about Andropov's death, Wiatr indirectly, but unmistakeably, answered his Soviet critics. "We shall always appreciate," he wrote, "Andropov's understanding and support for the efforts of the Polish state under Communist leadership, for socialist renewal. . .".[40] And at the conference on the future of Europe held in Warsaw in June 1984 he reasserted that it is necessary to blend ". . . the universal features of socialism with Polish traditions."[41] Apparently what the Soviet Marxist theoreticians tend to forget is that in 1984—unlike in 1948—an ideological reprimand no longer suffices to bring the foreign Communists into line.

Russia's cultural advance in Europe historically has been checked by the Finns in the north, the Romanians in the south and the Poles in the centre. For despite their common Slavic roots the Russian and the Polish national traditions are quite different.* The Soviet Union has reached a *modus vivendi* with Finland and Romania, and sooner or later it will have to seek some viable accommodation with Poland too.

---

* The reasons it was easier for the Russians to arrive at an agreement with the Finns and the Romanians than with the Poles are inherent not only in Poland's more important strategic position, but also, paradoxically, in the fact that the Poles are Slavs. While their ethnic, linguistic and cultural differences with the Finns and the Romanians are readily apparent, the Russians—as Ryzhov's contemptuous statement about the Poles wanting to be Latins testifies—do not understand the Poles' commitment to western values and tend to view them as traitors to Panslavism.

NOTES

1. For the role of China in Albania's and Romania's quarrels with Moscow see Chapter V.

2. J. T., "Realpolitik—The Politics of Realities", *Res Publica* Warsaw, Samizdat publication, No. 7, 1980), in Abraham Brumberg (ed.) *Poland, Genesis of a Revolution*, (Vintage: New York, 1983), pp. 266-7.

3. For the upheaval in East Germany in 1953 see: Stefan Brandt, *The East German Rising, 17th June 1953* (Thames & Hudson: London, 1955).

4. Sergei Kovalov, *Pravda*, September 25, 1968.

5. Adam Bromke, *Poland, The Protracted Crisis* (Mosaic: Oakville, 1983). pp. 216, 222.

6. For the changes in Poland in 1956 see: Konrad Syrop, *Spring in October, The Story of the Polish Revolution 1956* (Weidenfeld and Nicolson: London 1957); Flora Lewis, *A Case History of Hope, The Story of Poland's Peaceful Revolutions* (Doubleday: New York, 1958); and Adam Bromke, *Poland's Politics, Idealism vs. Realism* (Harvard: Cambridge, 1967), Ch. 6.

7. See: Paul Maurer, "Has Eastern Europe Become a Liability to the Soviet Union?", in Charles Gati (ed.), *The International Politics of Eastern Europe* (Praeger: New York, 1976).

8. Jan Vanous, "East European Economic Slowdown", *Problems of Communism*, No. 4, Vol., July-August 1982. p. 6.

9. Andrzej Korbonski, "Eastern Europe" in Robert F. Byrnes (ed.), *After Brezhnev, Sources of Soviet Conduct in the 1980s* (Indiana: Bloomington, 1983). p. 331.

10. For the Gomulka and the early Gierek years in Poland see: Richard Hiscocks, *Poland, Bridge for the Abyss? An Interpretation of Developments in Post-War Poland* (Oxford, 1963); Hansjakob Stehle, *The Independent Satellite, Society and Politics in Poland Since 1945* (Praeger: New York, 1965); Nicholas Bethel, *Gomulka, His Poland, His Communism* (Holt, Rinehart and Winston: New York, 1969); Adam Bromke and John W. Strong (eds.), *Gierek's Poland* (Praeger: New York, 1973); M. K. Dziewanowski, *The Communist Party of Poland* (Harvard: Cambridge, 1976, Second edition); R. F. Leslie, *The History of Poland since 1963* (Cambridge, 1980), Chs. 14-16.

11. For an account of the congress by one of its participants see: Jerzy J. Wiatr, "Poland's Party Politics: An Extraordinary Congress of 1981", *Canadian Journal of Political Science*, no. 4, Vol. XIV, December 1981.

12. For the events in Poland in 1980-81 see: William F. Robinson (ed.), *August 1980, the Strikes in Poland* (Radio Free Europe: Munich, 1980); Neal Ascherson, *The Polish August* (Penguin: London, 1981); Daniel Singer, *The Road to Gdansk* (Monthly Review Press: New York, 1981); Jean Poter, *The Promise of Solidarity* (Praeger: New York, 1981); Steven Steen, *The Poles* (MacMillan; New York, 1982); Lawrence Weschler, *Solidarity, Poland in the Season of Its Passion* (Simon and Schuster: New York, 1982); Timothy Garton Ash, *The Polish Revolution* (Cape: London, 1983); and Bromke, "The Protracted Crisis", *op. cit.*, Chs. XVI-XIX.

13. For a western view of what would have been feasible changes in Poland in 1981 see: Charles Gati, "Polish Futures, Western Options", *Foreign Affairs*, No. 2, Vol. 61, Winter 1982-83. Pp. 296-7; and Richard Spielman, "Crisis in Poland" *Foreign Policy*, No. 49, Winter 1982/83. p. 34.

14. Teresa Rakowska-Harmstone, " 'Socialist Internationalism' and Eastern Europe—A New Stage", *Survey*, No. 1, Vol. 22, Winter 1976. p. 52.

15. For the best account of political institutions and processes in Eastern Europe see: H. Gordon Skilling, *The Governments of Communist East Europe* (Crowell: New York, 1966); and Ghita Ionescu, *The Politics of the European Communist States* (Weidenfeld and Nicolson: London, 1967).

16. Edvard Kardelj,*Pravci Razvoja Politickog Sistema Socijalistickog Samoupravljanja* (Komunist: Belgrade, 1978).

17. Adam Bromke, "Workers' Councils in Poland", *Slavonic and East European Studies*, No. 4, Vol. I, Winter 1956-57.

18. For post-Tito Yugoslavia see: Slobodan Stankovic, *The End of the Tito Era* (Hoover Institution: Berkeley, 1981); and Fred Singleton and Bernard Carter, *The Economy of Yugoslavia* (Croon Helm: London 1982).

19. *RAD Background Report*, Radio Free Europe, November 7, 1983. p. 3.

20. Louis Zanga, "Grooming Ramiz Alia by Hoxha", *RAD Background Report*, Radio Free Europe, September 30, 1982. p. 3.

21. *Trybuna Ludu*, March 19, 1984.

22. Andrei Ryzhov, "When Bearings Are Lost, Scanning the Warsaw Weekly Polityka", *New Times*, No. 19, May 1983.

23. *Ibid.*, p. 19.

24. *Ibid.*, p. 18.

25. *Ibid.*, p. 19.

26. *Ibid.*, p. 20.

27. *Ibid.*

28. A. V. Kuznetzov, "O teoreticheskikch kontseptsiiach odnogo polskovo politologa", *Voprosy Filosofii*, No. 12, December, 1983.

29. *Ibid.*, p. 39.

30. *Ibid.*, p. 27.

31. *Ibid.*, p. 28.

32. *Ibid.*, p. 29.

33. *Ibid.*, p. 32.

34. *Ibid.*, p. 34.

35. *Ibid.*, p. 30. Italics by the author.

36. *Ibid.*, p. 31. Italics by the author.

37. *Ibid.*, p. 33. Italics by the author.

38. "Andriej Ryzhow o 'Polityce' ", *Polityka*, May 14, 1983.

39. Kuznetzov, *op. cit.*, p. 38.

40. "Zal spoleczenstwa polskiego: sprawy bezpieczenstwa i pokoju byly jego nadrzednym celem", *Rzeczpospolita*, February 11, 1984.

41. Jerzy J. Wiatr, "Poland's Place in Europe", a paper delivered at the Conference on Human and Social Developments in Europe within an Inter-regional and Global Perspective", Warsaw, June 4-8, 1984. (Mimeographed). p. 11.

IV
THE LIMITS OF POLYCENTRISM

There are various ways by which the USSR can restrict the spread of polycentrism in Eastern Europe. These, however, are not just linked to the Communist ideology, but are rather inherent in the geopolitical model. So far, popular explosions in the region have been confined to a single country at a time. The closest that ferment in one country came to spreading into another was in 1956, when the upheava inl Poland served as a spark for the revolution in Hungary (it is also possible that, in turn, the explosion in Hungary influenced the Soviets' adopting of a moderate stance in the Polish crisis). In 1968 the Prague Spring contributed to the students' rebellion in Poland (their slogan was: "We want a Polish Dubcek") and made Gomulka support the Soviets in suppression of Czechoslovakia. In turn, in 1978 the Polish Committee for the Defence of the Workers tried to establish cooperation with the "Charter 77" movement (their representatives actually held a meeting in the Tatra mountains), though little came of it.

Conceivably, if all the Eastern European peoples were to rise at once, they could shake off the Soviet domination. It would be next to impossible for the 270 million Soviets (even if all of them supported the effort wholeheartedly) to suppress over 100 million East Europeans. The very heterogeneity of the region, however, militates against such a development. It helps Moscow to apply the principle *divide et impera* by exploiting the animosities among various Eastern European nations. The problem, of course, is not new; it was already very much in evidence during the inter-war period. At that time Poland under Marshal Pilsudski toyed with the idea of organizing a bloc of nations— all the way from Finland to Greece—which would provide an effective countervailing force to both Germany and Russia.[1] The plan, however, ran into several obstacles. First, Eastern Europe was torn apart by internal rivalries and territorial disputes, including those between Poland and Czechoslovakia as well as Lithuania. Second, the danger to them posed by Nazi Germany and Soviet Russia was perceived in different ways by the different countries in the region, ; indeed, some of them looked for support from either one or another of the two neighbouring great powers to foster their local ambitions. Finally, there was a suspicion, particularly evident in Czechoslovakia, that

Poland's objective in promoting regional cooperation was to enhance its own international position.[*]

Persistent animosities in the area have been consciously exploited by the USSR. Lingering fear of Germany among the Poles has been effectively used to win them over—including many non-Communists—to support Poland's alliance with the Soviet Union.[†] Whenever Yugoslav-Soviet relations deteriorate, Bulgaria is there, ready to assert its territorial claims to Macedonia, and the suppression of the Magyars in Transylvania continues to be a sore point in Hungarian-Romanian relations. Even the Czech-Slovak dispute surfaced anew in 1968, and the participation of the Slovaks in the "Charter 77" movement has been noticeably smaller than that of the Czechs.

There is another, even more perverse way in which the national diversities could help the USSR to perpetuate its dominant position in Eastern Europe. By allowing more freedom to some nations in the region, it could aggravate the cleavages among them. Those peoples who enjoy, even if only temporarily, a privileged position in the Communist bloc (occupying "the freest barracks in the prison", as the Hungarian saying has it) are unlikely to risk it by helping the others. Yugoslavia watched with evident sympathy the strivings for greater freedom of both the Hungarians in 1956 and the Czechs and Slovaks in 1968, and yet, when these failed, nevertheless resumed proper, and even, on occasion, warm relations with Moscow. The Poles and the Hungarians have been historically linked by close bonds of friendship, yet they each failed to come to the other's assistance at a time of need: in 1956 the Poles were unwilling to risk their newly won, modest political liberties by starting an uprising of their own to aid the Budapest freedom fighters; and in 1980 the Hungarians did not want to prejudice their economic comforts by supporting "Solidarity."

Indeed, the differences among various East European nations can also produce opposite effects: the envy of the less privileged peoples

---

[*] An echo of the apprehension about Poland's intentions was still present in the early 1980s. Reportedly one of the reasons why "Solidarity" produced little response in Lithuania was that some of its leaders openly espoused the Pilsudskiite ideolgy. (V. Stanley Vardys, "Polish Echoes in the Baltic", *Problems of Communism*, Vol. XXXII, No. 4, July-August 1983. pp. 31-32).

[†] There were even rumours in Poland in 1981 that as a reprisal for the rise of "Solidarity", after a joint Soviet-East German invasion, Moscow would return the Polish western territories to the GDR. These, however, can be easily discounted, as the USSR would clearly be the last country likely to re-open the issue of boundaries in Europe determined by the outcome of World War II.

can be effectively channelled to aggravate the traditional national animosities against the more fortunate ones. In 1968 there were some Poles who, under the influence of the Communist propaganda, genuinely believed that Czechoslovakia not only tried to extricate itself from Soviet domination, but was ready to enter into an alliance with West Germany. All members of the Warsaw Pact (except Romania) participated in suppressing Czechoslovakia in 1968; and, had it been necessary, no doubt they would have also followed the Soviet lead in invading Poland in 1981.

Time, moreover, is not all on the Eastern Europeans' side. During their forty years domination of the region the Soviets have come to understand the region better. They have realized that the crude Stalinist ways of imposing uniformity by brute force do not work, and can even be counter-productive. Instead the modern Kremlin leaders are more likely to use more subtle methods: to employ the different leverages of power which they command in the area, and especially, to exploit its heterogeneity—the internal as well as external cleavages—to their advantage. Their patient, but persistent handling of the recent Polish crisis—which enabled them to achieve their political aims without being directly involved militarily—has clearly demonstrated a degree of growing political sophistication on their part.[*] In the wake of the Polish upheaval the USSR is likely to try to consolidate its control over Eastern Europe to prevent an outbreak of similar events somewhere else.

The prospect of the Eastern Europeans' early attainment of their goals of independence and democracy, thus, does not appear promising. The peoples in the region cannot do it by themselves; and if the Western democracies could not, or did not want to, help at the end of World War II when they commanded decisive military superiority over the USSR, they are even less likely to try it today when the Soviet Union has reached nuclear parity. And an internal collapse of the USSR is not in the cards wither; while its internal evolution is painfully slow.

In those circumstances polycentrism, with all its shortcomings, is still the most sensible course for the Eastern Europeans to follow. In the short-run it offers them the best chance of averting sovietization. The fact that their strivings for democracy and independence—along the lines followed by Finland—was cut short by the introduction of

---

[*] There is a parallel between the handling of dissent in Eastern Europe and in the USSR itself. Since the 1970s, in suppressing its own dissidents the Soviet government has relied less on force and has often used other, but no less effective, methods of intimidation.

martial law was undoubtedly a bitter blow to the Poles, but it will not be helpful to them if they were to adopt an "all or nothing" attitude. They will be better off if the Jaruzelski regime succeeds in steering towards a freer Communist system, such as exists in Hungary, rather than towards a more oppressive one, as in Czechoslovakia.

In the long run polycentrism, by bringing Communism more into line with local needs, also reduces the dangers of new, potentially costly, popular explosions. As such it provides the Eastern European nations with the best available opportunity to survive until the optimistic part of the geopolitical model, namely, the attainment of their independence, eventually comes true.

*   *   *

The most important force in Eastern Europe committed to the preservation of traditional values has been organized religion. The position of the different churches has reflected the heterogeneity of the region and it has fluctuated with the ups and downs in the Communist regimes' policies. During the late 1940s and the early 1950s there was religious persecution everywhere; subsequently, however, relations between the various churches and the Communist governments have gradually improved. Only in Albania has a militantly anti-religous course continued, and during the "ideological and cultural revolution" in 1967 all of the churches and mosques were closed there. Albania has been declared "the first atheistic state in the world" and religious practices have been ruthlessly suppressed.

The only predominantly Protestant country in the region (excluding Estonia and Latvia) has been East Germany, where the Protestants represent some 47 per cent of the total population and the Catholics about 8 per cent.[2] Relations between the Communist government and the Evangelical churches improved in the 1960s, but the Ulbricht regime still insisted upon their complete separation from their counterparts in the FRG. After the separate Synod of Evangelical Churches in the GDR was established in 1969, and especially under the Honecker regime since 1971, religious tolerance has been further expanded. The churches have been permitted to carry on their spiritual functions relatively freely. Their leaders have addressed themselves, at times quite candidly, to various social and even political issues (such as peace), and Christians have been admitted into minor administrative positions.

In the predominantly Orthodox areas in the Balkans a reconciliation between Communism and religion has also been gradually ad-

vanced. Although through systematic atheistic propaganda its following has been substantially reduced, the Bulgarian Orthodox Church
has been tolerated, and in 1969 Zhivkov even praised its patriotic
tradition.[3] At present the Church has about 6 million followers representing about two thirds of the total population.[4] Atheism has
also made substantial inroads in Yugoslavia, but since the 1950s the
Serbian Orthodox Church (and since its separation in 1967 the Macedonian Orthodox Church also), have not been molested in any major
way by the Communist authorities, and they have jointly retained
some 9 million followers. In Yugoslavia there are also approximately
4 million Muslims, and in Bulgaria some 700,000 (mostly Turks).[5]

In Romania the forcible union of the Transylvanian Uniate Church
with the Orthodox Church in 1948 brought it closer to the Communist
government (although it left a scar on Bucharest's relations with the
Vatican). Subsequently, the merger of the Communist and nationalist
ideology in the 1960s has helped the Orthodox church in that country to assume an even more favourable position. The Church remains
under strict government control, but conducting its spiritual functions
has not been hindered, and in 1969 Ceausescu commended it for
contributing to progress in the country.[6] It has at present some 16
million followers.[7]

The major religious force in Eastern Europe has been Catholicism.
It has occupied a dominant position in Croatia, Slovenia, Hungary,
Czechoslovakia and Poland, with its influence stretching into Lithuania and Eastern Galicia (where the forcible merger of the Ukrainian
Greek Catholic Church with the Russian Orthodox Church in 1946
has been a particularly painful problem). The authority of the Catholic
church in the various countries in the region, however, has been
weakened by its cooperation in the inter-war period with the right-
wing regimes, and, particularly in Croatia and Slovakia, with the German occupant during World War II. In the early post-war years Moscow
was especially fearful of the Catholic church in Eastern Europe's preserving its ties with Rome, where Pope Pius XII followed a strongly
anti-Communist line. In 1949 the Holy Office issued a decree forbid-
ding the Catholics, under a threat of excommunication, to cooperate
in any way with the Communists; and the Communist regimes responded with outright persecution of the Catholics. In 1955 some
5,000 priests in the region—including the Primates of Hungary and
Poland—were imprisoned.[8]

With Khrushchev's ascendancy to power and the pontificate of
John XXIII, the frigid relations between Moscow and the Vatican

thawed. Some Lithuanian prelates were permitted to attend the Vatican Council and in 1963 Archbishop Josyf Slipyj of the Ukrainian Uniate Church was released from imprisonment and allowed to go to Rome. In exchange the Vatican abandoned its view of Communism as a "temporary evil" and in a symbolic gesture John XXIII granted a private audience to Khrushchev's son-in-law Alexei Adzhubei. The Vatican's "Eastern policy" was launched, aimed to improve its relations with the Communist governments in Eastern Europe (with Franz Cardinal König of Vienna acting as its main emissary), and it was continued during Paul VI's pontificate.

These Vatican efforts produced at least some tangible effects. After Cardinal Mindszenty left the American Embassy (where he sought refuge in 1956) for the West, an agreement regulating the status of the Catholic church in Hungary was signed in 1964, and a similar accord was concluded with Yugoslavia in 1966. In Czechoslovakia there was an expansion of religious freedom during the Prague Spring, though subsequently the Husak regime resumed efforts at restraining the influence of the Catholic church. An effort was even made to split the clergy from the Vatican by luring some of them into the government-sponsored group "Pacem in Terris". Nevertheless the church's influence especially among the Slovaks, has remained substantial.

*   *   *

The Catholic church in Poland has been in a stronger position than anywhere else in Eastern Europe. With the loss of the Ukrainians and the Byelorussians in the east, the fleeing or expulsion of the Germans in the west, and the extermination of the Jews by the Nazis, by the end of World War II the Polish state emerged remarkably homogeneous. There were no longer any significant minority groups in the country, and the overwhelming majority of the Poles were Catholics. It is estimated that at that time (at least nominally) 98 per cent of the Polish population was Catholic, with corresponding figures for Hungary being 74 per cent and Czechoslovakia 69 per cent. Out of some 50 million Catholics in the region, 23 million, i.e. almost half of the total, were located in Poland.[9]

The Catholic church has traditionally occupied a prominent role in Polish political life. In the 17th and 18th centuries, when the Polish kings were elected, during the interregnum between the death of one monarch and the coronation of the next, the Catholic Primate ruled as regent. And during the partitions era—faced with Protestant Prussia to the west and Orthodox Russia to the east—Polish nationalism became closely identified with Catholicism. The Polish church, moreover, was not tainted by collaboration with the Germans during World War II; if anything, it was submitted to brutal persecution by the Nazi occupants. Some 1,200 priests perished in the concentration camps—one of them being Father Maksymilian Kolbe who was later canonized for sacrificing his life for another inmate.[10] And the new Polish Primate appointed in 1948, Archbishop Stefan Wyszynski, during the war was an underground chaplain.

Wyszynski, who was elevated to Cardinal in 1953, became not only a spiritual leader, but, in fact, until his death in 1981, was also a towering political figure on the Polish scene. With the Poles withholding popular legitimacy from the Communist regime, he was widely regarded as their true national leader: an *interrex* linking the past independent Polish state to that which was to arise in the future.*

Indeed, Wyszynski never betrayed the ultimate geopolitical goal of Poland's independence—he steadfastly upheld not only the principle of religious freedom, but also respect for human rights and national sovereignty. In 1953 this led to his detainment by the Communist government, but following the popular upheaval in 1956 he was triumphantly restored to his office.[11]

Cardinal Wyszynski, however, was a political realist. He was aware that for the time being Poland's complete independence was unattainable; so, without compromising his long-range political goals, he strove to expand the country's internal autonomy along the lines of the polycentrism model. In 1950 he signed an agreement with the Communist government in which he strove to achieve a *modus vivendi* (and which, incidentally, was not enthusiastically welcomed by the Vatican) between the church and the state. In 1956, and again in 1970—when the danger of Soviet intervention in Poland arose—he appealed to the Poles for calm and restraint. After the rise of "Solidarity" he took the same stand and, early in 1981, shortly before he died, he was alarmed by its manifest extremist tendencies.[12]

Meanwhile, however, the Polish Primate relentlessly continued to press for concessions from the Communist government. He won substantial gains for the church in 1956, and again after the ouster of Gomulka in 1970. And in the wake of the workers' upheaval in 1976, the faltering Gierek regime openly turned to the Catholic church for

---

*In a conversation with this author in the spring of 1980 when the subject of his political role as a *de facto* regent of the country came up, he neither confirmed nor denied it, thus indicating that he was aware of such an image being deeply ingrained in the minds of the Poles.

support. Wyszynski responded to the Communist leader's overtures favourably—contacts between the Catholic Episcopate and the Communist government (including regular meetings between the Primate and the First Secretary) were intensified. Poland's relations with the Vatican improved too—in 1979 Gierek was received by Pope Paul VI. In exchange, not only was the church's position consolidated, but Wyszynski used his influence to moderate the government's political course as well. He effectively blocked the unpopular constitutional amendments in 1975, defended the persecuted workers in 1976, and, subsequently, threw a protective shield over the activities of the democratic opposition.

Under Wyszynski's leadership the Catholic church in Poland went from strength to strength. Despite repeated atheistic drives by the Communist party, and ignoring the secularizing impact of social modernization, the Poles' commitment to their faith remained very strong. About 50 per cent of the population continued regularly to attend Sunday masses and over 90 per cent of the dead were buried with Catholic rites.[13] The election of the Arbishop of Cracow, Karol Cardinal Wojtyla, to the Throne of Saint Peter in 1978 strengthened the traditional bonds of the Poles to their church even further. The next year, when John Paul II went on a pilgrimage to his homeland, millions of the faithful greeted him everywhere. His visit served not only to deepen the Poles' religious sentiments, but also to enhance their national pride. As such, no doubt, it contributed to the popular upheaval in 1980.

The new Primate of Poland, Jozef Cardinal Glemp (who, incidentally, was Wyszynski's personal choice for that position), has continued the line of his predecessor. In the fall of 1981 he desperately tried to forestall the ultimate clash between "Solidarity" and the Communist government by arranging a meeting, in which he also took part, between General Wojciech Jaruzelski and Lech Walesa. When martial law was imposed Glemp deplored the curtailment of personal freedoms and called for its early lifting. The church also undertook extensive assistance to the victims of persecution. At the same time the Polish Primate appealed to his compatriots for reason and prudence and warned them against carrying out futile, and possibly costly, all-out resistance. He unmistakeably distanced himself from the underground "Solidarity", and cautioned the priests not to get involved in the clandestine activity.[14]

In exchange, the church was spared from any reprisals under martial law. Freedom of religious services has been fully upheld, and even the broadcasting of Sunday mass on the state radio, which was initiated during the "Solidarity" period, has been resumed. Construction of new church buildings—in fact over 600 of them—throughout the country has not been interrupted. Catholic publications have proliferated; Contacts between the Episcopate and the Communist officials—including regular meetings between Cardinal Glemp and General Jaruzelski—have stayed close, and proper relations between the Vatican and Poland have been preserved.

In June 1983 John Paul II for the second time arrived in his native land.[15] In his statements there the Pontiff adopted the same carefully measured centrist position that characterized the Polish church under the leadership of Cardinal Wyszynski. Symbolically the Pope proceeded directly from the airport to the Warsaw Cathedral, where his former mentor is buried, to pray at his grave. At his side was Primate Glemp.*

In his homilies in Poland John Paul II did not refrain from criticizing the Polish Communist regime. He forcefully restated the need not only for religious freedom, but also for respect of human rights. He minced no words in expressing his sympathy with the victims of political persecution. He paid tribute to the workers' rebellion in 1980-81, and called for a renewed dialogue between the Communist government and the Polish people. Indeed, he strongly underlined the right of the Polish nation to independent existence, free from any foreign interference. At the same time, however, the Pope scrupulously avoided giving the impression that he sided with the political opposition. Referring to international issues he pointedly reminded his compatriots of the limitations inherent in Poland's difficult geographical position. And, although he insisted upon meeting with Walesa, it was a quiet affair, basically a private audience granted by the Pontiff to a devout Catholic.

During his stay in Poland the Pope held two private meetings with General Jaruzelski. No doubt, John Paul II used these occasions to urge the Polish leader to lift martial law, as indeed happened a month later. Among the subjects discussed was an infusion—under the aegis of the Catholic church—of western aid to private farmers in Poland. The Pontiff may have also used Jaruzelski as a sounding board for his plans to improve relations between the Vatican and the Communist

---

* In an interview granted to Wyszynski's biographer, well-known Polish Catholic historian Andrzej Micewski, Cardinal Glemp explicitly underlined his predecessor's influence in shaping the political views of the Pope: "Even though he is today the head of the Universal Church, the Holy Father's sensitivity to the national and the church issues belongs to the school of Primate Wyszynski". ("Zadania Kosciola w Polsce", *Niedziela*, March 4, 1984).

states, including possibly the USSR. In any case, in the next few months the Holy See launched a broad, and well-coordinated, effort to expand the dialogue with several Communist governments in Eastern Europe.

In the fall Cardinal Glemp went on an official visit (the first such visit by a Polish Primate since 1938) to Hungary. He was not only received in Hungary's ecclesiastical capital in Eszterdom by Laszlo Cardinal Lekai, but upon his arrival in Budapest was greeted by the Communist officials responsible for state-church relations. At the same time there were reports about a possible visit by Cardinal Glemp to the USSR. If this were to come true, he would be the official guest of Patriarch Pimen at the seat of the Russian Orthodox Church in Zagorsk, but on his way he would visit the newly appointed Latvian cardinal, Julijans Vaivods, in Riga.

Primate Glemp also would like to visit Lithuania, where a strong Catholic community in 1984 celebrated the 500th anniversary of its patron, Saint Casimir. Until recently the Catholics in Lithuania were subjected to persecution and some of them even went underground to practice their religion.[16] In 1982, however, an agreement was reached between Moscow and the Vatican to appoint two Lithuanian bishops and, after having been prevented for a quarter of a century, Bishop Vincentas Sladkevicius was permitted to take charge of his diocese in Kaisiadorys. When the Holy Father visited Warsaw a delegation of the Lithuanian Catholics was there. His desire to visit Lithuania is well known, so Cardinal Glemp's mission may be to pave the way for a future papal visit. This would bring John Paul II into direct contact not only with Patriarch Pimen, but also with the Soviet head of the state.

Since the 1970s there has been a marked revival of religion in general, but of Catholicism in particular, in Eastern Europe. It has been manifested both in a growing participation in the traditional liturgical rites and in a turning to Christianity for a spiritual guidance and deeper sense in life. Various developments have contributed to this. The apparent decline of the Communist ideology and the widespread social malaise, has made the Eastern Europeans, and especially the younger ones, search for new values. In Hungary small prayer and meditation groups, known as "basic communities", have spread. In Czechoslovakia, including the traditionally more secularized Bohemia, some unofficial Catholic groups have sprung up and religious *samisdat* publications have appeared. And in Poland the "Oases"—the high-school students' Catholic movement—claimed in 1984 some 200,000 members.[17]

The elevation of a Pole to the Throne of Saint Peter, no doubt, has inspired the Catholics in Eastern Europe, and especially those in the Slavic lands, with great pride and stronger attachment to their religion. In Czechoslovakia the church has taken a bolder stand. After the Vatican's ban on priests' participating in political organizations, many of them left the "Pacem in Terris" organization. And Frantisek Cardinal Tomasek has formally invited John Paul II to visit the country. Despite all the historical animosities among the Catholic, Orthodox, and the traditional as well as non-Protestant churches, there is also a feeling of community among them. They know that when they are faced with an atheistic state, the expansion of religious rights is of benefit to them all. It is rather significant that some of the junior Orthodox clergy in Romania have advocated the restoration of the Uniate Church. The Pope's vigorous defence of human rights, moreover, has won him respect among many non-believers.

* * *

Meanwhile, the Vatican's diplomacy has succeeded in improving relations with some other Communist states in Eastern Europe. In Yugoslavia in the 1970s the Communist government blamed the Catholic church for inflaming Croat nationalism and championing the human rights' movement. Yet, Belgrade's relations with the Vatican were preserved and in 1983 Msgr. Franjo Kuharic was elevated to Cardinal. In Czechoslovakia until recently the Husak regime submitted the Catholic church to strict restraints. After John Paul II ascended to the papacy the Communist authorities accused him of trying to transform the position of the Czechoslovak church along the Polish pattern. And after 1980 all contacts between the Vatican and Prague were suspended, and Frantisek Cardinal Tomasek was not allowed to go to Poland during the papal visit there. At the end of 1983, however, John Paul II received the Czechoslovak Foreign Minister, Bohuslav Chnoupek, and the contacts were restored. On the agenda of negotiations are appointments of bishops in the 10 out of 13 dioceses which are still vacant as well as the plans for a visit by John Paul II—in response to Primate Tomasek's invitation—to Czechoslovakia.

Simultaneously, the Vatican's relations with Romania also improved. The position of the relatively small Catholic community in that country has been complicated by the fact that it is largely composed of two national minorities: the Hungarians and the Germans; it has, therefore, been exposed to double chicaneries: religious as well as nationalistic. Nevertheless, the Vatican's special envoy, Archbishop Luigi Poggi, has been a regular visitor to Bucharest and in June 1984 an official Romanian government representative (the first since World War II) visited the Holy See. At the same time the Romanian Catholics were permitted to go on a pilgrimage to Rome to participate in the beatification of the first Romanian saint, a Capuchine monk from the end of the 16th century, Jeremiah of Wallachia. Even in Bulgaria the restrictions on the miniscule Catholic community has been eased. Since Archbishop Poggi's visit to Sofia in September 1983 their religious rights have been upheld.*

The Vatican's peace initiative, thus, has been a vigorous and a broad effort, and it has evoked a positive, and apparently well-orchestrated, response from the Communist side. In 1983 all over Eastern Europe (except in still militantly atheistic Albania) relations between the Catholic church and the Communist governments have undergone substantial improvement. And the Pope's efforts may, although just may, still be crowned by his visiting the USSR. In May 1984 the Pontiff did not conceal his desire to go to Moscow. The Russians, he said, "are also my brothers. They are Slavs, like the Poles, and these two nations understand each other's tongue".[18]

In seeking an improvement in relations with the Communist states, John Paul II has also been concerned over deteriorating East-West relations and the danger of a nuclear conflict. In the fall of 1983 he wrote both to the American and to the Soviet leaders urging them to persist in arms control talks. He reiterated his appeal early in 1984 in an essay entitled, "Peace is Born in Man's Heart", in which he argued that it is a man who kills, be it by a sword or a rocket. "The horrible risk inherent in the weapons of mass destruction must lead to evolving the process of cooperation and disarmament which will make war practically impossible".[19] Apparently as Supreme Pontiff he feels strongly that it is his duty to protect mankind from a nuclear disaster. And with its large following in the East and the West the Catholic church is in a unique position to try to bridge the gap between them.

In his belief that a coming together of the East and the West is possible John Paul II may well have been influenced by his Polish experience. For, after all, under the Communist system, as his own elevation to the Throne of Saint Peter eloquently testified, the

---

* The Bulgarian government's positive reaction might have been prompted by its desire to counter the widespread western reports (which may not have been without at least some substance) about its involvement in the abortive assassination of John Paul II in 1981).

Catholic church has done very well. Yet, there is certainly more to the Vatican's diplomacy than just the current Pope's personal beliefs. The Catholic church is a repository of historical experience and knows that ideologies come and go, while religion stays. The Communists have already moved a long way from their early, militantly atheistic stance. The Vatican's objective, then, is clearly to accelerate this evolution of Communism by internally humanizing it. On his deathbed Cardinal Wyszynski prophesied a new role for Catholicism in the east.[20]

There are, of course, still many Communists who are adamantly opposed to religion and who resent the growing influence of the Catholic church in their countries. There are also those who approach the rapprochement with the church in a purely Machiavellian fashion—and by developing cooperation with it hope to mitigate, and perhaps even to compromise, its temporal political influence. Yet, there are also some Communist leaders who are prepared to accept the church's new role—along the lines of the de facto recognition of polycentrism—since for various reasons it is advantageous to them too.

First of all the Pope's unequivocal commitment to peace is beyond doubt even in the Communists' eyes. In a period of declining East-West relations the Vatican's diplomacy may be useful in defusing at least some international tensions. John Paul II's balanced denunciation of the curtailment of personal freedom not only in the East, but also in some western countries, as well as his stress on the need for more equitable distribution of global wealth, with its implicit criticism of capitalism—make it easier for the Communists to accept him as a genuine partner in the international dialogue. Some of them even profess to share his humanist values which, they claim, are inherent in the Marxist vision too. Finally, with the Communist ideology on the decline in Eastern Europe, the various governments there may welcome the revival of religious values among their people for purely practical reasons. Commitment to hard work, honesty, and family and social ties may be helpful in overcoming the sloth, corruption and alienation which are widespread in the Communist societies.[*]

In the last instance, however, whether the Communists like it or not there is little they can do about the growing influence of Catholicism

---

[*] A striking example here is offered by the coincidence between the Catholic church's conservative views on family planning and the Ceausescu regime's drive to increase the Romanian population. "Solidarity" bridged these two positions and for both religious and nationalistic reasons advocated greater support for families with many children.

in Eastern Europe. Short of returning to the Stalinist terror there is
no way they can overcome the church. Evidently the Pope, and a Polish one at that, commands many more divisions than Stalin once
used to believe.

The rapprochement between Catholicism, and religion in general,
and Marxism in Eastern Europe will be a drawn-out and tedious process. Philosophically, of course, the two doctrines can never come
together; the best that could be achieved would be an uneasy co-
existence based on mutual tolerance of continuing differences. Psy-
chologically, however, removing the barriers between the Catholics
and the Communists could have far reaching repercussions in the
region. It could enable the church's followers, without abandoning
their ultimate goals, to participate in the existing political system by
trying—along the lines recommended by Cardinal Wyszynski—to
change it from within.

*   *   *

The crisis of 1980-81 forced not only the Communist party, but
also the opposition in Poland, to re-think its strategy. A debate over
the consequences of "Solidarity's" suppression and the future political programme for the Poles has been carried out in the underground
press. A former leader of KOR, Jacek Kuron, took the most adamant
stand. Writing from internment in the spring of 1982, he expressed
the belief that an ultimate showdown between the Communist government and the Polish people is inevitable and, in fact, will take
place shortly. If by nothing else, the new popular explosion will be
brought about by the deteriorating economic conditions and will
lead to the overthrow of the Jaruzelski regime. To prepare for such
an eventuality the underground should evolve a strong, centralized
organization and clearly warn the Communist authorities that, if necessary, ". . . it will not refrain from violence."[21] Kuron recognized
that such a development could lead to a Soviet intervention. But this,
he argued, could be forestalled if the Poles were to reassure the Soviet
leaders that even without the Communist government their security
interests in Poland would be respected.[22]

Other underground "Solidarity" leaders were less sanguine. In contrast to Kuron, a leader of the "Solidarity" Warsaw region, Zbigniew
Bujak, anticipated a prolonged struggle—"trench warfare", as he
labelled it—and favoured, if only to avoid easy detection by the police,
a decentralized form of clandestine activities. He also rejected violence

on the part of the Polish society because it would only provoke more violence by the Communist authorities. And should this fail to pacify the country there would be a Soviet intervention.[23] A member of the "Solidarity" national commission, Wiktor Kulerski, was even more circumspect. He called merely for the development of an "underground society". It would be a popular movement, he explained, ". . . decentralized, informal, composed of independent, loosely connected groups, circles, committees, etc., all of which could enjoy considerable autonomy and freedom of decisions. It would provide regular assistance to persecuted people, assure the circulation of free information and thought, establish a network of social contacts, create educational opportunities, and offer moral and psychological encouragement."[24]

A former leader of the Movement of Young Poland and later a "Solidarity" activist from Gdansk, Aleksander Hall, went even further. He took direct issue with Kuron over the question of Soviet intervention. There is no reason to believe, he wrote, that the USSR would tolerate an overthrow of the Communist regime in Poland. The underground's objective, then, ". . . should not be to remove the Communist party from power, but to compel it to extend concessions to the Polish people. This is not because we love the present government or accept its moral right to rule Poland, but because there is no other way. Anyone who fails to see this is indulging in lunar politics."[25]

In any case Kuron's prediction did not come true. Despite the continued difficult economic conditions there has been no new popular upheaval in Poland. For a while the underground "Solidarity" still claimed to be preparing for a general strike, but its date has been relegated further and further into the future. And after the fiasco of the appeal for massive street demonstrations following the formal dissolution of "Solidarity" in the fall of 1982, even this form of expressing dissatisfaction with the Jaruzelski regime has markedly declined. The clandestine publications still flourish, but the underground leaders have admitted difficulty in recruiting new members.[26] The boycott of the local government elections in June 1984 did not work either.

In January 1984 Hall resigned from "Solidarity". In an article significantly entitled: "The time has come to follow one's own road", he explained the reasons for his decision.[27] He did not repudiate his motives for initially joining the underground. "I believed, and still believe, that after December 13, 1981 it was necessary to undertake the struggle for 'Solidarity' and protest against the imposition of martial law." He also argued that the normalization of the situation by the Jaruzelski regime has failed. "The greatest and most significant demonstration of the Poles' emotions took place during the papal pilgrimage to Poland in June of last year. This was not the behaviour of a defeated, but of a proud, fighting and still hopeful nation."[28] And the existence of the clandestine "Solidarity" helped to maintain the morale of the Polish nation.

But, argued Hall, as time went on, the underground "Solidarity" has largely outlived its usefulness. "The internal logic" of this type of resistance inevitably "pushes it towards spectacular, massive actions... I regard this model of social resistance as not suitable for the present situation.... In my opinion there is no opportunity, and most likely none will occur in the next few years, to bring about a radical change in the situation in Poland... through a general strike or street demonstrations."[29] Furthermore, "the more the underground "Solidarity"... assumes the character of a national-liberation movement, the more difficult will become "Solidarity's" revival as a trade union acting openly in the People's Poland. And, after all, at some future point a new August may occur."[30] The most urgent task ahead for the Poles, concluded Hall, is to evolve a new political programme which, without abandoning the ultimate goal of the country's independence, will serve as a guide to action in the existing conditions. "Everywhere one hears the demands for a programme."[31]

Hall responded to these calls by submitting to the Poles a comprehensive programme for political action of his own. In the fall of 1982 a new *samizdat* quarterly, significantly called: *Polityka polska* (Poland's Politics), made its appearance. Its first issue included a programmatic manifesto, which bore the unmistakable personal imprint of Hall's previous ideas as well as a lengthy analysis of the activities of the Polish democratic opposition in 1976-80 signed by A.H.[32]

Hall's essay in *Polityka polska* is one of the most interesting and profound statements to have emanated from Poland in recent years. It is a comprehensive document dealing with international as well as domestic affairs, and it includes an analysis of the historical background as well as a prescription for the future presenting both the short- and long-range goals for the Polish nation. It is cogently argued— revealing the political maturity of its author—and written in a powerful, at times moving, prose. Yet, at the same time it is a detached, almost a scholarly evaluation of Poland's current circumstances.

The author stresses the urgent need for critically re-examining the events in the past few years. Without detracting from the greatness of the "Solidarity" period, which was marked by the political re-awakening of the entire Polish nation, he also admits to its weaknesses. He rejects the apologetic explanations for "Solidarity's" failure, and, in order to avoid repeating them in the future, he underlines the need for their critical assessment. "Precisely because the struggle goes on", he emphasizes, "we must search for the errors which we committed in the past."

Poland's position in the international sphere is presented in a thoroughly realistic, almost brutal fashion. Various illusions current among the Poles that somehow, for no particular reason, their dependence upon the USSR will ease are demolished one by one. As long as the Yalta system remains in force in Europe, and there is no reason why this should change soon—observes Hall—Poland will remain in the Soviet sphere of influence. The hopes that Moscow would tolerate an overthrow of Communism in Poland, or even a sharing of power between the Communists and the genuine representatives of the Polish nation, are completely unfounded. And there is little that the West—even if it wanted to—can do to change this situation.

In the domestic sphere it is not only the aspirations to overthrow the Communist system by a national uprising or a general strike that are illusory. For the time being, the opportunity for going back to the situation as it was in August 1980 and trying to create at least some social organizations independent of the Communist government, has been lost and is unlikely to arise again in the near future. Even the programme of creating an "underground society" is unrealistic. For it is impossible over the long haul for an entire people to operate clandestinely. The underground endeavours, then, should be confined only to those activities which cannot be conducted openly, particularly to the continuation of the *samizdat* publications and the political education of the Polish society.

In those circumstances, should the Poles abandon their goal of independence and passively submit themselves to their fate as captive people? By no means, asserts the author. They should remain faithful to their ultimate goal of life in freedom and, in the meantime, engage in the activities which will bring this prospect nearer. While admitting that for the time being the Poles cannot regain control over their state, he argues that they should strive to build a "sovereign society". They should avoid exposing themselves to unnecessary losses and concentrate on developing their national strength so that when the right moment comes they will reach for their independence.[*]

The concept of a "sovereign society"—continues Hall—is not novel. It was already developed during the Stalinist period by Cardinal Wyszynski. The Polish Primate recognized that as long as the Yalta system remains in force it will be impossible for Poland to regain its independence. He, therefore, evolved a programme designed not just for the immediate future, but for generations. What he strove to achieve was to develop "... the internal, spiritual sovereignty of the nation. If this could be accomplished the Polish national identity would be saved", and when a suitable opportunity would arise, the Poles "... could once again resume the struggle for their national rights."

Cardinal Wyszynski's national and religious programmes were inseparably linked together. In his teaching he emphasized "... close links between Catholicism and the Polishdom and the intimate links between the Polish and western values and traditions...". Yet, his designs were not only directed at the future; he also encouraged, and in fact often spearheaded, all sorts of social pressures to restrain the Communists' oppressive policies in the realm of religious freedom, as well as in upholding human rights and personal freedoms.

The Polish nation heeded the advice of its Primate. The upheavals in 1956, 1968, 1970 and 1976 were just the flashpoints, but the social pressure upon the Communist government was persistent. Faced with it the Communists retreated. Both the Gomulka and the Gierek regimes offered substantial concessions to the people. Combined with the dissatisfaction over the deteriorating economic situation, the popular pressures culminated in the explosion in 1980-81 and the rise of "Solidarity".

Faced with the new retrogression on the part of the Communist regime after 1981, the Polish people ought to revert to their efforts to build a "sovereign society". "Its essence is the defence and the

---

[*] The concept of avoiding both the costly revolutionary road and concentrating upon building the nation's strength, while waiting for the opportune time to regain independence, is not new in Polish political thought. It was advanced almost in the same terms in 1908 by the National Democratic leader, Roman Dmowski: "While in the past, it was understood that the nation had only two alternatives, either military uprising or complete surrender and reconciliation with the existing conditions... the Polish nation has found a new way, excluding both of these possibilities.... It has grasped the importance of political struggle carried out every day and everywhere; a struggle in which its forces gain in enlighenment and strengthen their morale; a struggle which, even if it does not secure gradual successes, at least protects the nation from constant losses". In Adam Bromke, *Poland's Politics, Idealism vs. Realism* (Harvard: Cambridge, 1967. p. 254).

development of the national community in the context of a non-sovereign, alien state. The nation which is internally sovereign is conscious of its goals, and is consciously shaping its fate. It is a nation of free people in the deepest Christian understanding of freedom. It is a nation faithful to its own historical heritage, cultivating and ready to uphold its own identity. . . ."

"Is this a realistic programme?"—asks Hall. "Certainly it is not an easy task. Yet, it is within the realm of our possibilities"—he answers. In advancing these goals the Polish nation can count on continued support from the Catholic church, whose authority has been additionally strengthened by the fact that there is now a Polish Pope in Rome. In the past few years there have also emerged influential lay moral, social and political elites. Indeed, during the "Solidarity" days social consciousness spread throughout the broad masses. By now ". . . millions of people are aware of their duties towards their country, they share common ideals and are, if necessary, ready to make sacrifices for the sake of their goals."

Concentrating upon the progress of "national sovereignty", however, must not prevent the Poles from trying to attain more immediate political goals by exerting pressures upon the Communist government. At present there is no prospect of a repetition of the situation of 1980, but in the future this may change. Should at one time or another a "new August" occur, its goals should be more clearly defined, and also more realistic than the last time. The Poles should not strive to wrest the state away from the Communists, but in exchange for preserving the existing political system, they should modify it by winning within it tolerance for the autonomy of national life. Social organizations and institutions genuinely independent of the Communist government should be established.

In practical political terms, then, Hall's essay is not far from the ideas advocated on the Communist side by Wiatr, Toeplitz, Reykowski and others. It endorses the polycentric model, but with an important difference. It makes it clear that the goal of the Poles is not just a "new August", but ultimately—this way subscribing also to the geopolitical-optimistic scenario—the restoration of Poland's independent statehood. And should favourable external circumstances develop, the Poles will undoubtedly reach for this goal.

*   *   *

Yet, even if, at one time or another—due to some, as yet unforeseen, international changes—the geopolitical-optimistic scenario is realized and Poland regains its independence, in reality the outcome might not be that much different from an expanded version of polycentrism. For the cloak of history cannot simply be turned back to 1945. Some features of Communism—good as well as bad—will undoubtedly survive. After forty years of existence the Communist system just cannot be eradicated instantly, and democracy and capitalism instituted overnight. The present political and economic institutions, without provoking utter chaos, can be dismembered only gradually. And at least some of the manifold ties with the USSR, notably in the economic sphere, would probably be preserved too.

No less importantly, popular habits developed under Communism, and now deeply ingrained in the Poles' patterns of behaviour, can change only over time. The cultivation of entrepreneurial talents will be a tedious process, and meanwhile the administrative skill of the new class—geared to the old socio-economic structures—will be needed. Likewise, the welfare state mentality of the workers and, above all, their reliance on the government as an easy employer, will endure. Indeed, more likely than not the labourers would insist upon preservation of the basically socialist character of their state. Developing a political culture fitting parliamentary democracy would require time too. And the expansion of viable economic bonds with the West, which occasionally might be quite painful, would also proceed gradually.

Last but not least, it should not be forgotten that despite all their yearnings to rejoin the West, which in their eyes poses such an attractive alternative to Russia, Poland is not just another western nation. Historically, and especially through its close ties with Rome, it belongs more to the West than the East. Yet, it is also a borderland between these two civilizations, and a strong eastern influence is present there too.* The way of life in Warsaw remains somewhere halfway between those of Paris and Moscow. The autocratic style of Gomulka and Gierek was not altogether different from that which had been displayed by Pilsudski and his followers in the inter-war period, although the latter adopted it not at the instigation of their Russian bosses, but of their own volition. And similarly the new class

---

* There is nothing wrong with belonging to both the East and the West: on the contrary it may offer fascinating cultural opportunities. As Kamil Dziewanowski observed it may lead to such challenging paradoxes as the existence side by side of an outstanding school of mathematical logic and the thriving of the theatre of the absurd. (*Poland in the 20th Century*, Columbia: New York, 1977. p. 253).

is not just the product of Communism, but manifests many of the unattractive features which characterized the bureaucracy, both foreign and native, which ran the country during the partitions as well as during its short-lived independence.[34]

Some eastern influence was even evident in the activities of the democratic opposition in the 1970s. The model adopted by its activists was affected not only by the Poles' own conspiratorial traditions, but also by the legacy of the 19th century Russian revolutionary movement with whom the Poles were closely associated.[35] The Polish dissidents' proclivities towards moralism, speculating in utopian terms divorced from all reality, and the inability to compromise, all largely stemmed from this source. In their theoretical writings some of the leaders revealed an affinity to Trotskiism; and the KPN sought its inspiration in the Pilsudskiite ideology, despite its less than impeccable democratic record. Thus, paradoxically, even in their strong anti-Sovietism, the opposition leaders were not free from the Russian influence.

"Solidarity", where the KOR and the KPN activists had significant roles, displayed some eastern influences as well. Its demands for wage increases when the Polish economy was crumbling revealed a strong though convoluted belief in Soviet-like state welfarism. "Solidarity's" organizational structure was basically patterned after that of a Communist party. And the "all or nothing" attitude of its leaders was more typical of the heroic Eastern European revolutionaries than of the pragmatic western trade unionists.

Under the impact of the crisscrossing influences from the West and the East, from their own historical traditions and Soviet Communism, new societies are emerging not only in Poland, but throughout all of Eastern Europe. As Aleksander Gella sagely observed, if they were free to select their own system it would probably be somewhere in the middle between the Yugoslav and the Swedish socialism.[36] The region, then, continues to occupy its historic place as a "transitional zone" in Europe.

NOTES

1. Adam Bromke, *Poland's Politics, Idealism vs. Realism* (Harvard: Cambridge, 1967), p. 41.

2. "Eastern Europe: Toward a "Religious Revival'?", *RAD Background Report*, Radio Free Europe, May 23, 1984, p. 19.

3. Bohdan R. Bociurkiw and John W. Strong, (eds.), *Religion and Atheism in the USSR* (Toronto: 1975), p. 342.

4. RAD Report, *op. cit.*, p. 10.

5. *Ibid.*, pp. 10, 39.

6. Bociurkiw, *op. cit.*, p. 325.

7. RAD Report, *op. cit.*, p. 33.

8. Bociurkiw, *op. cit.*, p. 208.

9. M. K. Dziewanowski, *The Communist Party of Poland* (Harvard: Cambridge, Second Edition, 1976), p. 241.

10. M. K. Dziewanowski, *Poland in the 20th Century* (Columbia: New York, 1977), p. 240.

11. For a comprehensive biography of Cardinal Wyszynski see: Andrzej Micewski, *Kardynal Wyszynski, Prymas i maz stanu* (Edition du dialogue: Paris, 1982).

12. Adam Bromke, *Poland, The Protracted Crisis* (Mosaic: Oakville, 1983). Pp. 178-80.

13. Bociurkiw, *op. cit.*, pp. 245-6.

14. For the role of the church in the "Solidarity" period see: Stefania Szlek-Miller, "Church and Catholic Opposition in the Polish Political System", in Ajit Jain (ed.), *Solidarity, The Origins and Implications of Polish Trade Unions* (Oracle: Baton Rouge, 1983). Pp. 115-148; and Bromke, "The Protracted Crisis", *op. cit.*, pp. 193, 197, 210, 216-7, 237, 245.

15. For this author's personal impression of John Paul II's visit to Poland in 1983 see: Adam Bromke, "The Delicate Dance of Pope and General", *Newsday*, July 1, 1983.

16. V. Stanley Vardys, "Polish Echoes in the Baltic", *Problems of Communism*. No. 4, Vol. XXXII, July-August 1983), pp. 32-3.

17. RAD Report, *op. cit.*, p. 31.

18. *Glos Polski* (Toronto), May 23, 1984.

19. "Pokoj rodzi sie z serca nowego", *Mysl Polska* (London), No. 1, Vol. XLII, January 1984. p. 3.

20. Ks. Bronislaw Piasecki, *Ostatnie dni Prymasa Tysiaclecia* (Dom Polski Jana Pawla II: Rome, 1982). p. 75.

21. Jacek Kuron, "Macie zloty rog", *Tygodnik Mazowsze*, reprinted in *Informacja* (Montreal), No. 5, July 21, 1982, p. 7.

22. Jacek Kuron, "Tezy o wyjsciu z sytuacji bez wyjscia", *Tygodnik Mazowsze*, reprinted in *Trybuna* (London), No. 41/97, 1982, p. 21.

23. Zbigniew Bujak, "Walka pozycyjna", *Tygodnik Mazowsze, Ibid.*, p. 27.

24. Wiktor Kulerski, "Trzecia mozliwosc", *Ibid.*, p. 30.

25. Aleksander Hall, "Polemika z Kuroniem", *Solidarnosc* (Gdansk), *Ibid.*, p. 28.

26. Adam Bromke, "Poland's underground crumbles", *Toronto Star*, August 27, 1983, and "Poland settles into depression", *The Spectator*, June 30, 1984.

27. Aleksandr Hall, "Nadszedl czas isc wlasna droga", *Glos Polski* (Toronto), March 9, 1984.

28. *Ibid.*, March 9, 14, 1984, p. 10.

29. *Ibid.*

30. *Ibid.*, March 14, 1984, p. 10.

31. *Ibid.*, March 9, 1984, p. 10.

32. "Proba spojrzenia"; and "A.H.", "Opozycja demokratyczna: wielkosc i slabosc", *Polityka polska*, No. 1, September-October, 1982. Typed.

33. *Ibid.* For selected excerpts see Appendix II.

34. For the continuity of the old bureaucratic tradition in Eastern Europe and the new class see: Peter F. Sugar, "Continuity and Change in Eastern European Authoritarianism: Autocracy, Fascism, and Communism", *East European Quarterly*, No. 1, Vol. XVIII, Spring, 1984.

35. Bogdan Cywinski, "Rodowody niepokornych". (Biblioteka "Wiezi": Warszawa, 1971).

36. "Poland in the Last Quarter of the Twentieth Century: A Panel Discussion", *Slavic Review*, No. 4, Vol. 34, December 1975, p. 785.

V

EASTERN EUROPE AND THE WORLD

Since the end of World War II the relative significance of Eastern Europe in the international sphere has declined. In the immediate post-war years it was the major theatre of East-West confrontation: it was over the Communisation of the region that the Cold War started, and it was there, in the civil war in Greece, where the first proxy war between the two superpowers was fought. It was, moreover, inseparably linked to the unresolved question of Germany. With the rise of the Third World, and its growing penetration by the USSR, however, the primary attention of the United States has shifted. Eastern Europe, of course, remains an integral part of the balance of power in Europe, and as such still occupies an important place in East-West relations, but in terms of its urgency it has been overshadowed by many other areas in the world.

The Third World countries, except for trade and technical assistance, have no direct stake in Eastern Europe. Despite their commitment to the principle of national self-determination, they are indifferent to the Soviet domination in the area, and in any case there is little they could do about it. Preoccupied with their own problems, they have taken little interest in the recurrent crises there. Among the Eastern European countries only Yugoslavia, as a co-founder of the non-aligned movement, has cultivated relations with the developing countries, although Romania, proclaiming itself a developing country, has in the last decade also made some progress. The other WTO states have focused mainly on maintaining ties with those Asian and African countries which have been close to the USSR. [*]

Japan is far away. It showed some interest in Poland in the late 1930s when that country was courted by Germany to join the Anti-Comintern Pact, and, subsequently, it took exception to the signing of the German-Soviet Pact of 1939 (not because of Poland, but be-

---

[*] In the 1970s the Gierek regime cultivated good relations, evidently to gain easier access to Iranian oil, with the Shah of Iran. Yet, little came of this effort economically, and politically it has proven quite embarrassing to Poland . .

cause it resented the rapprochement between Berlin and Moscow).[*]
Since its return to the international scene in the post-war years, Japan
has been marginally interested in Eastern Europe—only inasmuch as
the USSR could be weakened by the tensions at its western border—
but basically it has been satisfied with the balance of power in Europe being preserved by NATO. The Japanese, of course, would welcome expanding their trade with Eastern Europe, but in the present
state of the economies in the region the prospects for this are poor.

During the Stalinist period the Eastern European states (except
Yugoslavia) maintained little contact with the outside world. They
supported the North against the South in the Korean War—in fact,
the conflict prompted them to accelerate their drive to develop heavy
industry, particularly in armaments. After the Communist revolution
in China in 1949, they also established close ties with that country.
As long as China remained closely aligned to the USSR, and Beijing
dutifully adhered to Moscow's leadership in the Communist bloc,
however, this made little difference in their position.

The first differences between Moscow and Beijing actually developed over events in Eastern Europe. It seems that it was not that the
Chinese were particularly interested in the fate of the Eastern Europeans, but it offered a convenient way for them to demonstrate
their growing independence from the Russians. In 1956 China dis-
creetly supported Poland's strivings to expand its freedom from the
USSR,[1] and it ostentatiously endorsed the Soviet declaration of
October 30 promising more equal relations with the smaller Communist states. Although the Chinese subsequently approved the Soviet
suppression of the Hungarian revolution and abandoned the "let a
hundred flowers bloom" course at home, the Poles and the Yugoslavs
still hoped they would champion the transformation of the Communist bloc into a community of equal partners. At the world Communist conference in Moscow in 1957, however, Mao Zedung strongly
supported Khrushchev's claim to the leadership in the international
Communist ranks.[2] In doing so Mao was clearly striving to assume
the role of kingmaker in the international Communist movement.

With Moscow evidently believing that its leadership should apply
not only to the smaller Communist partners, but to Beijing as well,
the Sino-Soviet dispute flared up anew. Thus, some opportunities

---

[*] The first attempt to draw Japan into Eastern European politics came, in
fact, from the Polish side. During the Russo-Japanese war in 1904, Pilsudski—
then a socialist leader—went to Tokyo to obtain Japanese assistance for an uprising in the Russian-occupied provinces of Poland. He was countered by the
National Democratic leader, Dmowski, who also went to Tokyo and prevailed
with the Japanese not to get involved in such a dubious military venture.

opened up for the Eastern European states. In the geopolitical sense they were marginal. China remained a regional power, considerably weaker than the USSR, and clearly unable to challenge the Soviet military supremacy in Eastern Europe. In this sense only Albania succeeded in exploiting the Sino-Soviet rift much to its advantage. During the 1960s and in the early 1970s, Chinese diplomatic support and economic aid was of considerable help to Tirana in maintaining its independent course from Moscow.[3]

Occasional hopes for China's support were expressed in some other countries. Paradoxically, they came mainly from the ranks of the non-Communist opposition. In 1969 the students in Prague, in their anger and helplessness, shouted at the Russian soldiers: "The Chinese will teach you a lesson." And in the late 1970s similar sentiments were voiced among some groups among the Polish democratic opposition.* Beijing, incidentally, was not above playing up nationalisms in Eastern Europe. In its diatribes against Moscow in the early 1960s it accused the USSR of an outright suppression of the different nations in the region, and even enticingly raised the issue of Soviet territorial annexations there at the end of World War II, but it was careful not to commit itself to any specific action in that part of the world.[4]

More important for Eastern Europe were the effects of the Sino-Soviet split in the ideological realm. Until then, only Yugoslavia had consistently subscribed to the concept of different roads and its example undoubtedly contributed to the upheavals in Poland and Hungary in 1956; but after the abortive Hungarian revolution Belgrade's influence was once again contained, by Moscow—and with Beijing's full support. As long as the two major Communist parties, the Soviet and the Chinese, stood together, the Yugoslavs' separate course had posed no major danger to the unity of the international Communist movement. With the conflict between the USSR and PRC flaring up once more, however, this situation changed.

Beijing's defiant stance vis-à-vis Moscow vindicated polycentrism in the Communist ranks. The Chinese missed few opportunities to denounce the Soviets for pursuing the policy of "great power chauvinism" and "national egoism towards fraternal socialist countries", and of treating the "fraternal parties as pawns on their diplomatic chessboard."[5] After coming to power in 1964 Brezhnev reacted to these

---

* This was particularly evident in the ranks of the KPN, whose leader, Moczulski, may have been inspired here by the example of his idol's, Pilsudski's, mission to Tokyo in 1904.

charges defensively. "It would be wrong", he declared, "to thrust the example of one party and country on the other parties and states. The choice of one or another method of socialist building is the sovereign right of each people."[6] The Soviet efforts to use the international Communist movement to condemn the Chinese line came to naught. The Yugoslavs, the Romanians and even the Poles, as well as many non-ruling parties, would not have it.[7] When the third (following those in 1957 and 1960) world conference of Communist parties gathered in Moscow in 1969 only 75 of 88 invited parties attended, and, moreover, 14 of them did not subscribe to the joint statement. The document contained no condemnation of the CPC and it failed to recognize any special role for the CPSU in the international Communist ranks. Since that time proposals for a new world Communists' meeting have been occasionally floated, but none has been implemented.

The Chinese's own model of militant Communism, especially during the aberrations of the Great Cultural Revolution in the late 1960s, had little appeal to the Eastern Europeans. Only Albania, and to a limited extent Romania, responded to it favourably. In the era of "goulash Communism", all other countries in the region were moving in exactly the opposite direction.* It was the Chinese espousal of the concept of different roads which had the greater impact in Eastern Europe. In 1964 the Gheorghiu-Dej regime shrewdly exploited this occasion to expand Romania's independence from the USSR. By adopting an overtly neutral position in the Sino-Soviet rift, he managed to transform the Romanian-Soviet dispute over the functioning of the CMEA into a more general one, concerning the overall political relations between the two countries. In April 1964 a Romanian party statement, emphasizing the country's right to a different road, declared: "It is the exclusive right of each party to independently work out its political line, its concrete objectives and the ways and means of attaining them, by creatively applying the great truths of Marxism-Leninism. . . . No party has or can have a privileged place, or can impose its line or opinions on other parties. Each party makes its own contribution to the development of the common treasure store of Marxist-Leninist teaching."[8] Gheorghiu-Dej's course was

---

* In Poland in the early 1960s the Chinese course won support from a group of unrepentant Stalinists who opposed Gomulka. One of them, Kazimierz Mijal, went so far as to actually to leave for Albania from where he broadcast appeals to the Polish workers to revert to the true revolutionary course as it was prior to 1956 (sic!). After the Sino-Albanian rift, Milaj left for China where (although still claiming to be the leader of a truly Marxist-Leninist movement in Poland) he lives in obscurity.

continued under Ceausescu, and even though Romania simultaneously proceeded to expand its relations with the West, relations between Bucharest and Beijing stayed close.[9] And Romania did not take part in the suppression by the WTO of the Prague Spring in 1968.

Despite its dislike of the reformist course of the Dubcek government, Beijing came out strongly against the WTO invasion of Czechoslovakia. "The act of naked armed aggression", it declared, "has brought to the full the growing fascist features of the Soviet revisionist renegade clique.... The Soviets claim," it continued "... that this action was taken for the unbreakable solidarity of the 'fraternal countries'.... You do not want really to build any socialist community!" it exclaimed. "What you really want is to found a colonial empire with the Soviet revisionist clique as the overlord...".[10] At the same time China unequivocally repudiated the Brezhnev doctrine and warned the USSR not to intervene in Romania. Significantly, from then on Sino-Yugoslav relations started to improve.

Following the Sino-American rapprochement in 1972, and the death of Mao Zedung in 1976, China's relations with Romania remained close, although in the Sino-Soviet rift Bucharest carefully emphasized its equidistance from both Moscow and Beijing. At the same time China's relations with Yugoslavia continued to improve to the point that after 1977 the leaders of the two parties exchanged regular visits. Beijing's moderate stand vis-à-vis Washington, however, irked Tirana, and with Hoxha vehemently denouncing the Chinese leaders for abandoning true Marxism-Leninism, in 1978 the Sino-Albanian alliance was terminated. The attitude of all other Eastern European states towards China remained lukewarm. They acknowledged Beijing's more moderate course under Deng Xiaoping, but in the dispute between the PRC and the USSR they sided firmly with Moscow.[11]

In a striking contrast to its position over the ferment in Czechoslovakia in 1968, China offered no encouragement to the Poles in their strivings for freedom in 1980. Despite Washington's prodding, Beijing ostentatiously stayed silent during all phases of the Polish crisis. Evidently, the Chinese leaders had no use for the free trade unions. They may have also been motivated by broader international concerns: the aggravation of the dispute with the United States over Taiwan under the Reagan administration, and the desire to improve relations with the USSR which gained momentum in the late stages of Brezhnev's rule and continued under Andropov and Chernenko.

The prospects for a Sino-Soviet rapprochement, if it is to come at all, are at best that it is going to be a drawn-out process. Ideologically, although in recent years their polemics have been toned down, the two Communist parties remain far apart. Moscow, moreover, clearly does not accept Beijing as an equal in the international Communist movement, and any lesser role does not seem to be attractive to China. And China's model of Communism—with the regimentation of its society even more strict than that of the USSR—has little appeal in Eastern Europe. From the Eastern Europeans' point of view—and particularly to the Romanians and the Yugoslavs—China may still play a useful role on the fringes of the international Communist movement in supporting the concept of different roads. But lately, as its attitude towards the events in Poland has demonstrated, Beijing's interest in international Communist affairs has largely waned and its major preoccupation has been with the progress of modernization at home.

Yet, even if at one stage or another Beijing decides to again challenge Moscow's supremacy in Eastern Europe—as it did in the 1960s—it would be mainly rhetorical. The Chinese themselves reocgnize this, for as Zhou Enlai put it to a Yugoslav correspondent in 1971: "distant water cannot quench fires."[12] China is and will remain for quite some time to come merely a regional power. Even in Asia it has been largely contained by the USSR. To the north it is flanked with vastly superior Soviet forces, and to the south it is flanked by Soviet allies: Vietnam and India. It has not been able to uphold the independence of two nearby states: Kampuchea and Afghanistan. There is no reason to believe, thus, that it could exert any meaningful political influence in Eastern Europe.

*   *   *

In the ideological domain, and, from the Eastern Europeans' point of view, more important than the changes in China, has been the movement of several Western European Communist parties in the direction of what has been labeled Eurocommunism. To a large extent this tendency originated in Eastern Europe, and notably in Yugoslavia. In May 1956, shortly before his advancing the idea of polycentrism, the Italian Communist leader, Palmiro Togliatti, visited Yugoslavia and was impressed by its interpretation of the concept of different roads. The process of Communist evolution in Western Europe was interrupted by the Hungarian revolution. All of the Western European Communist parties, including the Italian, approved of its suppression. The Yugoslavs adopted a more sophisticated approach. In a speech in Pula on November 11, 1956, Tito upheld the Hungarians' desire to reform the Communist system, but he disapproved of the attempt to overthrow it, and ultimately concluded, therefore, that the Soviet intervention was necessary.[13]

Despite the fact that the USSR did not like Tito's interpretation of the Hungarian events and Soviet-Yugoslav relations declined once more,[14] contacts between the Yugoslav and the Italian Communists were maintained. The Italian party, moreover, continued to adhere to the idea of polycentrism. At its Congress in 1981, it took the position that in the international Communist movement: "There is not, and there cannot be, a leading party or state. . . what is needed in the present conditions is the greater individuality and full autonomy of each party."[15] This Italian stand met with full approval from the Yugoslavs. Defending the Italians against attacks from other parties, a Yugoslav writer argued: "The criticism of 'polycentrism' stems from dogmatic conceptions of the parties which have not freed themselves as yet from the complex of a 'single vanguard', the 'leading party', etc., and who are apprehensive about the Italian Communists' bold initiative. . . to search for new forms of relations within the Communist movement."[16]

In the mid-1960s the Italian Communists were joined in their support for polycentrism by the then exiled Spanish Communists; and, after the death of Maurice Thorez, although still more cautiously, by the French Communists. Among the more important non-European parties the Japanese moved in the same direction. The evolution of the Eurocommunists coincided with the ferment in Czechoslovakia—both proceeding along the same lines in the search for a Communism more compatible with democratic freedoms. The Western European Communists, then, watched the Prague Spring with interest and sympathy. The suppression of the Czechoslovak "socialism with a human face" by the WTO intervention came as a great shock to them and they all condemned it roundly.

The Eurocommunists continued their opposition to the repressive measures in Czechoslovakia undertaken by the Husak regime in the late 1960s and the early 1970s. They offered encouragement to the exiled Czechoslovak (and also Polish) Communists. This, in turn, inspired hopes on the part of the opposition in Czechoslovakia that the support of the Western European Communists would lead to the alleviation of conditions in the country. In 1976, in an open letter addressed to the Communists and socialists in western Europe, a leading

Czechoslovak refugee, Zdenek Mlynar, pleaded for their help. The aspirations of the Czechoslovaks, he underlined, ". . . are very similar with the tendencies that are increasingly and positively asserting themselves in the European working class movement, especially in the recent political evolution of the Communist parties in Italy, France, Spain, Great Britain, Sweden, Belgium and elsewhere."[17] Mlynar's appeal evoked a sympathetic response among the Eurocommunists, but their protests were to no avail, and the Husak government stayed on course.

The invasion of Czechoslovakia, however, solidified the Eurocommunists' ranks and they also stuck to their guns. At the Conference of the European parties in East Berlin in 1976, acting shoulder to shoulder with the Yugoslavs and the Romanians, they firmly rejected the Soviets' attempts to restore their dominant position in the Communist ranks, and re-affirmed the principle of polycentrism. In the conference's final document there was no condemnation—which had been the original purpose for its convening by the Soviets—of the Chinese Communists. There was also no reference to proletarian internationalism, and, instead, a distinctly polycentric formula of relations among the Communist parties was accepted. The "internationalist, comradely and voluntary cooperation", the document declared, will be developed by "strictly adhering to the principle of equality and sovereign independence of each party, non-interference in the struggle for social change of a progressive nature and for socialism."[18]

Meanwhile, the Eurocommunists continued to moderate their domestic political programmes. They repeatedly professed their commitment to democracy and emphasized that, instead of by revolution, the only way they would come to power would be through parliamentary elections. They also expressed willingness to participate in coalition governments with other parties: in France with the socialists, and in Italy even with the Christian democrats (corresponding to Seton-Watson's stage one).* Once in power the Eurocommunists pledged to uphold the democratic liberties, including freedom of religion and respect for human rights. They also declared their strong support for the Helsinki accords. In foreign policy they supported East-West détente, but did this unconditionally without even

---

*The Italian Communists' proposal to enter into a coalition as junior partners with the Christian democrats—a "historic compromise" as they call it—is particularly interesting for it is the most radical offer yet on the Communists' side towards overcoming their differences with the Catholics. It could be usefully replicated à rebours in Poland, with the Communists remaining as the dominant party and the Catholics occupying some influential posts in the government too (corresponding to the intermediate phase between Seton-Watson's stages one and two).

demanding the withdrawal of their countries from NATO.[19] Indeed, in 1976 the Italian Communist leader, Enrico Berlinguer, bluntly stated that Italy's continued participation in the western alliance could be a useful protective shield against his country's sharing the fate of Czechoslovakia.[20]

The change in their political programmes by the Western European Communist parties, of course, was primarily inspired by their trying to improve their electoral chances at home, and, after many years in opposition, to come to power. Doubts were expressed whether this was not just a tactical manoeuvre on their part, and whether once in government they would not break their promises and follow in the footsteps of the Eastern European parties in perpetuating themselves in power (along Seton-Watson's scenario). Obviously the degree of their commitment to democracy differs—along the polycentric lines—from one party to another; but at least in the case of the Italians and the Spaniards, it seems to be genuine. And in any case the prospects of the Communists coming to power in any Western European country as a dominant party so far appear to be remote; and if they do join governments as junior partners—as, in fact, they did in France in 1981-84—reneging on their promises would not be possible.

During the Polish crisis in 1980-81 all of the major Eurocommunist parties, as well as the trade unions dominated by them, threw their support behind the programme of reforms, and they repeatedly warned the Soviet Union against intervening in Poland. The Yugoslavs shared these positions, and the Romanians, while remaining conspicuously silent about the rise of free trade unions in Poland, also upheld the principle of non-interference in Polish internal affairs. As the Polish crisis advanced and "Solidarity" adopted more adamant positions, however, there was evident concern among the Eurocommunists. The Yugoslav trade unions' delegation to the "Solidarity" Congress disassociated itself from the message issued on this occasion to the workers in the other Communist countries and the leading Yugoslav daily criticized it as "provocative, unnecessary and harmful."[21]

The suppression of "Solidarity" by Polish rather than Soviet forces—touching upon the major ambiguity in their programme—blunted the Eurocommunists' response to it. On the one hand the restricting of human rights under martial law was incompatible with their democratic assertions; on the other hand, however, since this step was taken by the Polish Communists themselves (even though it obviously conformed with the Soviet wishes), it fitted into the concept of internal autonomy of each party. The Eurocommunists' confusion was compounded by their allies in Eastern Europe, the Romanian

Communists, throwing their support firmly behind the Polish military regime, and by the Yugoslavs' taking a more critical approach, while not being outrightly challenging.

The Eurocommunists, then, adopted a middle course, urging their Polish comrades to release the political prisoners, restore personal freedoms and resume the course of internal reforms. The admonishments of the Jaruzelski regime administered by the Italian Communists were stronger than those by the French (despite the fact that at the same time their socialist partners in the government condemned the imposition of martial law in Poland as a Soviet intervention by proxy). Generally, however, the reaction on the part of the Eurocommunists to the forcible suppression of the popular ferment in Poland was not as strong as it had been in the case of Czechoslovakia.

The muted reaction to the Polish events illustrated well the limits of the Eurocommunists' role in Eastern Europe. By espousing a more moderate brand of Marxism-Leninism they can set an example for those Eastern European countries which are attracted to it (and are willing to follow this course even at the risk of Moscow's wrath); but they cannot claim that their model should be universally binding for this would be incompatible with the doctrine of different roads. Yet, the Italian and the French parties (and less so, despite its heroic past, the Spanish), do command a certain influence in Eastern Europe, and, even more importantly, in the USSR. They can serve, thus, as a useful channel for conveying western opinions about the developments in the area, without being dismissed outright as subversives. This way they can occasionally restrict Moscow's heavy hand in Eastern Europe or mitigate the excesses of the local Communist regimes.

The Eurocommunists' bargaining position vis-à-vis the USSR and its allies, however, is weak. After all, they are not in government, but only in opposition in their own countries. And the more they distance themselves from the USSR, in order to win electoral support at home, the less attractive the prospect of their coming to power becomes for the Soviet Union. Participation of the French Communists in the government under Mitterand in no way mitigated that government's antagonism towards the Communist bloc; in fact Franco-Soviet relations under Giscard d'Estaing were distinctly warmer. Likewise, should the Italian Communists join the Christian democrats in a coalition government in Italy, there is no reason to believe that this—as Berlinguer himself admitted—would favourably affect Italian-Soviet relations. The death of Berlinguer in June 1984 was a blow to Eurocommunism, although there is little reason to believe that the Italian party will abandon its own independent course.

The Spanish and other smaller Western European Communist parties which do not even command substantial electoral support in their own countries, are not taken seriously by Moscow. If they cannot be used as pawns, they can be dismissed—as the Soviet contemptuous treatment of the Spanish Communist leader, Santiago Carillo, illustrated. Indeed, its support of the Spanish Communist splinter group suggests that Moscow prefers smaller, but disciplined parties in Western Europe. The Eurocommunists are simply not regarded as equal partners by the Soviet party. Their influence in Eastern Europe, thus, remains restricted. For it is not just ideology, but power which counts in that region.

*   *   *

Only the position taken towards the region by the West, then, is of a major political significance for Eastern Europe. In formulating their policies there the western powers have used both geopolitical and ideological models. Their avowed objective has been the realization of the geopolitical-optimistic scenario, i.e. the attainment of independence by all the Eastern European nations. In reality, however, the West has often looked at the area as a "shatter" zone prone to outside influence, and has tacitly accepted foreign domination there.

A foretaste of this ambiguous western attitude towards Eastern Europe was already evident in the inter-war period. Italy, in fact, tried to carve out a zone of influence for itself around the Adriatic and the Aegean. At the end of World War I it annexed Istria, in 1939 it conquered Albania, in 1940 it attacked Greece, and the next year it tore away Dalmatia from Yugoslavia. With the collapse of the Fascist regime in 1943 Italy's expansionism came to an end, but the dispute with Yugoslavia over Istria continued for another decade. Only in 1954 was a compromise reached with Trieste remaining in Italy, while the surrounding territory was assigned to Yugoslavia.

After World War I, France entered into alliances with several Eastern European states designed to protect, under its leadership, the Versailles system. In 1920 the "Little Entente" composed of Czechoslovakia, Yugoslavia and Romania, was formed, aimed at keeping Hungary and Austria in check; and in 1921 the Franco-Polish alliance, aimed to counter Germany, was concluded. But France's commitment to the preservation of the status quo in Eastern Europe came into question when in 1925 it signed the Locarno Pact, which confirmed Germany's western border,[22] but left open the issue of its eastern boundaries; and in 1938, in fact, France agreed in Munich to the partitioning of Czechoslovakia. The Franco-Polish alliance was reactivated in the spring of 1939, but after Germany's attack against Poland the French did not keep their obligations to come militarily to the Poles' assistance. And with France's defeat at Germany's hands in 1940 its political role in Eastern Europe came to an end.

In the inter-war period Britain had little interest in the region—it was only in 1935 that the British foreign secretary visited Warsaw and Prague for the first time. The British also did not support the French efforts to keep Germany restricted within the Versailles system, for this undermined Britain's traditional role as the holder of the balance between these two continental powers. It acceded both to the Locarno Pact and the Munich agreement; indeed, on the latter occasion the British prime minister strongly disclaimed any interest on the part of his country in Eastern Europe. Britain's attitude changed only in the spring of 1939, when, after Germany occupied Czechoslovakia, the extent of Hitler's aggressive designs became apparent. It offered a unilateral guarantee to Poland and on the eve of World War II the Anglo-Polish alliance was formally concluded.

After the defeat of France Britain afforded haven to the Polish government-in-exile, and, subsequently, to the Czechoslovak, Yugoslav and Greek governments. Early in 1943 Winston Churchill advocated an Anglo-American invasion of Europe through the Balkans which would have anticipated the entry of Soviet armies there, but he dropped this plan when faced with American opposition. In Yugoslavia the British soon switched their support from the Chetniks, loyal to the government-in-exile, to the Communist partisans, who were winning. Only in the case of Greece, which had been traditionally important to Britain in protecting its communication routes through the Mediterranean, did the British intervene directly. In 1944 British troops were used to install a non-Communist government in Athens. Britain continued to support the Greek government against Communist insurrection until 1947 when—no longer being able to afford to continue—it passed this role to the United States.

An independent Eastern Europe was also conceived by some Western European statesmen as a *cordon sanitaire* preventing the spread of Communism throughout the continent. In 1920 the French and the British offered limited military support to Poland in its war with Russia; but the British were opposed to any eastward expansion of the Polish territory beyond purely Polish ethnic lands. The Western European support of Poland, Romania and the Baltic countries against possible Soviet encroachments, however, was not consistent. In the mid-1930s France even tried to expand its alliance with various Eastern European states by including the USSR—which would clearly have given Moscow a dominant political position in the region. Only Czechoslovakia—which had no direct border with the Soviet Union—responded favourably, while the remaining Eastern European states stayed cool to the French plan. The scheme was revived in the spring of 1939 during the military talks by the French and the British with the Soviets, but the signing of the Soviet-German Pact on August 25, 1939 brought it to naught.

During the Soviet-Finnish war of 1939-40 there was considerable sympathy for Finland in France and Britain and tentative plans were even made to come to its assistance, but these were not implemented before the hostilities ended. In 1942 Britain accepted the Soviet annexation of the Baltic countries; and at the Teheran Conference in November 1943 Churchill agreed to the incorporation of the Polish eastern territories (for which Poland was to be compensated in the west at the expense of Germany) into the Soviet Union. At the Yalta Conference in February 1945 the British conceded that the Polish government would be dominated by the Communists, and in July they formally withdrew their recognition from the Polish government-in-exile in London.[23]

Since World War II the Western European countries have played a secondary political role in Eastern Europe. As long as they are effectively protected from the USSR by the United States, they can live with the Soviet domination of the eastern part of the continent. Some of them, of course, have tried to preserve their historical bonds with the Eastern European peoples (Sweden with Finland, or Austria with Hungary), but only in the case of divided Germany has the problem been really acute. Generally, the Western Europeans tend to look upon the Eastern Europeans as their poor, and occasionally even troublesome, cousins, whose sad plight is to be regretted, but is of no major concern.

The United States played an active role in Eastern Europe for the first time at the end of World War I. President Woodrow Wilson's strong commitment to the principle of national self-determination helped the Poles and the Czechs to restore their independent states. But soon the United States returned to the policy of non-involvement in European affairs. In 1939-40 it tacitly accepted the partitioning of the northern part of the region between Nazi Germany and Soviet Russia. With the United States' entry into the war at the end of 1941, however, it soon became apparent that it would be an arbiter of the post-war settlement in Europe. Eduard Benes—mindful of the western betrayal of Czechoslovakia in 1938—strove to come to terms with the USSR. But the leaders of the Polish government-in-exile— Wladyslaw Sikorski, and after his death, Stanislaw Mikolajczyk—sought American assistance in upholding their country's territorial integrity and independence. They made repeated trips to Washington to obtain personal support for their cause from President Franklin D. Roosevelt.[24]

At first the Americans seemed to be adhering to the Wilsonian principle of national self-determination, which was reasserted in the Atlantic Charter of 1941. By refusing to enter into any specific negotiations with the Soviets concerning the region's future, they conveyed the impression that they were ready to uphold its independence. Then, at the Conferences in Teheran and Yalta, Roosevelt, along with Churchill, for all practical intents and purposes accepted the Soviet sphere of influence in Eastern Europe. A "fig leaf" was afforded by provisions that the post-war governments there, while friendly to the Soviet Union, would somehow reflect popular aspirations, but the implementation of these provisions was left to Stalin. When the USSR proceeded with the Communization of Eastern Europe, the United States confined itself to purely verbal protests.

The Eastern Europeans, thus, have had the worst of both worlds. They were encouraged to oppose the Communization of their countries, but without, however, receiving any concrete support from the United States. When Mikolajczyk left for Poland in June 1945 to enter a coalition government with the Communists there, he believed that the western powers would provide him with appropriate diplomatic support. But when he lost the 1947 election—which was rigged by the Communists—the only assistance the Americans afforded him was to remove him out of the country.[25] The double standard which the United States used in its policy towards Eastern Europe—in theory adhering to the optimistic, but in fact subscribing to the pessimistic-geopolitical scenario—were also detrimental to Washington's relations with Moscow. The discrepancy between the words and deeds did not help the Eastern Europeans, while at the same time it aggravated the Soviet's distrust of the Americans. In this way the East-West friction over Eastern Europe, and over Poland in particular, became one of the main reasons for the rise of the Cold War.[*]

---

[*] There is a broad agreement among western scholars over the role of Eastern Europe in bringing about the Cold War. "According to Robert Divine, for example, 'Poland, more than any other issue, gave rise to the Cold War.' Adam Ulam agrees: 'The cold war began just as had World War II, with Poland providing the immediate cause of the conflict.' Admiral Leahy records that the United States' non-recognition of the governments of Rumania, Bulgaria and

The same attitude of moralism cum indifference vis-à-vis Eastern Europe was displayed by the Republicans in the early 1950s.* In the presidential elections of 1952 they—and especially the Secretary of State to be, John Foster Dulles—proclaimed a policy of liberation.[26] Yet, when the crunch came the Eisenhower administration abstained from any concrete steps to assist the Eastern Europeans. The United States passively watched the Soviet suppression of the uprisings in East Germany in 1953 and in Hungary in 1956. And during the second term of the Eisenhower administration the slogan of liberation was quietly shelved.

In the immediate post-war period for all practical intents and purposes the United States showed no major interest in Eastern Europe; apparently from the strategic point of view it considered itself to be sufficiently protected by denying the USSR access to the eastern shore of the Atlantic and the Mediterranean. Thus, in effect, the American policy towards Eastern Europe adhered to the pessimistic geopolitical model.

Hungary at the Potsdam Conference resulted in a 'complete impasse and might have been said to have been the beginning of the cold war between the United States and [the Soviet Union].' Walter La Feber argues that the immediate cause of the split in the wartime alliance was 'the dropping of the iron curtain by the Soviets around Eastern Europe, and the determination of the world's sole atomic power [the United States] to penetrate that curtain.'" (Lynn C. Davis, *The Cold War Begins: Soviet-American Conflict Over Eastern Europe*, Princeton: 1974, p. 3.)

---

* The recurrent American tendency to resort to moralism in Eastern Europe has apparently been inspired by the same belief which in the post-war years made the British law-givers think that democratic institutions could be effectively transplanted into various Commonwealth countries. It stems from the same roots of political idealism—in the case of the United States so deeply embedded in the Wilsonian tradition—which profess that democracy is the inevitable wave of the future in the world.

NOTES

1. See Zbigniew K. Brzezinski, *The Soviet Bloc, Unity and Conflict* (Harvard: Cambridge, 1961), p. 251.

2. For Poland's and Yugoslavia's maneuvering between Moscow and Beijing in 1957 see: Brzezinski, *Ibid.*, Chs. 12-13, *passim*; and Adam Bromke and Milorad Drachkovich, "Poland and Yugoslavia: The Abortive Alliance", *Problems of Communism*, No. 2, Vol. X, March-April, 1961.

3. For the Albanian-Soviet dispute see: William E. Griffith, *Albania and the Sino-Soviet Rift* (MIT: Cambridge, 1963); Harry Ham, *Albania, China's Beachhead in Europe* (Praeger: New York, 1963); Alexander Dallin (ed.), *Diversity in International Communism* (Columbia: New York, 1963); and Nicholas C. Pano, *The People's Republic of Albania* (Johns Hopkins: Baltimore, 1968).

4. For the role of Eastern Europe in Sino-Soviet polemics see: Donald S. Zagoria, *The Sino-Soviet Conflict, 1956-1961* (Princeton, 1962); William E. Griffith, *The Sino-Soviet Rift* (MIT: Cambridge, 1964); and Robert H. Neal, (ed.), *International Relations Among Communists* (Prentice Hall: Englewood Cliffs, 1967).

5. *The Peking Review*, February 7, 1964.

6. *Soviet News Bulletin* (Ottawa), November 11-12, 1964.

7. For the impact of the Sino-Soviet dispute in Eastern Europe see: H. Gordon Skilling, *Communism National and International* (Canadian Institute of International Affairs: Toronto, 1964); Adam Bromke (ed.), *The Communist States at the Crossroads, Between Moscow and Peking* (Praeger: New York, 1965); Ghita Ionescu, *The Breakup of the Soviet Empire in Eastern Europe* (Penguin: London, 1965); Kurt London (ed.), *Eastern Europe in Transition* (Johns Hopkins: Baltimore, 1966); and Jacques Lévesques, *Le Conflit sino-sovietique et l'Europe de l'Est* (Montréal, 1970).

8. "A Rumanian Manifesto", *East Europe*, No. 6, Vol. 13, June, 1964, p.29.

9. For the Romanian-Soviet dispute see: Stephen Fischer-Galati, *The New Romania, From People's Democracy to Socialist Republic* (MIT: Cambridge, 1964); and by the same author, *The Socialist Republic of Romania* (Johns Hopkins: Baltimore, 1969).

10. *The Peking Review*, August 23, 1968.

11. For China's role in Eastern Europe during and after the Czechoslovak crisis see: Adam Bromke and Teresa Rakowska-Harmstone (eds.), *The Communist States in Disarray, 1965-1971* (Minnesota: Minneapolis, 1972).

12, Harold C. Hinton, *An Introduction to Chinese Politics* (Praeger: New York, 1973), p. 285.

13. *Borba*, November 16, 1956. For the text in English see: Paul E. Zinner, (ed.), *National Communism and Popular Revolt in Eastern Europe* (Columbia: New York, 1956), pp. 516-541.

14. For the fluctuating of Yugoslav-Soviet Relations see: Vaclav L. Benes and others (eds.), *The Second Soviet-Yugoslav Dispute* (Indiana: Bloomington, 1959); and Robert Bass and Elisabeth Marbury (eds.), *The Soviet-Yugoslav Controversy, 1948-1958* (Prospect Books: New York, 1959).

15. *L'Unita*, November 22, 1961. For an early development of polycentrism in the Communist ranks see: *Polycentrism, The New Factor in International Communism*, Walter Laqueur and Leopold Labedz (eds.), (Praeger: New York, 1962).

16. Punisa Perovic, *Review of International Affairs*, April 20, 1962.

17. *Listy* (Rome), No.3, 1976, pp. 41-4. Quoted in Rudolf L. Tokes (ed.), *Opposition in Eastern Europe* (Johns Hopkins: Baltimore, 1979), p. 50.

18. *New Times*, No. 28, July, 1976, pp. 17-32.

19. For the Eurocommunists' programme see: Howard Machin (ed.), *National Communism in Western Europe. A third way to Socialism?* " (Methuen: London, 1983); Kevin Devlin, "The Challenge of Eurocommunism", *Problems of Communism*, No. 1, Vol. XXVI, January-February 1977; Charles Gati, "The Europeanization of Communism", *Foreign Affairs*, No. 3, Vol. 55, April 1977; and Jiri Valenta, "Eurocommunism and Eastern Europe", *Problems of Communism*, No. 2, Vol. XXVII, March-April, 1978.

20. Devlin, *op. cit.*, p. 14.

21. *Borba*, September 29, 1981.

22. For France's relations with Eastern Europe in the early 1920s see: Piotr S. Wandycz, *France and Her Eastern Allies, 1919-1925* (Minnesota: Minneapolis, 1962).

23. For British-Polish relations during World War II see: Antony Polonsky (ed.), *The Great Powers and the Polish Question, 1941-1945* (London School of Economics, 1976); and George Kacewicz, *Great Britain, the Soviet Union and the Polish Government-in-Exile (1939-1945)* (Martinus Mijhoff: The Hague, 1976).

24. For American-Polish relations during World War II see: Richard C. Lukas, *The Strange Allies: The United States and Poland, 1941-1945* (Tennesee: Knoxville,1978); and Piotr S. Wandycz, *The United States and Poland* (Harvard; Cambridge, 1980).

25. See: Stanislaw Mikolajczyk, *The Rape of Poland: Pattern of Soviet Aggression* Sampson Low, Marston: London, 1948); and Stanton Griffis, *Lying in State* (Garden City, New York, 1952); and Edward Rozek, *Allied Diplomacy: A Pattern of Poland*, (Wiley: New York, 1958).

26. For the original formulation of the policy of liberation see: James Burnham, *Containment or Liberation?* (Day: New York, 1953); and for a critical assessment: Bennett Kovrig, *The Myth of Liberation: East Central Europe in U. S. Diplomacy and Politics since 1941* (Johns Hopkins: Baltimore, 1973).

VI.

POLYCENTRISM AND THE WEST

There has been, however, another tendency in American policy towards Eastern Europe, namely, the encouragement of polycentrism. This was first applied when the Truman administration supported Yugoslavia's resisting the Soviet pressure in 1949. Following the changes in Poland in 1956, the Eisenhower administration also extended modest economic aid to that country.* The Communism-polycentrism model as a guide to the western policy vis-à-vis Eastern Europe known as "peaceful engagement" or "building bridges", was clearly formulated in 1961 in the celebrated article in *Foreign Affairs* by Z. Brzezinski and W. E. Griffith.[1]

The article bluntly admitted that hitherto the United States had no "realistic and effective foreign policy toward Eastern Europe." As a premise in formulating such a policy, the authors observed that there had been a basic change in the prevailing climate of political opinion in the region. The Eastern Europeans had come to believe that there would be no war between the United States and the Soviet Union, and consequently ". . . there will be no overthrow of their Communist regimes; and that further changes are likely to stem from evolutionary developments within their own countries and within the bloc."[2]

Brzezinski and Griffith, thus, proposed a policy of "peaceful engagement" which should ". . . aim at stimulating further diversity in the Communist bloc—increasing the likelihood that the Eastern European states can achieve a greater measure of political independence from the Soviet domination."[3] Although the authors admitted the

---

* In the mid-1950s an early proponent of polycentrism—inspired by the example of Yugoslavia—was Louis Gallantiere, a political dvisor to the Radio Free Europe in New York and well connected in Washington. His line, however, was not consistently observed for during the Hungarian revolution some RFE broadcasts, at least implicitly, encouraged the overthrow of the Communist system in that country. Gallantiere's close collaborator was William B. Griffith, then a political advisor to the RFE in Munich.

possibility of the region attaining neutral status, like Finland, the new United States' policy would deny ". . . that we plot to make it a Western outpost. In the long run, a gradual change in Eastern Europe which neither challenges Soviet suzerainty nor abandons the area to the Soviets, may also help to improve American-Soviet relations."[4] From then on the Communism-polycentrism model was consciously used as the most practical approach to promote constructive changes in the area, by several successive American administrations.[5] The desire to utilize the nascent American-Soviet détente as a means to reduce the division of Europe was already visible in the late stages of the Kennedy administration and this line was invigorated under the Johnson presidency. On March 10, 1964, testifying before the Subcommittee on Europe of the House of Representatives, the Undersecretary of State, Averell Harriman, made the new American policy quite clear. "We hope to see", he declared "and are trying to encourage, a progressive loosening of external authority over Eastern European countries and continuing reassertion of national autonomy and diversity. . . . Our policy is to encourage the evolution now in progress by using every kind of contact available."[6] This process was undoubtedly assisted by Brzezinski serving as a foreign policy councillor in the Johnson administration—there was an unmistakable imprint of his ideas upon the President's speech of October 6, 1966 on "peaceful engagement". The United States supported Romania's more independent stance in international affairs—helping it in the mid-1960s through the delicate transition of power from Gheorghiu-Dej to Ceausescu.

The process was interrupted by the Czechoslovak crisis. By the time the events in Czechoslovakia flowered into the Prague Spring in 1968, the attention of the United States had been diverted from Europe to South-East Asia, where the war in Vietnam had just entered into its most acute stage. Following the Tet offensive Johnson decided not to run for re-election and to open up negotiations aimed at peaceful termination of the conflict. In order to erase his bellicose image, he was eager to go to Moscow in September and to launch strategic arms limitations talks with the USSR. The WTO invasion of Czechoslovakia on August 20, 1968 played havoc with these plans.

During all the stages of the Czechoslovak crisis the United States' stand was one of studied near-indifference. John C. Campbell, who at that time succeeded Brzezinski in the State Department, explained the reasons for this American policy. The West, he argued, could not save freedom for Czechoslovakia ". . . if it would come to the test of force. The United States had every reason to want the matter settled without coming to this point and without a new East-West crisis. Its eye was on the existing crises elsewhere and on the global relationship with the Soviet Union". Washington, then, continued Campbell, was faced with a veritable dilemma: "It would not be wise to give public encouragement to the Czechs and Slovaks in what was in its nature an anti-Soviet course, and thus raise false hopes or give the Soviets some pretext for action. From a cold-blooded standpoint, a case could be made for discouraging the Czechs and Slovaks from going too far and too fast, but it is not easy to imagine who would take upon himself the responsibility for imparting this political piece of advice. The choice, accordingly, was to say nothing".[7]

In 1968, then, the United States was for the first time faced with the practical necessity to reconcile the potentially incompatible consequences of their pursuing both the policy of "peaceful engagement" in Eastern Europe and that of global détente with the USSR. American officials, wrote Campbell, "felt as deeply about the Czechoslovak tragedy as did their critics at home and abroad. Obviously there could not be business as usual with the Soviet Union after what had happened.... On the other hand, the menacing problems of arms race... required talking with Moscow, if any solutions were to be found. Even in its initial reaction to the invasion of Czechoslovakia, therefore, Washington made sure that its sense of outrage did not close off the channels which in its own interest, and that of a world peace, should be kept open".[8] At first the United States confined itself to a mere moral reprobation of the invasion and the symbolic cancellation of cultural exchanges with the Warsaw Pact countries. When the fears of a similar attack against Romania intensified, in a speech on August 20, 1968, the American President warned the Soviets against "unleashing the dogs of war", and the Johnson-Kosygin meeting was quietly cancelled. Yet, soon afterwards the American President indicated that, despite all that happened, he still would be ready to go to Moscow. But by that time the Soviets were not interested in talking with the lame-duck American president. [*]

---

[*] The Czechoslovak crisis had important repercussions on the American internal political scene for in seeking an early dialogue with the Soviets President Johnson was evidently motivated by domestic considerations too. "Had Mr. Johnson succeeded in holding a meeting with Mr. Kosygin in Moscow, a political climate much more favourable to the Democrats would have emerged in the United States. A first visit to Moscow by their President—something which eluded President Eisenhower in 1960—would have been regarded by the American people as a major breakthrough in East-West relations. . . . The war image of Mr. Johnson would have been erased and the popularity of the President and his party greatly increased. Considering the closeness of the presidential race in November 1968, it is reasonable to assume that with a political climate more favourable to the Democrats, Mr. Humphrey would have won the American presidency". Adam Bromke, "Aftermath of Czechoslovakia", *Canadian Slavonic Papers*, No. 1, Vol. XI. spring 1969. p. 25.

Efforts at American-Soviet détente not only continued, but, in fact, were intensified by the Republican administration. In the fall of 1969 the talks to reduce the nuclear arms race between the two superpowers were launched and in the spring of 1972—during President Nixon's visit to Moscow—the SALT I agreement was signed. In 1972-74 the American and Soviet leaders regularly exchanged visits. Pursuit of détente continued under the Carter administration. In the spring of 1979 Carter and Brezhnev met in Vienna to sign the SALT II Treaty. American-Soviet relations, however, deteriorated sharply after the Soviet invasion of Afghanistan in December 1979. Meanwhile, the American policy of "peaceful engagement" also proceeded apace. In the 1970s the United States preserved good relations with Yugoslavia and Romania, improved relations with Hungary and considerably expanded those with Poland.[9] Both Nixon and Ford visited Warsaw, and Gierek came to Washington in 1974. The Carter administration (with Brzezinski now in the position of National Security Advisor) initially also stayed on course. In fact, Poland was the first country President Carter visited, in December 1977. Brzezinski, who accompanied the President there, when asked in a television interview whether this gesture meant the United States' trying to tear Poland away from the Soviet Union, flatly denied it. On the contrary, he argued, it was part of an overall effort to advance East-West détente.[*]

The Western European countries—notably France under the Gaullists and West Germany under the Social Democrats—developed their own versions of "bridge building" into Eastern Europe. Bonn's *Ostpolitik* was particularly interesting in that it deliberately employed both the optimistic-geopolitical and the polycentrism models. In establishing formal diplomatic relations with the GDR (and assisting it in a substantial way economically), the short-term goal of the FRG was to ameliorate as much as possible the conditions of life in East Germany; but at the same time, West Germany never conceded its ultimate aim of re-unification in freedom of the German nation. Of great significance was also the West German-Polish treaty of 1970 which provided for the recognition of Poland's western boundary by the FRG and the normalization of diplomatic relations between the two countries—this way paving the way for an eventual reconciliation between these two traditionally hostile nations.[10]

---

[*]Brzezinski's statement (as recalled from memory by this author) was entirely consistent with his article in *Foreign Affairs* in 1961. Yet, there is little doubt that the Soviets were irked by the fact that the new American President chose to visit Poland before the USSR. Brzezinski's Polish background (although he left Poland as a child and had lived in North America ever since) clearly intensified the Soviet apprehensions.

The Helsinki accords of 1975 tried to apply the concepts underlying *Ostpolitik* to Eastern Europe as a whole. While they sanctioned the territorial and ideological status quo, they also strove, within that context, to promote constructive changes in the region. In a way the Final Act aimed at bringing the situation in Eastern Europe into line with what was envisaged at the Teheran and Yalta Conferences, where the West conceded the area as a Soviet sphere of influence, but still expected that the governments there would reflect genuine popular aspirations; except that in Helsinki, in contrast to the wartime conferences, the western powers also explicitly agreed that this would be carried out within the Communist, although polycentric, framework.

The western powers' goal in expanding their relations with the East European countries, in fact, was not only to encourage them to move towards greater freedom, but also to use them as an additional channel to cultivate cooperation with the USSR. While he was in Warsaw in 1977 President Carter appealed to Gierek to use his influence in Moscow to improve East-West relations. And in the spring of 1980, when Soviet-American relations deteriorated sharply after the invasion of Afghanistan, Giscard d'Estaing and Brezhnev met in Warsaw, at Gierek's invitation, to explore ways to salvage East-West détente. The western policy of "building bridges" to Eastern Europe, then, was not regarded just as an end in itself, but also as a possible channel to reach into the USSR in order to reduce the East-West conflict.

Yet, even during the climax of détente there were already some disquieting signs in Eastern Europe. In a speech delivered in 1976 Helmut Sonnenfeldt, who at that time was a counsellor in the State Department, pointed to the possibility of a growing popular unrest in the region and warned about its potentially detrimental effects in East-West relations. In order to forestall such a development he advocated evolving more normal—"organic," as he put it—relationships between the USSR and the different Eastern European Communist regimes, enabling them to undertake urgent domestic reforms. Sonnenfeldt's analysis, thus, emphasized that the progress of polycentrism and détente should go hand in hand.[*]

---

[*] Sonnenfeldt, however, was much maligned for his statement. The right-wing Republicans seized upon his expression of "organic" relationships and claimed (even though it was evident in the total context of his remarks that this was not the case) that, in order to protect détente, the Ford administration supported sovietization, or even an annexation of Eastern Europe by the USSR. The myth of the "Sonnenfeldt doctrine" persists in some quarters in the West, as well as in Eastern Europe, until today.

A British scholar, Philip Windsor, writing when the Polish crisis was already under way, elaborated upon Sonnenfeldt's apprehensions. The West has in Eastern Europe ". . . a fundamental interest, namely, that of trying to restore the unity of European civilization and to recover a degree of freedom from the East. . . [yet] in the geopolitical circumstances of the present, very little can be done to create the opportunity for full national independence. But something can be done to transform the conditions in which the peoples of Eastern Europe can lead their lives. . . . This is perhaps an unpleasant proposition, and could easily be confused with the notion of making life easier for the Soviet Union. . . . But history shows that the West is neither able nor willing to help when small nations come against the USSR and are defeated."[11]

To make it worse, argued Windsor, ". . . the West no longer knows how to approach the East. The effects of Western actions are unpredictable; there is no necessary connection between internal liberalization and experiment in any Eastern country and the closeness of its relationship with the West; too great a degree of Western enthusiasm for further room for manoeuvre or a higher degree of experiment, could lead to adverse social reactions—and possibly endanger the security of Europe as a whole."[12]

*   *   *

The Carter administration was aware of the dangers inherent in the Polish crisis. Brzezinski, although he advocated a tough American stance vis-à-vis the Soviet Union in some other parts of the world, remained faithful to the polycentric model in Eastern Europe. On December 8, 1980, when a Soviet invasion of Poland seemed imminent, Washington issued a strong warning to Moscow to refrain from doing so. Brzezinski explained that one of the objectives of this American move was ". . . to calm the situation in Poland by making the Poles aware that the Soviets may in fact enter. The Poles till now discounted this possibility and this may have emboldened them excessively. Here in effect we have a common interest with the Soviets for they too prefer to intimidate the Poles to a degree."[13] Had Carter remained in power and Brzezinski continued as his National Security Advisor the United States would probably have continued to follow a moderate course towards Poland—it would have relied more on diplomatic, and particularly economic, means to resolve the Polish crisis. But in January 1981 the Democratic administration was replaced by the victorious Republicans under Reagan.

The Polish issue was at first controversial in the Reagan administration. Secretary of State Alexander Haig, who, like Brzezinski, advocated a tough American posture towards the USSR in some other areas, took a moderate stand over Poland.* "For the Soviet Union," he argued, "Poland is a *casus belli*, a question on which she would go to war with the Western alliance. . . . The Poles themselves, though they have preserved a vibrant sense of nationhood. . . cannot be the masters of their own fate so long as the USSR disposes overwhelming power and wills otherwise."[14] In the councils of the Reagan administration Haig advocated ". . . discouraging direct intervention by Soviet troops." To some of the President's other advisers, these policies were not sufficiently red-blooded, despite the fact that the United States hadn't the military power or the interrelated diplomatic influence to go farther."[15] It was clear, added Haig, ". . . in the very first discussions of the Polish situation, that some of my colleagues [in the National Security Council] were prepared to look beyond Poland, as if it were not in itself an issue of war and peace, and regard it as an opportunity to inflict moral, political, economic, and propaganda damage to the USSR."[16]

When the army took over in Poland on December 13, 1981, Haig ". . . recognized at once that, for the time being at least, martial law, rather than something worse had been imposed upon Poland. [Yet] at meetings in the White House the hardliners spoke of draconian measures."[17] The President at first hesitated, at one time even speaking ". . . about offering the East a Marshall Plan for the eighties and suggesting to the Soviets a new era of cooperation."[18] Eventually, however, Reagan sided with his hardline advisers. The United States responded to the introduction of martial law in Poland with harsh economic sanctions, and after the formal disbanding of "Solidarity" in October 1982 these were even stiffened. Relations between Washington and the Jaruzelski regime deteriorated sharply. And when martial law in Poland was lifted in July 1983, the major American sanctions, denying that country most-favoured-nation status, and opposing its application to the International Monetary Fund, stayed in force.[19]

Meanwhile, after Haig's resignation in June 1982, the United States used the situation in Poland as a pretext to try to block the construction of the gas pipeline from the USSR to Western Europe.

---

* Haig, no doubt, profited from the advice of his Political Undersecretary and later his Deputy, Walter J. Stoessel, Jr., who in the late 1960s and the early 1970s served as Ambassador in Warsaw and knew, and understood, Poland extremely well.

However, faced with determined opposition from the Western European countries, this attempt was discontinued in the fall. By that time, significantly, Washington had conveniently forgotten the Polish issue. In the Polish crisis, thus, the Reagan administration returned to the posture of moralism cum indifference which characterized American policy towards Eastern Europe in the 1940s and the early 1950s. And, like its predecessors, it achieved doubly negative results—without helping the Poles in any tangible way, it contributed to the aggravation of American-Soviet relations.

The Polish events were significant not only because they demonstrated the rise of a new political consciousness among the workers as well as the continued strength of historical traditions—the two quickly merging into a formidable revolutionary moveement—but they also underlined the close interdependence between the progress of polycentrism in Eastern Europe and East-West détente. In the 1970s the Gierek regime deliberately exploited the more benign political climate in Europe to expand its relations with the western powers, in this way also obtaining access to western technology and credits. This, in turn, provided an effective shield over the activities of the democratic opposition in Poland. The Gierek government, especially after the signing of the Helsinki accords in 1975, was reluctant to suppress outright the Polish dissidents, for this could have adversely affected Poland's profitable relations with the western democracies.[*] In doing so, however, Gierek was courting political disaster for the organized political groups merged with "Solidarity" in 1980, rapidly transforming it from what was initially a vehicle for expressing the workers' economic discontent into a radical political movement.

The Polish experience, thus, has shown—as Sonnenfeldt and Windsor advocated—the need for coordinating the progress of détente and polycentrism; for abusing the former, to foster the latter, can be counter-productive. The American indiscriminate support of the Poles' demands for democracy and independence, transmitted to Poland by the western media, encouraged "Solidarity" to move too far and too fast, and in this way contributed to its ultimate demise.[†] An

---

[*]It is interesting to observe that, at first, many Czechoslovak and Polish dissidents opposed détente, including the convening of the CSCE, because they feared that by confirming the status quo in Eastern Europe it would amount to a Munich- or Yalta-like appeasement in that region on the part of the West; later on, however, most of them changed their position and tried to use the Helsinki accords to their advantage.

[†]The Poles did not actually expect that the West would come to their assistance militarily, but many of them—and particularly the younger ones, who did not remember the experiences of the late 1940s—genuinely believed that the United States would prevent Soviet intervention through diplomatic pressure, and that left to its own devices the Polish Communist regime would not be able to restore its control in the country. The imposition of martial law came as a crude shock to them.

opportunity to achieve more modest, but still substantial, reforms in Poland was lost.[20]

Polycentric and geopolitical goals, then, must not be confused by the West. While the principle of national self-determination should be maintained, conveying the impression that this goal is attainable in the near future should be avoided. The Brzezinski-Griffith evolutionary model still remains valid—in the sense that it prescribes striving for the optimum objectives feasible at each stage. It should, however, be updated and elaborated by inclusion of the Eastern European experiences of the last twenty years, and particularly the recent lessons of Poland. The delicate relationship between polycentrism in the region and East-West détente should also be carefully examined.

*   *   *

Continued commitment to changes in Eastern Europe along the geopolitical-optimistic scenario, even if perceived as a distant goal, is important to the western democracies if they are to stay true to their own values of democracy and national independence. There are also valid political reasons why the West must not stray off this course. As long as the FRG is a part of NATO, the western alliance cannot renounce the ultimate objective of reunification in freedom of the German nation, for if they did, the nascent nationalistic and neutralist snetiments in West Germany would be considerably strengthened. A lingering sense of all-European continental unity—as evidenced by the occasional statements by the German or French leaders blaming the Americans and the British for dividing the continent at Yalta— must not be overlooked either.*

Western upholding of the principle of national self-determination is helpful to the Eastern Europeans in reminding them that they have not been forgotten, and keeps alive their hopes for an improvement of their situation in the future. The Soviet Union, moreover, has not been altogether impervious to the western concern about the trends in the region. It was the Communization of Eastern Europe which gave rise to the Cold War in the late 1940s. The USSR's decision not to proceed with an outright annexation of the area, and its subsequent

---

* It is interesting to observe that the negative reaction in Western Europe was stronger to the suppression of Poland in 1981 than to the invasion of Afghanistan in 1979—despite the fact that the former was handled internally and the latter involved the use of Soviet troops, as well as the fact that Poland was a member of WTO while Afghanistan was a non-aligned state. The USSR, thus, must realize that if it wants to weaken bonds between Western Europe and the United States, the most effective way to do it is by relaxing its controls over Eastern Europe.

easing of sovietization there, were, no doubt, influenced by its desire not to aggravate even further the tensions with the Western powers. Moscow must also be cognizant of the fact that its acceptance of poly-centrism, by bringing Communism in several Eastern European coun-tries closer to popular aspirations, has helped to improve the climate in East-West relations.

In the southwest periphery of Eastern Europe there was actually an opportunity taken by the West to advance the cause of national self-determination. The United States' support of Yugoslavia helped it to withstand the Soviet pressure in 1949 (although that contributed to Stalin's drastic tightening of controls over the rest of the area). Any renewed attempt to bring Yugoslavia back into the Soviet orbit should be similarly resisted by the western powers. Indeed, Moscow's efforts to meddle in the internal affairs of Albania should also be op-posed. The obnoxious nature of the Communist regime there ought not stand in the way of such a western action, for it is to be hoped that, left to their own devices, eventually the Albanians will bring the regime there more into line with their wishes.

The paramount reason why the West has refrained from promoting changes in the region along the geopolitical-optimistic model, has been that this could precipitate World War III. In a nuclear era such a course would not only be hazardous to the western powers, it could also be fatal to the Eastern European nations by obliterating among them the oppressors and the oppressed alike. The West, however, has at its disposal various other means which could be used to advance polycentrism in the area. A western "peaceful engagement" in East-ern Europe, if advanced with imagination and skill, is entirely feasible.

Western broadcasts play an important role in shaping the political opinions of the Eastern Europeans. They should be used to cultivate the ideals of democracy and self-determination, but they should not encourage false hopes that these goals can be accomplished immedi-ately. Cultural and scientific exchanges and the broadest possible personal contacts should be developed to keep the window to the West open. Economic integration of Eastern Europe into the world economy—through the development of trade and the participation of various states from the region in international bodies, such as GATT or IMF—should be encouraged; and selective economic aid—particularly at critical junctures, such as was contemplated, although never implemented, by the United States during the Polish crisis in 1980-81—could be employed.[21] Finally, subtle western diplomacy, both bilateral and multilateral—such as within the CSCE—could assist polycentric trends throughout the area.

The pursuit of "peaceful engagement" in Eastern Europe by the West is more difficult in the adversarial international climate of a Cold War.[22] In such circumstances, if only as a defensive reflex, Moscow is more likely to insist upon closing the ranks in the WTO and preserving ideological unity among all its members. Avenues of cooperation between the different Eastern European countries and the western democracies will be blocked. The West could try to exploit unrest in the region to weaken the Warsaw Pact and to score some propaganda points over the USSR. In the long-run, however, such a course would be counter-productive. For in response Moscow would tighten its control over the restive peoples, if necessary by resorting to force, and outrage resulting from such an action in the western democracies would even further aggravate the Cold War. It was precisely such a vicious circle into which Poland was drawn in 1981. The introduction of martial law in that country, even though it averted a direct Soviet intervention, led to a sharp riposte from the United States; and the American diplomatic, and especially economic, sanctions pushed the Jaruzelski regime into even greater dependence on the USSR.

"Building bridges" into Eastern Europe, then, should be a constructive undertaking, carried out in conditions of, and conducive to, East-West détente. The West should repeatedly keep reminding the USSR that the tightening of its controls over Eastern Europe would result in the worsening of East-West relations; and, conversely, that the advance of polycentrism in the region, by bringing Communism in the various countries there closer to the popular aspirations, would be conducive to the progress of détente. In a relaxed international atmosphere the USSR is likely to be more tolerant of an opening by the Communist states in the region to the West; indeed, Moscow may find expanded contacts by its Eastern European allies with the western powers a useful channel in promoting the East-West dialogue. In the 1970s Poland effectively performed such a role until this was undermined by its domestic crisis; in the 1980s Hungary, where the internal situation remained stable, has assumed a similar, although somewhat more restrained, stance. And, despite the installation of the American cruise missiles in West Germany and the Pershing II rockets in 1983, the GDR has maintained its "special relationship" with the FRG, although by mid-1984 signs of Moscow's displeasure over this state of affairs were mounting.

*   *   *

The Polish experiences have clearly demonstrated that a stalemate exists today in Eastern Europe. Neither the pessimistic nor the optimistic geopolitical scenarios can be carried to their logical conclusions. After the "Solidarity" period the ideals of democracy and independence have been firmly implanted in the minds of the young Poles. If Moscow intends to persist in its efforts to sovietize Poland, it might as well start all over again; indeed, in view of the internal consolidation of the country, the chances of the Soviets' success are now poorer than they were in the 1940s. At the same time the United States' continued support for the Poles' maximalist goals has proved to be futile; if anything, by tacitly encouraging the activities of the underground "Solidarity", Washington's rhetoric has helped to prolong the political confrontation, possibly threatening a new popular explosion in the country.

The improvement of the situation in Eastern Europe should be sought, not along the lines of the geopolitical, but of the polycentric scenario. For it is polycentrism which offers the best opportunity to find a common ground among the three forces operating in the region: the Soviet security concerns, the Eastern Europeans' aspirations for expanded freedom, and the western desire to protect East-West détente. Such a reconciliation, however, should be approached not in a static, but rather in a dynamic fashion as a continuing political process. At each stage an optimum available solution should be sought; but it should not be regarded as an end in itself, but merely a step leading towards even further reduction of tensions in the future.

It is significant to observe that even the Reagan administration has remained formally committed to supporting polycentrism in Eastern Europe. The United States' relations with Yugoslavia and Romania have stayed close, and those with Hungary have continued to improve. This American policy, however, should be made consistent by including Poland. The United States should abandon its present adamant stance vis-à-vis the Jaruzelski regime and, instead, should try to encourage it to expand the modicum of freedom from the USSR which it, paradoxically, retained by suppressing "Solidarity" on its own rather than with the assistance of the Soviet forces. Above all, the American economic sanctions should be withdrawn, and perhaps even replaced with economic aid as was planned in 1981, rewarding Polish domestic reforms along the Hungarian pattern.

Examining the lessons of the Polish crisis for the United States in 1983, an American scholar, Jiri Valenta, admitted that ". . . the Soviet choice to intervene indirectly was less destructive to Poland, as well as to U.S.-Soviet relations, than invasion would have been." Washington, he argued, should draw the proper conclusions from this. It

". . . should forswear the empty rhetoric of the crusade for democracy. . . . Punitive measures to undermine 'the legitimacy of the Communist regime in Poland' could escalate conflict. [Their] success could push the Soviet Union into a corner, precipitate a Soviet backlash, and perhaps bring on an East-West confrontation."[23]

The United States, continued Valenta, "cannot hope to alter the Soviet East European security system, in which Poland plays a critical role. . . Washington does not have a military option in Eastern Europe, but it does have a number of economic and diplomatic instruments at its disposal." These should be used to encourage the Soviets ". . . to accept a moderate pragmatic course in Poland and to permit the reform of outmoded systems in at least some Eastern European countries. In return for this flexibility they would obtain less volatile allies as well as indirect Western aid." The negotiations to obtain this goal, given the Soviet tendency to regard Eastern Europe as their exclusive domain, would not be easy. But, ". . . in 1962 at the United Nations, the Soviet Union, Hungary, and the United States worked out such an understanding, ending a political boycott of then Hungarian Premier Janos Kadar's post-invasion regime in exchange for internal liberalization in that country. Subsequently, Kadar's liberal regime became one of the most popular in Eastern Europe."[24] Evolving a similar agreement should now be the goal of the West vis-à-vis the post-martial law Poland.

The polycentric model, thus, must not be used in a confrontationalist fashion. The purely rhetorical policy of liberation should be written off, as was the Vatican's concept of treating Communism in Eastern Europe as a "temporary evil". Instead, the West should patiently and persistently encourage the Soviet Union to accept peaceful evolution in Eastern Europe which—by promoting economic progress and political stability in the region, and in this way assisting East-West détente— is in its interests too. Polycentrism should not be regarded as an effort at *divide et impera*. Western efforts to tear away the Eastern European countries from the USSR should be recognized as not only futile, but counter-productive. It is not a question of destroying old ties, but rather of superimposing on them new ones. In such a way Eastern Europe could gradually return to its historical role as a "transitional zone"—not as a barrier, but a bridge—between the East and the West. Admittedly, especially in the tense international climate of the 1980s, such an evolution in the region remains a tedious and distant goal to achieve. But, at least for the time being, no other prospect to improve the situation in Eastern Europe seems to be in sight.

Efforts to advance peaceful changes in Eastern Europe are a task not only for diplomats, but for scholars as well. There is an urgent need, especially in the aftermath of the Polish crisis, for devising new concepts and new policies. So the good work by Hugh Seton-Watson, who has paved the way in our thinking about Eastern European history and politics in an analytical fashion, must be continued.

NOTES

1. Z. Brzezinski and W. E. Griffith, "Peaceful Engagement in Eastern Europe." *Foreign Affairs*, No. 4, Vol. 39, July, 1961.

2. *Ibid.*, p. 642.

3. *Ibid.*, p. 644.

4. *Ibid.*, p. 654.

5. For a re-evaluation of the United States' policy towards Eastern Europe in the mid-1960s see: John C. Campbell, *American Policy Toward Eastern Europe, The Choices Ahead* (Minnesota: Minneapolis, 1965); and Adam Bromke, "The United States and Eastern Europe", *International Journal*, No. 2, Vol. XXI, Spring 1966.

6. In Zbigniew Brzezinski, *Alternative to Partition, For A Broader Conception of America's Role in Europe* (McGraw-Hill: New York, 1965). p. 122.

7. John C. Campbell, "Czechoslovakia: American Choices, Past and Future," *Canadian Slavonic Papers*, No. 1, Vol. XI, Spring 1969. p. 14.

8. *Ibid.*, p. 20.

9. For the positions that the different Eastern European states adopted in the 1970s see: Adam Bromke and Derry Novak (eds.), *The Communist States in the Era of Détente* (Mosaic: Oakville, 1979).

10. For the assessment of the changing pattern of Polish-West German relations see: Adam Bromke, *Poland, The Protracted Crisis* (Mosaic: Oakville, 1983). Chs. IX-X.

11. Philip Windsor, "Stability and instability in Eastern Europe and their Implications for Western Policy", in Karen Dawisha and Philip Hanson (eds.), *Soviet-East European Dilemmas: Coercion, Competition, and Consent* (Heinemann: London, 1981). pp. 209, 211.

12. *Ibid.*, p. 219.

13. Zbigniew Brzezinski, *Power and Principle: Memoirs of a National Security Advisor, 1977-1981*, (Farrar, Strauss, Giroux: New York, 1983), p. 468.

14. Alexander M. Haig, Jr., *Caveat: Realism, Reagan, and Foreign Policy*, (Macmillan: New York, 1984), p. 238.

15. *Ibid.*, p. 239.

16. *Ibid.*, pp. 239-40.

17. *Ibid.*, p. 251.

18. *Ibid.*, p. 252.

19. For the official account of the Polish grievances towards the United States during the crisis in the early 1980s see: *Polityka Stanow Zjednoczonych Ameryki wobec Polski w switele faktow i dokumentow (1980-1983)*, (Polski Instytut Spraw Miedzynarodowych: Warszawa, 1984).

20. For what would have been feasible changes in Poland, see: Charles Gati, "Polish Futures, Western Options", *Foreign Affairs*, No. 2, Vol. 61, Winter 1982-83; and Richard Spielman, "Crisis in Poland", *Foreign Policy*, No. 49, Winter 1982-83.

21. For an early proposal on Western help for the Polish crisis see: Adam Bromke, "Poland: The Cliff's Edge", *Foreign Policy*, No. 41, Winter 1980-81.

22. The balance of advantages and disadvantages for Eastern Europe from détente and the Cold War respectively is well presented in Paul Marantz, "Poland and East-West Relations", *Canadian Slavonic Papers*, No. 3, Vol. XXV, September 1983, pp. 84-5.

23. Jiri Valenta, "The Explosive Soviet Periphery", *Foreign Policy*, No. 51, Summer 1983, pp. 97, 96, 98.

24. *Ibid.*, pp. 97, 96, 98, 97.

APPENDICES

APPENDIX I
THE THREE POLISH CRISES[*]

The founding of People's Poland, its present political system, its territory and its external alliances demonstrate the historical maturity and the correctness of political thought of the Polish Communists and the Polish revolutionary left. Its main goals have been realized by the working class in close alliance with the peasantry and the working intelligentsia. The rightness of its choice of the socialist road has been in time confirmed by the lasting and irreversible accomplishments of the nation, regardless of the errors which were committed along this road and the accompanying tensions and social conflicts.

The working class was prepared for its hegemonic role in the struggle for an independent, socialist Poland through decades of difficult experiences in the class and national-liberation struggle. The organized revolutionary movement of the Polish working class is over a hundred years old. And 35 years have passed since the historical moment of the fusion of the working parties and the founding of the Polish United Workers' Party.

The direct beginnings of socialist socio-political changes go back to the wartime and the Hitlerite occupation. This was assisted by the bankruptcy of the political conceptions of the bourgeoisie and the gradual maturing of the working class as it assumed the role of the basic political force in society, and as at the same time it received support from the progressive elements among the peasantry and the working intelligentsia. The main role in laying down the new foundations was played by the Polish Workers' Party. Its programmatic declaration "What are we fighting for?" of November 1943 and the Manifesto of the Polish Committee of National Liberation of July 22, 1944, represented the major documents determining the future of Poland. Poland's liberation by the Soviet Army, and the Polish military units fighting by its side, created objective conditions enabling the seizing and defending of power in the state by the working class and its close

---

[*] Chapter II. "The Characteristics of the Conflicts and Social Crises in the History of People's Poland", *Nowe Drogi*, special issue distributed in the fall of 1983. pp. 16-58.

allies. The social revolution marked a decisive turn in Poland's history. As a result of the profound social reforms which liquidated economic and social rule by the propertied classes the existing class structure was also profoundly transformed.

In the countryside the basic transformation was accomplished by agricultural reform, erasing the effects of the German colonization and resettling population in the western and northern provinces, and distributing the unowned lands. As a consequence of these changes as well as of the nationalization both of the forests and of a substantial number of land estates, the foundations of socialist agriculture were laid.

As a result of nationalization of the large and middle-sized enterprises and of the banks there emerged a socialist sector in the economy. In the reconstruction of industrial enterprises and putting them back into production, the major role was played by the workers, who became their actual owners. The workers took part in the implementation of the agricultural reform too. They also played an important role in defending and strengthening the people's authorities. They suffered the greatest sacrifices and carried the major burdens during the revolutionary transformations.

At first only a part of the old intelligentsia consciously supported the revolution. Yet, as the process of rebuilding the country, and of developing the economy, education and culture was advanced, more and more substantial segments, and, then, the overwhelming majority of the old intelligentsia found their place and became involved in the realization of the patriotic aspirations and their own professional aspirations. At the same time the ranks of intelligentsia were increasingly supplemented by the people already moulded by the new conditions, coming from workers' or peasants' families.

The reconstruction and the revolutionary changes very broadly affected education and culture. A historic benchmark in this process was the liquidation of illiteracy as a social phenomenon, the offering of free and universal education at all levels, the effective efforts to popularize book reading, etc. These created real opportunities for a civilizational advancement of the broad working masses and their active involvement in the socio-political and economic life of the country.

The reconstruction of Poland from the unprecedented ruin of war, the struggle against profound backwardness, the revival of the economy, the takeover, settlement and economic revival of the Recovered Territories, as well as the process of socio-political restructuring of the country and opening the educational and cultural opportunities-all of these changes released the energy of millions of Poles. In the first few years after the war the Polish society displayed a special readiness for sacrifices and a creative enthusiasm, a strong will to rebuild their working places, and for the strengthening of the country and its place in the international arena. This way, side by side with the growing patriotic activism of the nation, there progressed the realization of the people's democracy—by the workers and the peasants—of which the main characteristic was a broad participation by the people in resolving the manifold social problems.

In the principal matters the democratic camp had undeniable successes. Yet, they were neither easy nor attained without pain. An acute class struggle was under way against the adversaries of the people's authority—the reactionary forces forming anti-state underground organizations and applying terror against the emerging government organs. Thousands of members and activists of the PWP, as well as of the other parties of the democratic bloc, the activists of the Union of Fighting Youth and other leftist youth organizations, militiamen, functionaries of the security apparatus, and soldiers of the people's army were killed. The opposition, represented mainly by the Polish Peasant Party and supported by the activities of the armed underground, aimed at preventing the revolutionary transformations.

Despite all the attempts on the part of the counter-revolutionary underground, a civil war on a national scale was avoided and gradually social support for the new people's authority was consolidated. The overcoming of the contradictions and resistance was accomplished through various military and political means. Among others there was that of attracting former soldiers from the Home Army and other formations, who had demonstrated their patriotism and democratic convictions through work for People's Poland; while at the same time a sharp struggle was carried out against the anti-people and anti-Soviet commanders and the political activists of the London camp. After several years of struggle against political clericalism aligned with the political opposition, and after the adoption of the principle of separation between the Church and the State, an agreement was reached in 1950 between the government and the Episcopate. The wartime political divisions were diminishing. The process of integration of the society, its basic classes and strata gathered by their common and overriding goals, was advancing. These goals were articulated by the people's authorities and the political parties participating in the democratic camp. At the centre there was the political thought of the PWP, which in decisive matters was shared by the Polish Socialist Party and the bloc of democratic parties.

In 1947, after elections to the Constituent Assembly, a marked stabilization was attained in the country. The Three Year Plan of 1947-1949, the first great plan of socio-economic development, was launched. Along with the overcoming of the profound backwardness of the country and economic recovery, the plan envisaged an increase in the working people's standard of living above the pre-war level. The plan was successfully fulfilled, and ahead of time. It deepened the changes in the social and economic structure of the country and essentially consolidated the socialist sector in the economy.

The difficult tasks of reconstruction, development and the revolutionary transformations were implemented in international conditions that were worsening, because of activities of the imperialist centres. The cold war was gathering momentum and the division of the world into two antagonistic blocs was emerging. The internal political opposition was increasingly becoming an instrument of global anti-Communism.

The international conditions, the acute class conflicts and the severe experiences of the struggle imposed by the counter-revolutionary underground, did not make it easier to avoid some incorrect moves in the political and economic sphere. These incorrect moves also stemmed from a lack of properly educated cadres, from then short administrative experience, and from the very earliness of the then current stage of formulation of the conceptions of socialist development in Poland as well as of the roads and the means of their realization. Over these problems there were discussions and disputes both between the PWP and the PSP, and within each of these parties. Yet even though the programmatic conceptions were still not fully developed—nevertheless—and especially at the I Congress of the PWP in December 1945—its important elements, loosely called the Polish road to socialism, which meant a way of socialist construction that would take into account both socialism's universal features and the actual Polish conditions which had already come into being.

It is against this background that the weaknesses and the shortcomings of the years 1944-1948, and especially those of the following period, must be viewed. Apart from the situation among the cadres which has already been mentioned, there were the facts that some segments of the PWP leadership did not appreciate the role of the allied political forces that had joined with them during the struggle for the liberation of Poland, and the experiences involved in the patriotic understandings which were reached at that stage, that the rapid growth of the party ranks was not accompanied by a corresponding advance in their ideological consciousness, etc. And in the economic sphere, in planning and cooperatives. the views of Hilary Minc gradually began to dominate. Other studies, research and discussions were abandoned.

1. The political turn in 1948 and the crisis of 1956

In 1948 a rapid and a surprising change in the political line of the PWP took place. The essence of this change—which was preceded by a crisis in the leadership—was the dogmatic-sectarian turn. It was expressed in a departure from the hitherto accepted conceptions and methods of gradual socialist adaptation of the political and socio-political structures, in favour of a considerable acceleration of this adaptation with a substantial resorting to non-economic, repressive measures. It was mainly around these problems that serious differences arose in the PWP leadership.

An important role was played by the external circumstances and, above all, by the changing situation in the Communist and the workers' movement in Europe. It took place in the context of the imperialist war threats, of the intensification of the "cold war" and the anti-Communist psychosis, and, against this background of a conflict between the leadership of the All-Union Communist Party (Bolsheviks) and the Communist Party of Yugoslavia which considerably influenced the parties grouped around the Information Bureau of the Communist and Workers' Parties founded in 1947. This situation was exploited by the PWP Politbureau majority, composed of Boleslaw Bierut (who was recalled in August 1948 to party work), Jakub Berman, Roman Zambrowski, H. Minc and others, to remove Wladyslaw Gomulka from the leadership and to introduce the above-described changes in the party line. B. Bierut became the party leader. He enjoyed respect for his activities in the cooperative and the workers' movement, and above all for his role as the chairman of the Home National Council during the underground struggle against the occupant. In People's Poland he had been president of the Home National Council, and since February 1947 had occupied the greatly respected office of the President of the Polish Republic. He won acclaim for upholding Poland's interests and its boundaries, for his dynamism in encouraging the reconstruction and development of the country, for his ability for a dialogue with different groups, and for his concern for development of the national culture.

W. Gomulka was accused of a far-reaching—going back, in fact, to the war times—so-called rightist-nationalist deviation. This was used to justify the necessity of the changes in the party, and also among that part of the PSP which was soon to join the PWP. An additional argument used by the supporters of the new line was the thesis, presented as a universally binding principle, that in the conditions of an advanced socialist construction the class struggle is accelerated. This also provided a rationalization for restricting democracy and in the first half of the 1950s it became one of the main reasons for violating the law. Accusations similar to those against W. Gomulka were also advanced against his closest collaborators from the occupation days, and were presented at the III Plenum of the Central Committee in November 1949. At that time the positions of the accused were characterized as supportive of the anti-socialist forces, to justify the arresting of and the preparing of political trials for the leading party activists.

An accelerated development of the country, its transformation from an agricultural-industrial into an industrial-agricultural state, and laying the foundations of socialism, was undertaken through a process of industrialization with priority being given to investments. In agriculture the collectivization of individual farms began—which was supposed to bring substantial increases in the agricultural production. In 1949-1955 the rise was supposed to be 50 per cent (while in industry the growth was to be 158 per cent). Side by side with the unusually rapid economic growth, education, culture and science were to be radically transformed. In the programme adopted by the Unity Congress in 1948 all of these plans were incorporated into the Six Year Plan, and in 1950 the targets of the growth were further raised. The plan's objectives were very ambitious and appealed to the imagination, especially that of youth. They offered enticing perspectives—among others, the anticipated growth by 40 per cent in the standard of living.

Many of these plans, however, exceeded the existing possibilities, especially since their realization took place in unusually difficult international circumstances. The West resorted to economic discrimination. It became necessary to intensify the armament efforts due to the establishment in 1949 of NATO—an aggressive military alliance composed of the United States and its Western European partners, the founding of the West German state committed to revanchism and border revisions, and the danger of a world war which was enhanced by the outbreak of hostilities in Korea in 1950.

From the start the plan was unfavourably affected by a subjective approach: the disregarding of economic realities. In particular it was erroneously assumed that the great leap was simultaneously feasible in all fields, i.e. in agriculture, the standard of living, etc. Restructuring the countryside, moreover, did not take into account the unavoidable need to supply agriculture with the means of production as well as the necessity to win over the peasants by offering them a convincing psychological motivation.

All of these factors produced various distortions and tensions. They led to growing dissatisfaction and undermined confidence that the party plans were realistic and correct.

In 1953 attempts were made to redress the profound economic imbalance by substantial price increases, and, then, in the last two years of the Six Year Plan, to modify the economic policy. Investments were substantially reduced. The rigorous—and often repressive—policy of collectivization was abandoned. More attention was paid to the economic principles of agriculture. The fact that agricultural production cannot be rapidly increased was accepted, though this meant that the realization of its social objectives—a major improvement in diet and the standard of living—also became questionable. These modifications partially restored the economic balance. Despite all the difficulties the overall economic objectives of the Six Year Plan in industrial production were attained. The achievements of that period were great. In six years the country was transformed into an industrial-agricultural one. In 1955 the share of industry in the national income was 44 per cent while that of agriculture was 27 per cent (in 1947 the corresponding figures were 34 per cent and 47 per cent respectively). In comparison qith 1938 the national income rose by 2.7 times. The productive capacity increased by 27 per cent. Nevertheless, none of the promises to increase substantially the national income, agricultural production, real wages or consumption, were completely fulfilled.

As a result of the Six Year Plan industry was restructured: the automobile and shipbuilding industries were established, while the iron, steel and chemical industries were largely expanded. Over 500 big industrial units were built. Together with those which were completed in the subsequent years they provided the foundations for industrialization. They were developed with the great, friendly assistance of the Soviet Union which provided supplies of equipment as well as advice by Soviet specialists in planning and construction, especially of the biggest projects.

The industrial map of the country included the territories of so-called Poland B.* Many city-centres were developed and urbanization was advanced. Warsaw as well as many other cities were rebuilt from ruin. There were profound changes in the social and professional structure of the population. The great migration processes were completed. The surplus of population in the countryside was relieved by moving many labourers to the cities to work in industry. As a result, during those six years the working class increased by over 2.5 million, predominantly young people.

There were truly revolutionary achievements in education, culture and science. These were marked, above all, by the liquidation of illiteracy, a great increase in book-reading (partly because books became so inexpensive) and the universal access to culture through construction of many cinemas, houses of culture, electrification and the making accessible of radio throughout the country, the support of mass cultural activities and of folklore creativity. The educational system, including students' residences, was greatly expanded. 438,000 students completed high school and university education, most of them of worker and peasant origin.

The accomplishments of the Six Year Plan had lasting effects upon social consciousness. They expanded and consolidated the social advancement of the workers and the peasants, strengthened the enthusiasm for work, which in the first post-war years was expressed in the system of socialist emulation, and especially appealed to the imagination of the younger generation among whom an important role was played by its mass organization: the Union of Polish Youth.

These were the social processes of historical significance. Yet, their effects and importance were reduced by the errors and deviations committed by the authorities, which led to the emergence of a rigid, bureaucratic system, and which, moreover, often unnecessarily resorted to repression. The gap separating the people and the authorities widened. This was particularly drastic in the realms having to do with social problems, conditions of labour, wages, etc., which fomented dissatisfaction and conveyed the impression that there was a discrepancy between the party's and the government's declarations, and their deeds and the existing reality. It was further deepened by the growing separation of the authorities and a part of the party apparatus from the working class and the society. Such legal categories as acts

---

* Poland B was composed of the poorest and predominantly agricultural areas located mostly in the east. (A.B.)

against the state and the political system, sabotage, etc., and the corresponding penalties, were broadened. The attitude towards the veterans of the Home Army and the Polish armed forced in the West, even those who actively participated in professional activities and worked for People's Poland, worsened. Indeed, repressions were applied against those who had been members of leftist groups during the occupation and the activists of the workers' movement. Disguised as being necessary in the conditions of the sharpening class struggle, the widening repressions resulted in abuses of their power by the security apparatus and the military intelligence as well as by the prosecutors and the courts.

The activities of the authorities responsible for security, which were necessary to prevent real political crimes—anti-state acts, espionage and diversions—in effect violated the constitutional norms. There emerged a specific, informal system of attributes and methods of operation of these organs. They even usurped the right to encroach into the party itself. The body which supervised them on behalf of the party leadership was the Politbureau's commission chaired by First Secretary B. Bierut. It also included the chief of the ministry of Public Security, Stanislaw Radkiewicz, and J. Berman, who as a Politbureau member and the party secretary directly supervised these matters. Without detracting from the responsibility of the top leaders for those activities, including the violations of the law (the appropriate steps in that regard were taken in 1956-1957), it should be noted that both in depth and in scope such violations in Poland were limited. It must also be stressed that the great majority of the security officials acted honestly, and, while fighting the real enemies, guarded with full devotion the young people's state.

In the process of selection of cadres in that period there was distrust, suspiciousness and a formalistic, mechanical application of the political and class criteria, often coupled with a failure to scrutinize the candidates' real ideological involvement, conscientiousness and professionalism. At the same time there emerged a network of informal connections depending on a common past or national origins. This restricted the access of new, valuable cadres to the top positions and a turnover there for better qualified people.

The ideological-political aggression by the western "cold war" centres and the acute class struggle in the broad realms of the spiritual life of the society, necessitated an intensification of the ideological activities. Yet, their effects were weakened by oversimplifications and superficiality and even incidents of dishonesty and disinformation.

From the first years of the existence of the People's Republic Marxism-Leninism has been gaining recognition in the ideological realm as a valid system of values and research tool. Owing to this, science in Poland was truly enriched. The Marxist cadres gained in knowledge and grew in number. A broad and intense ideological training undertaken among the party members, and especially among the party actiff, contributed to the spreading of basic Marxist-Leninist knowledge.

At the same time, however, a large number of Polish scientists were dismissed from their posts in a bureaucratic manner, and Polish science, including the applied sciences, was deprived of access to many world scientific achievements. In social sciences and pedagogy Marxism was often interpreted in an oversimplified fashion and the Marxists not infrequently paid for their shortcomings in scientific preparation by their rather contrived scientific careers. Hence, later on, during the painful period for the party, the ideological commitment of these people was easily eroded or even completely lost.

The period under consideration was characterized by the development of culture, its dynamic spread and true democratization—overcoming the barriers separating its creators from the broad masses, and especially the workers and the peasants. These achievements, however, were lessened by restricting creative styles and expressions, imposing socialist realism as the only valid creative method, and by mechanically separating this artistic creativity from the current climate of world cultural achievements. This led not only to limiting the richness of artistic creativity, but also to stimulating the conformist and opportunistic trends which later resulted in politically dazzling, but morally ignoble, twists by some individuals when they found themselves faced with situations requiring difficult ideological and political choices.

The negative phenomena in that period included oversimplifications of national traditions regarding patriotism. These produced a renewal and consolidation of the old divisions and the opening up of new spheres of distrust towards the party and the people's authority. They also negatively affected the climate in Polish-Soviet relations and the internationalist consciousness of the Polish working class and the society. The alliance and friendship with the USSR and its manifold assistance were of a decisive significance in restoring Poland's independence, protecting its state and national security, the integrity of its territory and its new and just borders. The manifold, brotherly Soviet aid helped Poland during the most difficult moments of restoring life in the devastated country, and, then, in advancing the great process of industrialization. Nevertheless, the cult of Stalin and its consequences assisted in preserving the historical prejudices and complexes in the Polish society. This was basically changed only after new leaders took over in the CPSU and in the PUWP in 1956. An exceptionally important role was played here by the Declaration of the Soviet Government on the developing and strengthening of the friendship and cooperation between the USSR and other socialist states of October 30, 1956.

It was during that period, starting with the historic Unity Congress, that the PUWP acquired its own character—its programme based on Marxism-Leninism, its internal life, its structures and its methods of performing its leading role. These were not just simple continuations of the traditions of the PWP and the left wing of the PSP. However, side by side with the positive there were also negative features. First of all the party's methods of performing its leading role relied less on inspirational than on institutional means. The arrangement of the party apparatus was made to exactly parallel that of the state and its administration. This contributed to the practice of substituting the party apparatus for state organs and of the party's directly intervening in an resolving detailed problems.

The party apparatus—which was its great asset—was recruited primarily from among the workers and the peasants. They obtained their organizational qualifications through practical experience and supplemented them by many courses at the party schools and by adult education, compensating for their theoretical shortcomings with ideological commitment. At the same time there grew up a tendency for the party apparatus to replace the collegial, elected organs of the party. A one-sided centralism developed while democracy—particularly as expressed through collegial, open and sincere discussions and uninhibited voting—became restricted. Internal criticism was formalistic, general and directed "from above", and less and less "from below". In the activities of the party as a whole a special role, even above the party statutes, was assumed by the Central Committee Secretariat and the First Secretary around whom a cult of the unique and an atmosphere of charisma were created. The role of the Central Committee as well as of the lower party organs was restricted; the independence of the provincial, district and basic organizations was similarly limited.

At the highest level of the Politbureau and the government, various functions of the party and the state were often merged. This was final confirmation of the party's assuming consolidated, detailed responsibility for everything that was happening in the state, which burdened the party with all the day-to-day problems. A similar situation existed in the provinces and the districts. This manner of performing the party's leading role also produced a feeling of being discriminated against among the allied parties and the non-party people.

In 1954 the party membership was lower than at the time of the Unity Congress. Participation by the workers and the peasants declined, while the proportion of the intelligentsia increased. In 1956 the party numbered 1,137,000 members and candidates. In 1957 the membership declined again due to the new situation in the party and the country. Strenuous efforts were made to maintain a majority of workers and peasants in the party.

The strong party presence in the state structures and social organizations, however, was not necessarily a measure of its real influence in the society, and, above all, among the working class—or of the development between them of mutual two-way information and inspiration and mutual understanding and confidence. The natural, but declining, enthusiasm manifested at the beginning of the Six Year Plan, was now encouraged through formalistic means and oversimplified propaganda, instead of through real discussions with the working class including the presentation of hard truths. As a result there began to emerge a gap between the party and its organs and the working class as well as other groups of working people; there even appeared distrust towards its correct pragmatic slogans.

The trade unions, the youth union and other social organizations, whose functions were to serve as the party's transmitters to the masses, performed their role in a more and more perfunctory fashion. The transmission was increasingly one-sided. The trade unions supported production efforts and carried out intense social and cultural-educational activities, and in those realms they had considerable accomplishments. Yet, they stopped short of performing the protective role which was also their natural duty. The unions' involvement in the determination of working conditions and wages became purely formalistic which—in view of the not always just and socially understandable administrative decisions—produced resentment among the labourers and entire professional groups.

The whole complex of socio-political practices presented above contributed to the accumulation of tensions which at one time or another had to break out.

It was at that time that the Communist Party of the Soviet Union—after the death of Stalin in March 1953—initiated the process of significant changes in the USSR. Through a determined struggle against so-called Beriaism the violations of legality were elminated, economic policy was modified and Leninist principles were restored in the internal party life. This, undoubtedly, had a great influence over the revival of criticism in other Communist parties, including the PUWP, and their own launching of political changes.

The leadership of the PUWP introduced the changes in economic policy which were adopted at the II Congress in March 1954. The need for political changes were first raised at the meeting of the party actiff in 1954, and was formally confirmed at the II Plenary Meeting of the Central Committee in January 1955. Criticism of the violations of legal norms and of insufficient supervision over activities of the security organs led to the dissolution of the Ministry of Public Security— and its replacement with the Committee of Public Security—which was at that time an event of great significance.

At the same time, however, the excessive restraint which was shown, especially in the half-hearted personnel decisions, evoked growing criticism among the party actiff, and diverse reactions among the persons who wanted to evade responsibility for their participation in the erroneous line and its effects. It is fair to say that the Politbureau and Secretariat of the Central Committee failed to anticipate the consequences of these phenomena in the party, and especially the ultimate contradictions in all spheres. Probably, while being aware of their responsibility for the past line, they feared its consequences and, therefore, clung to the non-Leninist methods of socialist construction.

In effect, then, the implementation of the correct resolutions of the III Plenum was slowed down. Liquidating the consequences of the violations of legal norms, withdrawing the false accusations and reviewing the unjust sentences, was carried out only reluctantly and sluggishly until October-November 1956. The most striking example was the case of W. Gomulka, who was arrested in 1951 and released in 1954, but against whom the old accusations were upheld until the VII Plenum in July 1956, and who was re-admitted into the party leadership only in October 1956.

The same position was taken by the Politbureau—headed after the death of B. Bierut in March 1956 by Edward Ochab as the First Secretary—regarding other urgent problems. There were many changes, but they were piecemeal and half-hearted; there were no major personnel changes in the government and those which were carried out were not sufficiently credible.

The ideological and moral shock which was produced by the revelations of the XX Congress of the CPSU coincided with the period when the political crisis in Poland was greatly accelerating. In practice it was affecting all spheres of political life as well as of culture, science and the management of the economy. In the party, and especially among its actiff, there were divisions over what its course should be and the ways to overcome the crisis. These divisions, however, were not as acute as they were perceived to be at that time. The group interests, dictated by the desire to avoid responsibility for the errors and deviations, also came to the surface. There was an attempt by some intellectual and journalistic groups linked with the revisionist circles in the Warsaw party actiff, to take over the initiative. Such tendencies emerged particularly, alongside of an understandable desire to overcome the deviations, in the editorial board of the two weeklies: *Po prostu* and *Nowa Kultura*.

The party leadership did not look up to the working class and the workers' party organizations. It did not search there for support and inspiration to lead the country out of the political crisis and to strengthen its bonds with the masses. Meanwhile, the dissatisfaction of the working class grew, especially over the economic problems and the declining standard of living as well as over the accumulated consequences of the illegalities and violations of the socialist principles.

On June 28, 1956 in Poznan, as a result of a prolonged regulating of the work norms and wages, which was unsatisfactory for many groups, there erupted a strike at the Cegielski factory. The direct cause for this was that on June 27 the Minister of Machine Industry, Roman Fidelski, temporized on some promises which he had made to the delegates of the Cegielski factory only a day earlier. The promises dealt with the reimbursement of unjustly collected taxes, overtime pay, the liquidation of the consequences of slowdowns caused by the co-producers, and other matters of interest to the labourers. The strike at the Cegielski factory produced a chain-reaction among other enterprises which advanced both specific demands and some of a general character.

Early in the morning of June 28 the workers took to the streets. About 9 a.m. tens of thousands of people gathered at and around Zamkowy Place. At first the mass demonstration was peaceful. Soon however, it became uncontrollable and became transformed into a destructive force. This was clearly inconsistent with the goals of the workers' protest, for this large and highly emotional gathering became influenced by hooligans and criminals as well as by people hostile to the socialist system. They fomented aggressive and destructive instincts and the robbing of social property. They also inspired and organized the acquisition of arms, attacks against public buildings and an assault upon the prison. About 10 a.m. a group of adventurers took over a broadcasting vehicle, using it to spread the false information that the Cegielski factory workers' delegates had been arrested. This information, bordering on provocation, intensified the aggressive mood of the crowds. An attack upon the prison at Mlynarska Street was organized, the guards were disarmed, 257 prisoners were released and the arms' depot was taken over. Next there came attacks against the court and the prosecutor's office as well as against the building of the Provincial Office of Public Security. The last was defended by its functionaries and a platoon of soldiers from the Corps of Internal Security. The building was stormed and attempts were made to set it on fire with Molotov cocktails. There was an exchange of fire and there were the first casualties. Armed groups attacked posts of the Citizens' Militia throughout the city and seized the arms' depot used in military studies at the university. Altogether 245 weapons were stolen. Looting of the public buildings and shops also started. As a result of the avalanche of events the situation in the city was becoming more and more dangerous—it had caused casualties and material losses and threatened still further grave consequences. It required the government to take immediate and decisive action.

The local authorities were not able to cope with the grave situation even in its initial stages. They did not have at their disposal sufficient forces to discipline the demonstrators and to disperse them before extreme, unfortunate dvelopments occurred. The appearance of some militiamen, who in any case were not properly equipped, only aggravated the participants. In this situation around 11 a.m. the small units of the Poznan officers' schools were introduced into action, also with little effect. Since the soldiers were ordered not to use firearms, the aggressive crowds attacked them with impunity and even tried to disarm them.

Faced with the necessity to bring to an end a situation which was acquiring dangeous proportions, the Politbureau decided to resort to military force. The command was taken by the deputy minister of National Defence, General Stanislaw Poplawski, who, together with the premier, Jozef Cyrankiewicz, responsible for the entire operation, arrived in Poznan at 1 a.m. General Poplawski used the two local officers' schools and military units from the nearby training centres to soon bring the situation under control. Around 5 p.m. order was restored around the building of the Provincial Office of Public Security, and on June 30 in the evening and through the night the military units were withdrawn from the city, leaving only temporary guards around some public buildings.

It must be underlined that the military received permission only about 1 p.m. to use firearms. Firearms, moreover, were to be used only in self-defence and to silence the armed groups' firebases, as well as to prevent the looting and the devastation of public buildings. The soldiers and militiamen—even though they were attacked with various objects, attempts were made to disarm them, and they were the targets of fire from the commandeered weapons—responded in a restrained fashion. This way the scope of the tragedy was restricted, but there were casualties, including some innocent ones.

During the events in Poznan 55 persons were killed and, subsequently, 19 died as a result of injuries. Among them were 66 civilians, 3 workers of the security apparatus, 1 militiaman and 4 soldiers of the Polish Army. There were 575 wounded including 15 security apparatus workers, 5 militiamen and 37 soldiers.

The Poznan events represented an extreme case of the long-building tensions and conflicts. The government did not search energetically enough for a way to remove the danger by taking appropriate socio-economic and political measures, and in particular by gaining the support of the working class. The leadership of that time lacked the ability to make a proper analysis and to strike at the roots of the existing situation. It assumed that the events were exclusively due to the new diversions and provocations by the enemy centres. This was an erroneous appraisal—which does not mean, of course, that the anti-socialist forces did not participate in the Poznan events and did not instigate and organize their extreme, confrontationist forms. Yet, it was not they who were responsible for the sources and the massive character of those demonstrations.

In connection with those events the prosecutor's office put forward charges against 54 persons and among them 27 were sentenced. However, only 3 persons, guilty of assassinations of public order functionaries, served their full sentences. By the decision of the Prosecutor General all other cases were dismissed and all the prisoners were released.

A fuller account of the June events was presented at the VIII Plenum in October 1956. In his programmatic speech the First Secretary asserted that the leadership of the party at that time was wrong and that the workers had compelled it to abandon its course. The workers, by giving the party a "painful lesson", protested against the wrongdoing and the deviations from the basic principles of socialism. The architects of the wrong course or those responsible for its implementation, however, were not named. No one in the government suffered official consequences, except that Minister R. Fidelski was transferred to another post in the central administration.

The events of June 1956 were a warning-signal against the attempts to arrest the changes which were underway. But they also contributed to the sharpening of the crisis. A progressive paralysis of the main political centres, which failed to establish contact with the working class, was manifested in various spheres. In particular it was demonstrated in the sphere of legality and democracy, in the system of economic planning and management, in the relations with the other parties and the youth movement as well as in the efforts to revive the Leninist norms in the internal life of the party. As a result of this paralysis the correct resolutions of the VII Plenum, which contained many new solutions and proposals, could not be realized. Only the cumulative effects of the tensions and conflicts, and their spread in the next few months, influenced the Politbureau to undertake basic decisions; above all, in the political and personnel sphere.

The final overcoming of the crisis became possible due to the position of the working class which, like all working people, believed that the solutions should be sought only within the framework of socialism and with decisive participation by the party. And there were forces in the party which helped it to restore its bonds with the working class and the society.

Of great assistance was the legendary person of W. Gomulka. The firm position which he had displayed when faced with unjustified accusations and during his imprisonment, brought him appreciation and respect in the party and the society. Ignoring the personal injustice and accepting the postponement of the resolution of the controversial issues from 1948, he agreed to assume the responsibility for the party's leadership. At the VIII Plenum, which was held on October 19-21, 1956, he was elected to be and took over the duties of the First Secretary of the Central Committee.

In the consciousness of the Poles the VIII Plenum represented a watershed. It elected—for the first time by secret ballot—the new Politbureau and the Secretariat. The line adopted by the VIII Plenum showed a determination and a realistic intention to break off the crisis and to restore in the country the principles of socialist democracy. This included relations with the USSR, which became governed by Leninist principles at the XX Congress of the CPSU. These relations were adopted during talks with the Soviet delegation led by Nikita Khrushchev, which arrived in Warsaw on the opening day of the VIII

Plenum. W. Gomulka participated in the Polish delegation. These talks were continued during the visit in Moscow by the party-government delegation, led by W. Gomulka, in November 1956, when appropriate declarations and agreements were signed. These made provision for, among other things, a Soviet loan to Poland, a moratorium on the Polish debts (compensating for past deliveries of Polish coal to the USSR), the determination of the conditions for stationing of Soviet troops in Poland, and the repatriation home of many thousands of Poles.

The innovations in the party after the VIII Plenum were quite extensive. There were basic changes in the composition of the provincial and the district committees. In most cases these were carried out in response to strong, and even emotional, pressures by the party rank and file and even by non-party people. The party apparatus was also changed. After its final reorganization in 1958 its size was reduced by 44.4 per cent. The structure and the activities of the party apparatus were now fitted to serve political, and not administrative, needs. The decisive role was given to the elected organs: 33 members of the Central Committee, 51 provincial secretaries, 35 ministers and deputy ministers and 23 chairmen of the Provincial National Councils, were dismissed.

The IX Plenum in May 1957 expelled from the Central Committee and the party former Politbureau members J. Berman and S. Radkiewicz (S. Radkiewicz was dismissed from the Politbureau at the VI Plenum in July 1955, and J. Berman at the VII Plenum in July 1956), who had been responsible for the direction and supervision of the security apparatus. The Plenum also expelled from the Central Committee a former deputy minister of Public Security, Mieczyslaw Mietkowski.

The Deputy Minister of Public Security, Roman Romkowski who was also a former Central Committee member), and the department directors there, Anatol Fejgin and Jozef Rozanski, were sentenced to long-term imprisonment. Other functionaries of the security organs responsible for improper methods of investigation were also sentenced to imprisonment by the courts.

Towards the end of October 1956 Stefan Cardinal Wyszynski was released from detention in a monastery, where he had stayed since September 1954. After resuming activity he played a positive role in arriving at an understanding between the state and the Church on the basis of the church's recognizing the Polish, socialist *raison d'état*.

The process of restoring the unity and effectiveness of the party took longer. It was only completed by the III Congress, which was postponed several times and was eventually held in March 1959. It included the verification of the party ranks and a struggle against the proponents of revisionism and dogmatism.

The new party line sketched at the VIII Plenum was theoretically developed and supplemented in an address at the IX Plenum in May 1959 by W. Gomulka. He presented there the most developed conception hitherto of socialist construction in the Polish conditions. The programme and the general line were upheld by the III Congress of the party in March 1959, although even at that time a retreat from at least some post-October changes was visible. This affected particularly the workers' councils and the economic reforms which had been launched, inspiring great hope among the working class, in 1956.

The line of the VIII and IX Plena included many new priorities and tackled many new problems: undertaking the political and ideological struggle against both revisionism and opportunism as well as dogmatism and conservatism; adopting the changes devised jointly with the United Peasant Party in agricultural policy; deepening legality in the state; determining the conditions of understanding with the Church; reviving the cultural policy; renewing and enriching the forms of Polish-Soviet relations which offered new incentives towards a true class understanding and the effective realization of the ideals of both patriotism and cooperation among the PUWP, the UPP and the Democratic Party and an increase in participation in the government by the allied parties.

The new platform of national cooperation, called the Front of the Nation's Unity, expanded the scope of its participants and activities. The electoral procedures were changed even before the parliamentary elections in January 1957. They provided for the opportunity to choose among candidates. Composition of the parliament shifted in favour of the workers and the peasants as well as the non-party people, including representatives of the Catholic groups.

There were difficulties in the youth movement, which underwent an ideological, political and organizational crisis. The Union of Polish Youth, deprived of political guidance, could not withstand the tendencies towards its liquidation present within the Main Executive. This led to the unfortunate disbanding of the Union. An independent Polish Boy Scouts' Association was revived. With the assistance of the PUWP and the allied parties it was possible to create two new organizations representing special social strata: the Union of Socialist

Youth and the Union of Rural Youth. Then began the long process of their development which, however, in terms of numbers and the scope of their activities and, above all, of their ideological involvement never matched that of the UPY.

Most important was the fact that the new party line was introduced from the start—even though many innovations had not yet been properly legislated—and was supported by the new actiff as well as that part of the old one which constructively involved themselves anew in the changed circumstances. The post-October policy of the party, and the authority of W. Gomulka, gained support among a substantial part of the society in all its strata. The best illustration of this was the results of the elections in January 1957, and especially the positive response to the appeal not to cross out candidates, and thus to endorse the announced policy directives.

Motives for this support varied a great deal. They included not only a positive acceptance of the party line and its programme, but also speculation by the opposition group about the second stage of the changes which was to lead to so-called full liberalization; in other words it was conceived by the political opposition as merely a step towards ultimate eroding of the foundations of the socialist system. This was even more so since there appeared ideological differences in the party itself over the understanding and interpretation of the new line. They were manifested by the hesitant struggle against revisionism, which had not been fully crushed, and which in reviving was weakening the party, and at the same time in the abandonment of the struggle against dogmatism, which was perceived as not dangerous since it had few opportunities for advancement.

The confirmed adversaries of socialism, including the remnants of the reactionary opposition from the mid-1940s, manifested their presence during the crisis, but failed to win any visible support. At the time of the VIII Plenum calculations for the so-called second stage—which came into the surface in the context of the Hungarian events, where they were transformed into a counter-revolution—ended in a fiasco. The Polish society as a whole displayed prudence and supported the party line. This does not mean that the struggle against the adversaries was conducted with sufficient determination. There were instances of relenting to the alien pressures, of ideological confusion and of various frustrations stemming from its lasting too long, of a lack of sufficient energy in educating the youth, and in resistance against the slander campaigns carried out by the diversionary centres.

Yet, all in all, the line adopted by the new PUWP leadership was generally accepted as a correct one and for many years it assured a harmonious development of the country.

2. *The events in March 1968 and the crisis of 1970*

The Polish economy still lagged far behind the rich countries which had been developed earlier, were considerably less devastated by the war, and which, because of the scientific-technical revolution, were continuing to develop more rapidly. Yet, in that period there emerged in Poland new opportunities for economic growth and for satisfying the new needs of the society. These required greater efficiency and profitability as well as improvement in the quality and modernity of production through changing the structure of the national economy, its methods of planning and management, and the adoption of more effective social incentives. Such a chance was inherent in the conception of a general economic reform advanced by the Economic Council appointed in 1956. Its main feature was to reconcile the increased independence of enterprises with the corrected system of central planning. This conception, however, was not given sufficient attention and, consequently, was never properly considered and realized.

The lack of resolution and the weakness adversely affected future developments. Nevertheless, the growth of national income in the 1960s amounted to 80 per cent and as such was relatively high in the world. Considerable progress was made in developing the coal and energy industries, which proved to be particularly profitable during the sharp oil crisis (which, incidentally, was not originally anticipated) in the 1970s. Unfortunately, this was not coupled with the development of investments and technologies which would lead to saving coal and energy (as well as the other raw materials) in production.

Mining of copper ore and its refinement was initiated and developed. Exploitation of sulphur, which today represents an important export item, increased dramatically. Side by side with the development of the nitrogen and sulphuric acid industries, the production of chemical fertilizers was increased from 480,000 to 1,630,000 tons. Efforts were made to develop and modernize tractor production, and the automobile and shipbuilding industries.

Yet, the exploitation of the essential material base (and also the steel, rolling mill production, aluminium, cement and oil products) to diversify and modernize the final production of large-scale products of a high quality was obviously unsatisfactory. In investments not enough attention was paid to consumer industry or to agriculture and the agricultural industry.

Generally, then, the economic growth was one-sided, which reduced its positive effects and the quality of functioning of the economy as a whole. Ineffectiveness in mustering the forces contributing to technical progress prevented the development of greater export capabilities in manufacturing, and perpetuated, with only slight improvements, the pattern of raw material-agricultural exports to the developed countries. Although the balance of payments was preserved and debts were avoided (which undoubtedly was very positive), the opportunities inherent in international trading and specialization—which could have facilitated production for exports as well as modernization, and this way could have contributed to the reduction of tensions in the home market—were not sufficiently utilized.

So the policy of intensive development, already recognized as indispensable, was not actually implemented. The growth was not based on decreasing the material-energy input, increasing labour efficiency and developing profitable foreign trade. Only a small part of the surplusses attained in the economy could be used to increase consumption.

Starting from a low level, the rate of agricultural production increase somewhat exceeded the world average, but it remained subject to substantial fluctuations. Food consumption increased (for instance average meat consumption rose from 50 to 61 kilograms p.a.). Increased exports of meat more than compensated for some increase in the imports of grain and fodder. Nevertheless the fluctuations in the breeding of pigs resulted in serious difficulties at the meat market. A characteristic feature of the development of agriculture in that period was the slight effectiveness of the investments. This was due to the small size of the farms, which had no prospects for modernization and integration.

An increase in employment in the 1960s, as a result of the demographic rise and the greater number of women at work, amounted to 250,000 - 500,000 people annually. As a result an increase in consumption reflected more the increased employment in the socialized economy (39 per cent), and less the rise in real wages (19.5 per cent). The increase in real wages, especially towards the end of the decade, amounted to less than 2 per cent and tended to decline.

Individual wages were determined exclusively by central regulations for the different branches of the economy. They were not linked to the economic achievements of those branches and the enterprises, and not infrequently they represented just the results of the pressures exerted by various branches upon the central decision. This, in turn, led to disproportions in wages and evoked feelings of injustice. The divorce between wages and efficiency produced a negative, pessimistic view as to the prospects of economic growth and the already quite modest increase in consumption.

The discrepancy between social expectations in the realm of consumption and the degree of their fulfillment—which increased slowly, and at times even periodically decreased—together with limited choices at the market, the difficulties in obtaining apartments and furnishing them, as well as in purchasing automobiles and other durable goods, was manifested not only in a quantitative, but also in qualitative fashion. It began to weigh heavily upon the atmosphere of that period.

The 1960s were characterized by great transformations of the working class: it increased by over 2 million to over 6 million in 1970—which made it the most numerous class in Poland; it was concentrated in the big enterprises—over one-third of the industrial workers were concetnrated in enterprises with over 2,000 employees; there was also an improvement in education and professional qualifications of the workers—the proportion of labourers who completed elementary school rose in the decade from 43.4 per cent to 56.3 per cent, and those who completed the trade schools from 9.7 per cent to 18.1 per cent, leading to growth in their socio-political expectations.

At the same time among the working class there took place a visible generational change. Towards the end of the 1960s over half of the workers had been employed for less than 5 years, while the young workers with an elementary or trade education were especially heavily concentrated at the Coast, in Warsaw, Lodz and Wroclaw. For this generation of labourers, in contrast to their fathers, working in industry did not represent social advancement, for they had been brought up in a different social and cultural environment with higher incomes. They were influenced, moreover, by foreign, and often one-sided foreign, living patterns (which was particularly strongly accentuated on the Coast). In that decade there also emerged a stratum of people who worked both in industry and on the farms: the peasant-workers, who amounted to about 2 million.

There was also a rapid growth of the white collar workers, among them many with high school or higher technical education. Development and modernization of the schools was carried out jointly by the central and local governments as well as through social outlays. For example, the incentive put forward by W. Gomulka and adopted by the Front of the Nation's Unity to construct one thousand schools to mark [Poland's] millenium.

The post-October developments in culture and the arts, and the general revival of cultural and intellectual activity, were not accompanied by the development of a broad base—organized mass support for cultural-artistic endeavours, and an increase in the outlays for science and education. As the years went by and particularly towards the end of the decade, the level of cultural and educational infra-structure was one of the lowest among the socialist countries and seriously threatened the democratic principle of universality. There was painfully low—in contrast to the immediate post-war years—publication of books. Among some artistic circles there appeared ad-verse ideological trends—a vulnerability to the bourgeois system of values and manifestations of revisionism, which were not opposed energetically enough. At the same time the artistic circles were sub-mitted to confusing ideological and political criteria and growing arbitrariness in decisions as to which works should be published and popularized.

The general improvement in education led to the growth of social demands and aspirations not only in living conditions and the cultural sphere, but also with regard to the effective functioning of the econ-omy, the state organs and the social and political organizations. Wherever there appeared inability to resolve the growing contradic-tions in organizing production and developing social and cultural in-frastructure, the prestige of economic and local authorities suffered and even was undermined.

The deep qualitative and quantitative transformation of the social class structure reflected an objective and progressive socio-economic development in the 1960s. It influenced the strong aspirations of the working class and other social groups towards a better life, a more efficient economy and greater participation in the small as well as the large social communities.

An unsatisfactory response from the state and its organs to the as-pirations of the working class, and especially the younger generation—aroused by the progress in socialist construction—led to the accumu-lation of contradictions and tensions.

One of the main contradictions was the growing significance and the enhanced level of the working class (although many of its weak-nesses and immaturities still persisted) with the verbal acceptance and even emphasis of its social role, and the actual underestimating and even ignoring of the workers' aspirations towards greater influence over the activities of the party, the trade unions, management of the enterprises and local government.

Within the party throughout the entire decade the workers repre-sented about 40 per cent of the membership (the intelligentsia amounted to 42 per cent and the peasants 11 per cent), and, thus, they were situated in the second place behind the party and administration functionaries and the white collar workers. This was also reflected in the composition of the party leadership. Tendencies towards rapid growth in the number of the party members—and even a sort of competition among various territorial and local organizations in this regard—contributed to a decline in the admission criteria and the quality of the party ranks and this weakened its leading role in the ideological, political and social spheres. The foremost ideological and class character of the party, thus, was weakened.

The role of the basic party cells was gradually diminished and replaced by the higher party organs and their apparatus. The mechanism of intra-party democracy (democratic centralism) was undermined. The executive bodies (the first secretary, the secretariats, the executive) in practice dominated the elected bodies (the committees). Provincial and district executives were excessively composed—often by co-option—of members of the administration or their functionaries. This largely restricted participation by persons who did not occupy leading positions, but who nevertheless represented the party's major milieux.

Throughout the entire period of 1956-1970 the party activities and state policies were greatly influenced by the personality of W. Gomulka. In the party and state policies his views were of decisive importance and the new solutions in politics, ideology and the economy more often than not were undertaken on his initiative.

He had great leadership qualities and an immense and varied political experience. He was sensitive to class values and interests and he combined patriotic responsibility for the nation, its dignity and its state, with a profound internationalist sense. He displayed strong character, honesty, almost bordering on asceticism, an unusual capacity for hard work and an excellent memory. He did not care for popularity, although in the final years he did not resist sycophancy strongly enough. Yet, he was apodictic with increasing autocratic proclivities. Cooperating with him became more and more difficult and his popularity in the society declined and then evaporated. Not being able to appreciate the working of modern socio-economic mechanisms, he was afraid of the autonomy and initiative of the economic units and the enhanced position and activity of the socialist democratic institutions. This stemmed in part from his great concern for the existence of a stable state, which—he sensed from Polish history, as well as from his own life experiences—represents an indispensable pre-condition for the nation's existence and progress. His grasp of history as well as of modern needs enabled him to conduct an unmistakable, principled foreign and defence policy, and to uphold Poland's respected place in the socialist community, in Europe and the world. His achievement in winning recognition of the Polish western and northern boundaries from the FRG was historic. He never relented in the class struggle. At the same time the experiences of the international Communist movement and his own painful political trials made him wary of the excessive use of repression and he was patient and even magnanimous towards his political opponents. He understood the traditional, broad links between the masses of the people and religion, and he was concerned that the state policy towards religion should relfect the Polish *raison d'état*. He tended to resist the growth of current consumption in order to contribute more to future development and avoided dependence upon foreign debts.

The fate of this great leader is one more proof that even the greatest mind and the strongest character is not a substitute for collective wisdom and the combined strength of the party, and, consequently, that the development of democracy in the party and the workers' state is an absolute necessity.

Meetings of the Politbureau were called rarely (in 1961-1970 an average of 14 times a year) and rather irregularly (from 27 meetings in 1961 to 10 in 1970). Discussion at them was limited. The Secretariat of the Central Committee almost never met and its decisions were reached through the exchange of documents. This mode of operating enhanced the already extensive independence of the secretaries of the Central Committee, who were responsible for supervision of some specific spheres in not only the party, but, in effect, in the state. Among them particularly strong powers were concentrated in the hands of Zenon Kliszko, who was responsible for the cadres' policy, and Boleslaw Jaszczuk, responsible for overall economic affairs.

The Politbureau was practically beyond the control of the Central Committee. Its decisions were mechanically transmitted to all the state organs. This way the government, steered by the detailed directives from the Politbureau, and in fact from the Central Committee's secretaries, felt free of its constitutional responsibility to the parliament. In these circumstances the prestige and the competence of the parliament and the national councils were gradually more and more restricted.

The attempt after October 1956 to evolve new forms of cooperation between the PUWP and the UPP and the DP was half-hearted because it was more concerned with formalities than a real partnership.

This was not conducive to exploiting all of the opportunities and leverages of their cooperation and expanding the societal basis of the allied parties.

The III Congress took the position that the trade unions ought to actively participate in decisions concerning state matters, and particularly those dealing with the allocation of national income, wages and prices. It also postulated the participation of the executives of the unions in the various branches of industry, in the collegial bodies of the ministries and the associations of enterprises. But these principles were realized only to a limited degree.

In the 1960s, and especially in the second part of that decade, there was emerging a system of running the state and the economy which was incompatible with Leninist principles and the needs of developing socialism, and more and more rigid and overcentralized. At the same time the direct involvement of the party apparatus in the *de facto* administrative problems relegated into a secondary position its inspirational and follow-up functions. It also distracted the party's attention from ideological, political matters, from watching over the general social interest and justice, and from advancing initiatives to change the system in the direction of intensifgying its socioeconomic development. It also reduced the activity and involvement of the party in shaping the ideological consciousness of the working class and in attracting it to lead the state and economic affairs.

There was a serious lack of innovative approaches and of an understanding of development, including the changes indispensable in the structures and methods of the state and of economic activities, so they would correspond to the higher levels of production cadres' social milieux and their aspirations. As a result conclusions were not drawn when the period of extensive growth based on the increases in investment and employment was exhausted (although this fact was noted by the central party leadership). Only partial and quite ineffective reforms in the system of planning, management and material incentives were undertaken.

The party activities in that period suffered from insufficient attention to ideological matters, and from the proclivity of the top leadership to overlook acute differences and avoid ideological discussions. In 1960-1970 among 32 plena of the Central Committee only one (in 1963) was devoted to ideology.

Ignoring ideology and the development of social theory and underestimating the danger of dogmatism led to conservative tendencies and, this way, made the struggle against the real danger of revisionism, even more difficult. The lack of a creative Marxist-Leninist approach to the development of contradictions which appeared at that time facilitated the revisionists' penetration and attempts to introduce into the socialist society means and solutions characteristic of the bourgeoisie and capitalism. The anti-socialist ideologies in their different forms—from those openly hostile to those disguised behind demagogic phraseology—were spread by the opposition forces at home and by the outside diversionary centres, and had a definite influence in some segments of the society. The effects of this influence were generally greater wherever in the different milieux there was disillusionment over the lack of tangible improvement in the standard of living and in the broad expansion of socialist democracy.

There was also a deterioration in relations with the Church. Particularly in 1966—the year of celebrating the Millenium of the Polish state—the Church undertook activities incompatible with the accord and harmful to the interests of the state; the most glaring example of this being the letter by the Polish Episcopate to the West German bishops including the memorable passage: "we forgive and ask for forgiveness."

The first obvious signals of a growing crisis occurred during theso-called March events in 1968 and were strongly linked to revisionism and its carriers. The revisionist views had been nurtured, particularly in journalistic, literary and social science circles, since 1956. Their proponents were people who in the preceding period had been active as dogmatists and sectarians, such as the philosophers and sociologists from the University of Warsaw: Leszek Kolakowski or Bronislaw Baczko. Since the early 1960s they had been patrons of a group of Warsaw university and high school students, who often came from families of party activists who had been influential before 1956. After October 1956, these activists, although they claimed to be the leaders of the process of renewal, had been gradually deprived of influence. The main proponents of the movement of young oppositionists were Jacek Kuron, Karol Modzelewski and Adam Michnik. The activities and aggressiveness of these small groups visibly intensified after 1964. At first they tried to influence the party organizations at the Warsaw schools of higher education, and especially at the Warsaw University, and, then, they turned to developing independent structures of student political opposition and to provoking more and more serious political incidents.

In March 1968 in the conditions of a deteriorating material, cadre and ideological situation in higher education, and also not without influence from the developments in Czechoslovakia, they succeeded (by misinforming many students that they merely strove to improve social life and the workings of the higher educational institutions) in instigating disorders at the higher education schools in Warsaw and in several other Polish cities as well as street demonstrations. This produced indignation among the party organizations in the large enterprises and their support in extinguishing the disturbances. At the same time, however, there appeared on the part of the workers and in their party organizations sharp criticism of the party organs, and especially its leadership, stemming from dissatisfaction over economic conditions, the neglect of ideological conflicts and conservatism in the cadres' policy. In the shadow of the struggle against the revisionist and cosmopolitan tendencies there appeared, especially among the leading party actiff, the phenomena of factionalism and cliqueishness, including attempts to create artificial popularity of some persons.

The conclusions from the warning of 1968—heralding the forthcoming crisis in relations between the working class and the party or, to be precise, its leadership—were not properly drawn and utilized. The momentary ideological revival, partially in criticism of the economic system and the distorted relationship between the state and the party structures, and also the personnel changes in the composition of the Central Committee, the Politbureau and the Secretariat, which were undertaken at the V Congress in December 1968, were not deep enough to avert the growing conflict.

The last three years of the 1960s, thus, were characterized by the growing intensification of tensions in the economic, social and ideological-political developments. The contradictions, which the V Congress failed to resolve, were deepening. The authority of W. Gomulka was being exhausted—he proved to be increasingly helpless in coping with the tensions and the destructive activities within the central political and state leadership.

A violent explosion of social dissatisfaction took place after the announcement on December 12, 1970 of the decision to adjust prices, including an increase in prices of basic foodstuffs. The prices of meat and meat products and fats were increased by 17.6 per cent. The increases of other subsidized products were even higher. The prices of some unprofitable industrial goods were also raised. As a partial compensation the prices of highly profitable industrial commodities were reduced. Small wage compensations were also offered. At the same time the prices of purchasing [by the government] of livestock were raised.

From the economic point of view, especially in the light of a poor harvest, the adjustments were justified. But widespread social irritation and excitement was produced by the startling way they were introduced as well as by their unfortunate timing (just before Christmas when increased purchasing accentuated the shortage of money). The explosion, however, reflected above all the dissatisfaction of the working class and the entire society over the economic and political conditions in the country that had been accumulating for several years.

The mode of applying this decision and its implementation was as follows: after approving the government plan, the Politbureau sent a letter concerning this matter to the basic party cells to be read at their meetings on December 12. On the same day in the evening the price increases were announced on the radio and television, and next day a detailed communique appeared in the press.

On Monday, December 14, VI Plenum of the Central Committee was held (it should be noted that this happened only a few days after an important event—the signing of the treaty which normalized relations between the PPR and the FRG). The agenda of the Central Committee meeting did not include the price issue and no report was given on the results of the meetings of the basic cells where the Politbureau's letter was presented (while in the entire country these gatherings had been conducted in either an atmosphere of opposition or a universal, depressing silence, indicating that there was almost no support for the decision). None of the participants in the Plenum addressed himself to this subject. Until the end of the deliberations of the Central Committee its members were not informed about an explosion on the Coast.

During the Central Committee meeting, about 10 a.m., the first secretary of the party organization in Gdansk, Alojzy Karkoszka, and Politbureau member Stanislaw Kociolek, were informed about an interruption of work in several segments of the Gdansk shipyards and the gathering of several thousand workers demanding talks with the representatives of the Central Committee of the PUWP. S. Kociolek and A. Karkoszka immediately decided to go to Gdansk and they were joined by a few other participants in the Plenum: the Minister of Heavy Industry, responsible for shipbuilding, Franciszek Kaim; a secretary of the Gdansk provincial party organization, Wlodzimierz Stazewski, and the secretary of the party organization in the Gdansk Shipyards, Jerzy Pienkowski. After telephoning the director of the Gdansk Shipyards, S. Kociolek informed W. Gomulka about the developments in Gdansk and the decision of those comrades to go there. W. Gomulka, together with the Premier, J. Cyrankiewicz, approved of the plan.

Those comrades, receiving no additional instructions nor having any special powers, arrived in Gdansk at 1 p.m. and joined the local leading party actiff. About two hours later a thousand workers marched from the shipyard to the provincial party headquarters. At that time, however, the provincial party first secretary and the secretary responsible for economic affairs were still not present. The circumstances were also not conducive to talks with the delegates selected by the workers, especially after the masses were joined by incidental, hooligan and criminal elements and the crowd began to act in a typical spontaneous fashion.

The crowd, which quickly grew into several thousands, entered the Shipyards and the School of Engineering and occupied the Polish Radio broadcasting station, appealing for support in another demonstration before the Provincial Committee building in the afternoon to be followed by a strike and new demonstrations at 7 a.m. the next day.

At 2:50 p.m. there arrived in Gdansk the deputy minister of Internal Affairs, Henryk Slabczyk, to take command over the Ministry's forces. At 3:55 p.m. the first attempt to disperse the demonstration by force took place. The appeal to disperse failed and the cordon of Citizens' Militia was too thin to stop the crowd, which increasingly attacked it with stones, broke glass in the public buildings and continued to advance towards the Provincial Committee building. The demonstrators burned newspaper kiosks and buses, attempted to set the Provincial Committee building on fire, and, then, devastated the railroad station, halting train traffic. Only at 10 p.m. did the destructive activities stop and the crowd disperse.

In the course of the clashes about a dozen people were slightly hurt. Sixteen people who devastated public property and shops and committed theft were detained.

From the early morning on December 14 the party and economic actiff of the Gdansk Shipyards unsuccessfully tried to defuse the tense situation among the labourers and to stop, by persuasion, the strike and the demonstrations. In the evening the chairman of the Presidium of the Provincial National Council, Tadeusz Bejm, appeared on television appealing for reason and prudence and the protection of the property created in such difficult conditions by those who rebuilt Gdansk. Late in the evening there were consultations of the actiff of the Provincial Committee with the District Committee, the labourers' representatives and the party actiff of the local enterprises.

At 10:25 p.m. there arrived in Gdansk, with W. Gomulka's approval, two Politbureau members, Z. Kliszko and I. Loga-Sowinski, as well as, on W. Gomulka's order, the deputy minister of National Defence, General Grzegorz Korczynski.

Having present in Gdansk three Politbureau members, the deputy premier responsible for the shipbuilding industry, the deputy minister of National Defence and the deputy minister of Internal Affairs, was not conducive to effective managing of the state and party affairs. The authority of individual persons was not clear, there was no single state leadership responsible in a legal and constitutional fashion. Z. Kliszko, who was in Gdansk and whose advice had influenced W. Gomulka's decisions since he was the First Secretary's closest collaborator, was treated as representing the state-party leadership, although formally he neither had such powers nor was the chief of the local leadership.

The crucial decision which affected further developments at the Coast was reached next day, in the morning of Tuesday, December 15. At 9 a.m. in the Politbureau meeting room, there assembled a group of persons who in the existing circumstances occupied the most pertinent positions in the state and the party. Participating in this meeting were the First Secretary of the Central Committee of the PUWP—W. Gomulka; the chairman of the State Council—Marian Spychalski; the president of the Council of Ministers—J. Cyrankiewicz; and the secretaries of the Central Committee of the PUWP—B. Jaszczuk, responsible for economic affairs, Mieczyslaw Moczar, responsible for security and military affairs. There were also the persons especially invited to the meeting—the chief of the Administration Division in the Central Committee, Stanislaw Kania, the minister of National Defence, Wojciech Jaruzelski; the minister of Internal Affairs, Kazimierz Switala; and the Commandant-in-Chief of the Citizens' Militia, Tadeusz Pietrzak.

At the outset of the meeting the information about the grave, destructive events from the past day was already known, especially the devastation of shops and the looting of social property, the demolishing of vehicles, the attempt to set on fire the Provincial Committee building, and the devastation of the Gdansk railroad station. It was also known that earlier that morning events had already advanced in an avalanche-like fashion. The strikes had spread into the Gdansk harbour and the remaining shipyards in Gdansk and Gdynia as well as to other enterprises. Massive street marches were moving towards the Provincial Committee, the Gdansk National Council and the

Headquarters of the Citizens' Militia. Information arrived about attacks against the building of the Traffic Command of the Citizens' Militia and the prison, and, subsequently, against the Provincial Committee building. In its vicinity five militia and military vehicles and several trucks used as local delivery vans were set on fire. There were columns of smoke over the city. There were also reports of the first shots being fired from the crowds, wounding three militiamen. One militiaman was massacred.

In this situation W. Gomulka, taking into account the information which was arriving from the Coast and which testified to the violent and dangerous spread of the destructive current of events, made the decision to resort to arms by the forces of order and the army. Arms were to be used only in the event of a direct attack against the militiamen and the soldiers, the setting on fire or destroying of buildings and the posing of danger to human life. The rules of resorting to arms W. Gomulka determined in the following fashion: after a vocal warning the first shots should go into the air, then after 5-10 seconds—in the event of further advance by the attacking crowd towards the militiamen and the soldiers—a salvo was to be aimed at the legs. This decision took effect at 12 a.m. on December 15.

W. Gomulka's decisions were taken in the presence of the chairman of the State Council and the president of the Council of Ministers and therefore, became formal state decisions. W. Gomulka ordered J. Cyrankiewicz to convey these decisions to General G. Korczynski, which the chairman of the Council of Ministers immediately did.

At 1:50 p.m. on the same day in W. Gomulka's office there took place another meeting of the leading party and state activists; its composition was the same as in the morning (except for S. Kania), but it was expanded by the two party secretaries: Stefan Olszowski and Artur Starewicz as well as by the Chief-of-Staff, General Boleslaw Chochla. The meeting was already aware that in Gdansk the building of the Supreme Technical Council had been set on fire and the Provincial Committee building was burning, while the militiamen and soldiers had only with the greatest difficulty, risking their own lives, but without resorting to arms, evacuated its workers.

W. Gomulka, who was in a state of extreme agitation, accused the forces of order and the local authorities at the Coast of not undertaking sufficiently energetic and efficient activities. During that meeting W. Gomulka decided to establish in Gdansk a local staff headed by the deputy minister of National Defence, General C. Korczynski, and including S. Kociolek, A. Karkoszka, H. Slabczyk and the provincial commandant of the Citizens' Militia, Colonel Roman Kolczynski.

In addition, it was decided to send to Gdansk General B. Chochla to provide staff planning assistance.

The local staff did not include the two other Politbureau members already in Gdansk: Z. Kliszko and I. Loga-Sowinski. The staff did not work systematically and collegially. Z. Kiszko commanded the greatest, although informal, authority at the Coast, and in fact dictated some orders to the local staff.

At 2 p.m. on the same day there arrived at the Coast to organize a reserve position for the Ministry of the Interior forces, its deputy minister, Franciszek Szlachcic. In fact, however, this was never done.

On December 15 there was in Gdansk a very dangerous situation. Already at 7:30 the first shots had been fired from the crowd, wounding three militiamen. The crowd attempted to set public buildings on fire. The militiamen who tried to contain the crowd were attacked with stones, bricks, bolts, planks, etc. A fire brigade vehicle which was heading to help the people in a building set on fire, itself was burned.

In the course of the street disturbances on that day 6 people were killed and about 300 were wounded. Fifty-four shops were looted and 19 vehicles destroyed.

At 10:00 p.m. on that day there began in Gdansk a meeting of the executive of the Provincial Committee with the participation of S. Kociolek and F. Kaim. It was also attended by Z. Kliszko, I. Loga-Sowinski and the Central Committee secretary Ryszard Pospieszalski. During the meeting Z. Kliszko, worried that the street demonstrations with their dangerous consequences could be repeated, ordered a blockade of the Gdansk Shipyards. This was to be done by guarding the gates, so the workers could not come out of the Shipyard. In the event of such attempts arms were to be used.

On December 16 the labourers in the Lenin Shipyard as well as those from the Reconstruction and the North Shipyards declared occupational strikes. About 8 a.m., despite warnings, a large group of mostly young people, armed with iron bars, metal rods and other similar objects decided to move against the forces blocking Gate 2. Despite the calls to stop and the warning shots the group did not stop. After the salvos to the ground 2 people died from ricochetting bullets and 11 were wounded.

The wave of strikes, demonstrations and street disturbances continued. Only late in the evening did the authorities reach an agreement with the representatives of the Gdansk shipyards for the strikers to leave. Additional means of transportation were made available which took them home.

On December 17 the situation in Gdansk improved, but most of the enterprises remained closed. In various parts of the city there were continued clashes between the forces of order and, generally young people who acted aggressively and devastated public property. Particularly dangerous were the events in Gdynia. On December 14 there was quiet. On December 15 some of the labourers in the Shipyard of the Paris Commune, the Reconstruction Shipyard and the "Dalmor" abandoned work and marched to the City Committee of the PUWP and to the Presidium of the City National Council where their delegates held talks with the chairman of the Presidium, Jan Marianski. The chairman, after telephoning T. Bejm, agreed that he would convey a petition from the enterprises' representatives, demanding withdrawal of the price increases to S. Kociolek, provided that the demonstrators would go home or return to work, as in fact happened. It should be underlined that, although the above-mentioned enterprises manifested their solidarity with the Gdansk shipyards by interrupting work, there was in Gdynia no destruction, robberies, etc.

Nevertheless, at midnight all the delegates of the 31 enterprises in Gdynia, who formed a sort of strike committee, and who from 7:30 p.m. to 10 p.m. had negotiated with the chairman of the Presidium of the City Council in Gdynia, J. Marianski, were arrested. The decision to arrest the strike committee in Gdynia was taken by the local staff. The arrest had most unfortunate effects. The atmosphere in the Shipyard of the Paris Commune became even more tense and a new demonstration was announced, unless the arrested people were released.

On December 16, Z. Kliszko made two decisions concerning the Shipyard of the Paris Commune. The first was to dismiss all the labourers from work and to verify them before re-admission; and the second to blockade all the gates to the Shipyard. The blockade of the Shipyard was to prevent the workers from entering. On the basis of this decision, in the evening it was announced that work in the Shipyard was suspended and militia and army sub-units were placed to guard the gates. After this decision was made and implemented, S. Kociolek, who had not been informed about it, at 10 p.m. appealed on television to the workers at the Coast to return to work. After realizing the contradiction between his appeal and the blockade of the Shipyard, an informational activity was undertaken in the city and on the access routes confirming the shipyard closure and appealing to the labourers to stay home. This, however, was not very effective.

In the early morning of December 17 in front of the Shipyard of the Paris Commune, despite the calls and warnings, an attempt was made by an aggressive crowd to enter into the enterprise. The forces blocking the Shipyard were attacked with stones. After the first calls and warnings, with some soldiers already hurt and wounded, and after the warning shots into the air, the salvos into the ground in front of the attackers killed 4 persons by the ricochetting bullets and wounded several others.

In the next few hours in different parts of the city there were serious street disturbances, where soldiers and militiamen were actively attacked, attempts made to disarm them and to take over military equipment. In some cases the forces of order were compelled to resort to arms. The tragic consequences of all these clashes amounted to 18 killed and several tens of thousands wounded.

Another area of sharp conflict was Szczecin. There were violent protests and actions, especially by the workers from the A. Warski Shipyard and the Reconstruction Shipyard "Gryf".

On December 17 in all those enterprises there were work stoppages and mass gatherings and part of the labourers took to the streets. The shipbuilding workers were joined by hundreds of youth and especially the hooligan and criminal elements, as well as individuals hostile to People's Poland who shouted anti-state slogans. The crowd became aggressive towards the forces of order using Molotov cocktails, stones, and iron bars. The building of the Provincial Committee of the PUWP was attacked and set on fire, and aggressive groups entered inside and began to devastate it. The firefighters were prevented from taking action. Nevertheless the soldiers and militiamen guarding the building did not resort to arms.

Next the crowd attacked and set on fire the building of the Provincial Command of the Citizens' Militia and the building of the Provincial Council of Trade Unions. Nearby military vehicles were attacked with Molotov cocktails. In the burning building of the Provincial Command of the Citizens' Militia the attackers tried to break the door, and, climbing up the mouldings and gutters, attempted to reach the windows on the second floor. In this situation, after warnings, arms were used and there were the first killed and wounded.

The prison and the Prosecutor's Office were also attacked using, among others, incendiary means. In the prison there were several cores of recidivists whose release would threaten serious consequences. The forces of order, thus, were compelled to resort to arms. Again there were dead. It was also necessary to disperse the groups of hooligans and thieves, who broke into the stores and shops and were looting them (77 shops were damaged and 40 were completely or partially looted).

As a result of the events in Szczecin 16 persons were killed and well over a hundred wounded. There were also serious material losses. In Elblag the demonstrations and street disturbances took place on December 15-16. Buildings were set on fire. Shops and kiosks were devastated and robbed. On December 18 there were new attempts to set fires, and attacks took place with iron bars, bricks and stones against the forces of law protecting the bank, the post office and the telephone centre. After the calls to stop the aggressive acts and the warning shots, the ground slavos followed. As a result one person was killed and several wounded.

The events at the Coast produced many casualties and serious material losses. Altogether during these developments 44 persons were killed or died as a result of wounds, including 2 militiamen and 1 soldier, while 1164 persons were wounded including 600 from the forces of order. Nineteen public buildings were set on fire and were completely or partially demolished. Two hundred and twenty shops were looted and devastated. Tens of thousands of private, and many militia and military vehicles and pieces of equipment were destroyed or damaged. The losses caused by the destruction on the Gdansk Coast amounted in the prices of that time to 105 million zlotys, and in Szczecin to 300 million zlotys.

The events were adversely affected by the presence at the Coast of many leading activists from the central authorities, without, however, clearly determined hierarchy, competence and responsibility, which led at times to nervous, chaotic and contradictory decisions.

During the five dramatic and tragic days at the Coast, with the apparent tendency of their spreading into other cities, no meeting of the Politbureau was called and only on December 17 did the Council of Ministers reach a decision concerning the events in Gdansk, and in the entire Coast, to order the forces of the law to use all legal means of repression against persons engaging in violent acts, threatening the life or health of the citizens or looting and devastating public offices. The decision was made public on December 18.

The lack of unified and effective activities as well as the failure on the part of the government to provide quick and public information contributed to the spontaneous spread of demonstrations and their being dominated by the rowdy and criminal elements. On the other side the strikers' organizations were consolidated and the workers' distrust of negotiating with the managers of the enterprises and the representatives of the local authorities was increased.

After detailed analysis of the relevant materials, including the reports by the commissions working in 1971 which, among other things, examined the army involvement, the Commission concluded that in the unusually complex situation the leadership of the Ministery of National Defence undertook several decisions and issued many directives aimed at reducing to a minimum the resorting to arms. The use of heavy arms and the machine guns which were available in the military vehicles, even though these vehicles were not infrequently attacked, was categorically prohibited. While firing the warning shots, in order to avoid accidental casualties, the use of blank bullets was recommended. It was ordered, after the warning salvos, to shoot, not at the legs, but exclusively into the ground about 5 metres before the attackers. It was also essential that the soldiers acted in a disciplined fashion, controlled their emotions and did everything to reduce the tragic consequences. While guarding buildings which were burning or set on fire, and while preventing the looting and devastation of property, extreme situations occurred. There were also many instances of destruction of military equipment, including heavy pieces, of attempts to disarm the soldiers, and active attacks against the forces of order. Without the "safety valves" imposed from above, and the prudence displayed by the commanders of the military units and the militiamen, the dimensions of the misfortune would have been considerably greater.

Resolving the conflict ultimately led to the change in party policy initiated at the Politbureau meeting of December 19. W. Gomulka, depressed and showing signs of serious illness, could not take part in it. J. Cyrankiewicz was in the chair. After seven hours of discussions a decision was reached on the necessity of basic changes in the composition of the Politbureau. This included, above all, the departure of W. Gomulka from the post of First Secretary (during a talk at the hospital with the delegates of the Politbureau, J. Cyrankiewicz and Z. Kliszko, W. Gomulka submitted his resignation). The departure of Z. Kliszko, M. Sypchalski and R. Strzelecki were also recognized as indispensable. The second major change was the determination of the new core leadership. The Politbureau put forward E. Gierek as a candidate to be the new First Secretary.

E. Gierek had a reputation in the party and in the country as a good administrator, which he gained during his many years of leading the Silesian-Coal Basin party organization. He was a labourer-activist who knew the work of a miner, the workers' needs and living conditions. His understanding of modern production and its scientific-technical conditions and the structure of large city conglomerates favourably contrasted with the shortcomings in the socio-economic development in the second half of the 1960s. This contributed to E. Gierek's popularity and aroused hopes among the party actiff and the entire society.

For new Politbureau members there were proposed Piotr Jaroszewicz, as premier-designate, and Edward Babiuch, who as new secretary of the Central Committee would direct intra-party affairs. M. Moczar, S. Olszowski and J. Szydlak were also nominated to the Politbureau. In the next decade E. Gierek, P. Jaroszewicz and E. Babiuch, who gradually expanded his influence, in effect formed the party and the state leadership.

On December 20 the VII Plenum of the Central Committee received a report on the situation in the country and its consequences, which was submitted on behalf of the Politbureau by S. Kociolek. All of the nominations to the Politbureau were approved and an evaluation of the events as a conflict caused by the erroneous policy of the departing leadership and requiring major changes—above all, towards the working class—was adopted.

At the December 23 session of parliament the president of the Council of Ministers, J. Cyrankiewicz, and the chairman of the State Council, M. Spychalski, submitted their resignations.

The decisions taken at the VII Plenum brought to an end the strikes and demonstrations at Gdansk and Gdynia. They had already been discontinued on December 19. But there were recurrences in Szczecin. In these circumstances the decision to go to the Warski Shipyard by the First Secretary, E. Gierek, and the premier, P. Jaroszewicz—who were accompanied by the Central Committee secretary, Kazimierz Barcikowski, the minister of National Defense, W. Jaruzelski, and the deputy minister of Internal Affairs, F. Szlachcic—was a courageous and a correct one. After many hours of difficult discussions with the strikers, the strike in Szczecin ended. And the next day, on January 25 in Gdansk, during the meeting of E. Gierek with the workers' delegates from the shipyard and the associated enterprises in the Three Cities, the famous slogan: "We will help", originated;

The final wave of strikes, which came in February, and was particularly intense in Lodz, was brought to an end by the decision on March 1, 1971 to rescind the price increases.

The decision of the VIII Plenum held on February 6-7, 1981, about the suspension as Central Committee member of W. Gomulka, and the expulsion from that body of Z. Kliszko and B. Jaszczuk, closed the matter of their party responsibility.

Members of the Politbureau S. Kociolek and I. Loga-Sowinski resigned from their posts. S. Kociolek also resigned from the position of secretary of the Central Committee, which he had assumed only at the VII Plenum on December 20, 1981. I. Loga-Sowinski resigned from the position of chairman of the Council of Trade Unions.

A very important factor for the future was the attitude of the new party and government leadership towards the lessons and conclusions flowing from the critical events at the turn of 1970-1971 — when the social conflicts so abruptly came to the surface. On January 3, 1971 decisions were announced to allocate 8.6 million zlotys to improve the living conditions of the poorest families with many children as well as to increase pensions and to freeze for two years the prices of basic foodstuffs. They had significant political-psychological effects, although the freezing of prices, with their consequences intensifying in the following years, made the policy of effective and balanced economic growth difficult.

Under the influence of a prolonged strike of the textile workers in Lodz—with whom long talks were conducted by premier P. Jaroszewicz, the chairman of the Executive Council of Trade Unions, W. Kruczek, and the secretaries of the Central Committee: J. Szydlak and J. Tejchma—the price increases, introduced in December, were withdrawn. This decision, it appears, could have been replaced by a no less politically effective decision to increase wages in the textile industry, which in this respect was seriously discriminated against. But the withdrawal of the price increases strengthened the conviction in the society that prices were determined by the government's will, implying a complete divorce between prices and the costs of production. This became a permanent, destructive element in the economic system and mechanism.

Responding to the apparent expectations of the working class and the universally expressed will of the party masses, an evaluation of the December events and the conclusions flowing from them, were presented in a speech by E. Gierek at the VIII Plenum (February 6-7, 1981), and in the materials prepared for it by the commission chaired by J. Szydlak. They contained a more profound analysis than at any time in the past of the development of contradictions and conflicts in the economy as well as in the socio-political sphere and the cultural life.

The December conflict was characterized as the outcome of a long-term crisis of confidence in the party leadership among the working class and other social strata, especially stemming from the lack of concern about satisfying the society's needs. As to the opinions expressed by the party organizations and the enterprises that there was insufficient information about the events at the Coast and the responsibility for them of the leading party functionaries, the Politbureau decided to appoint a commission which, according to E. Gierek, was "to explain everything that still needs to be explained". The commission examining certain particular questions pertaining to the December 1970 events, worked under the chairmanship of W. Kruczek. It reviewed the documents and other relevant materials and it held many talks with activists and participants in the events on the Coast. In November 1971 the commission completed its work and its results were made available during the VI Congress (December 6-11, 1971) to those delegates who were the members of the outgoing Central Committee. Subsequently, on February 11, 1972 W. Kruczek and E. Babiuch also passed over the commission's findings to a small group of the Gdansk activists. From then on the events on the Coast were no longer mentioned in the party documents nor in the party propaganda, while the censorship also restricted or completely eliminated any references to this subject in the historical-scientific works.

At the VIII Plenum it was announced that a group of prominent specialists was to be appointed to evolve a proper conception of the functioning of the economic system, fitting the new strategy of socioeconomic development. Such a group, called the Party-Government Commission for the Modernization of Functioning of the Economy, was appointed and undertook its analytical-programmatic work which was supposed to lead to substantial systemic changes in the economy as well as in the methods of governing. Soon, however, the commission's work was restricted and, in practice, interrupted, at first in the sphere concerning the party and its role in the state and the society; and then in the mid-1970s it was altogether terminated.

Among the postulates concerning the systemic changes there remained only a not very clear and theoretically unelaborated slogan: the party leads, and the government governs. It reflected, however, not so much a will for democratic systemic changes as rather for the strengthening of the position of the premier, P. Jaroszewicz, in running the economy and the administration. In the first half of the 1970s an attempt was also made to reform the economic-financial structure of the economic organizations—by introducing the so-called big industrial organizations, which were based on the application of economic parameters and the net indices. Yet, the new principles of functioning of the enterprises were not correlated with the changes in central planning and management, and anyway they themselves were soon revised and then completely abandoned.

Soon after the December changes the discussion of the causes of the crisis became restricted, particularly with regard to the subject of intra-party control and the legal-state mechanisms of control over the so-called inner leadership. This informal institution was there to stay. The practice of combining the highest state and party posts continued, particularly in the Politbureau where the number of members also occupying key positions in the government actually increased. The widely popularized practice of meetings and consultations by the highest leaders with the labourers in the enterprises, people in the villages and in the other milieux, at first authentic, was gradually transformed into carefully staged spectacles where E. Gierek's directness and avuncularity were replaced by sycophancy around him personally. The apparent achievements in the first half of the decade led to an increase in self-confidence and even conceit. This was linked to the undertaking of various initiatives in socio-economic policy which were not preceded by a proper, keen analysis of their costs and without anticipating their long-term socio-economic consequences, as well as the launching on an unprecedented scale of what was later labelled as "the propaganda of success".

At the VIII Plenum and, subsequently, at the VI Congress, the 1970s were recognized as the decisive decade for the economic development of Poland—it was asserted that by harnessing the scientific-technical revolution the potential, inherent in the younger generation entering into productive life, could be released, securing in the international division of labour a high place for Poland among the developed countries.

Especially in the first few years of implementing this policy tangible and lasting results were achieved. In particular the inertia of the last years of the previous decade was overcome and far-reaching modernization of industry and the entire economy was advanced. Modern techniques and technology were introduced into many of its branches. As the scientific-technical progress gained momentum, the development of Polish science was accelerated and its contacts with world science were expanded. The challenging problem stemming fro from the entry into independent life and professional activity of three million young Poles—the greatest demographic increase in the postwar years—was successfully resolved. They were given a chance to obtain good education and, generally, to find employment in a modern environment. There was a good start in overcoming an impasse in developing the infra-structure of the big cities, and especially in constructing new housing—there was a substantial increase in the number of new apartments. Social services were expanded both in the cities and the countryside. There was also considerable progress in supplying individual households, and the number of private automobiles increased. Cultural and scientific contacts with the outside world were expanded (although not always in a thoughtful and prudent fshion), enhancing the international position of the Polish culture and artists; and tourism, both domestic and foreign, was developed. All of these achievements led to an improvement in the atmosphere and in the attitude of the society towards the government, producing at the same time the growth of further hopes and expectations.

The socio-economic situation in the 1970s, however, was more and more adversely affected by what appeared to be voluntarism in arriving at decisions, and, simultaneously, growing manifestations of their inconsistency and ineffectiveness. In particular the so-called policy of dynamic development, which was undertaken in the early 1970s, was based on accelerated, and often wrongly conceived, investments; and rested more and more on the thoughtless, and at times almost casual, use of foreign credits. At the same time the substantial growth in employment without improvement in efficiency favoured extensive economic development, instead of with more rational intensive methods of production.

It should be emphasized that in the period under consideration, as in the entire history of People's Poland, there were realms where the policy was entirely correct and was confirmed by life. This was particularly true in foreign and defence policy—crucial to the national existence. The international activities, especially with regard to the Conference on Security and Cooperation in Europe, gained for Poland, and E. Gierek personally, an undeniable popularity and prestige.

3. The events of 1976 and the crisis of 1980

In the first five years after the December change of policy, and especially in 1971-1973, there was high growth in production and national income as well as a substantial increase in real wages and consumption (in 1971-1975 the highest in the history of People's Poland). This was assisted by favourable weather conditions in 1971-1973, profitable opportunities for Polish goods in foreign markets, low prices of energy and raw materials, and easy access to foreign credits.

After 1973, however, the external conditions for development markedly declined—prices of imported raw material, and especially oil and its by-products, substantially increased, and the boom in the capitalist countries came to an end. In order to maintain balance, thus, it was necessary to reduce the growth of investments, incomes and indebtedness. Yet, in 1974 the original investment targets were riased and the wage increases planned for the next five years were implemented—and this was done through optimistic and voluntaristic decisions, often in response to pressures from various industrial and regional branches, which were also striving for "successes" of their own.

The tremendous resources obtained in foreign credits were not effectively invested (mainly because of demands from the heavy and machinery industries), contributing to the unsatisfactory structure of industry and preventing a rapid growth in exports. A tendency towards excessive economic cooperation with the western countries, with neglect of the possibilities of stable, long-term cooperation with the socialist countries, often led to erroneous decisions, such as the co-production with France of the Berliet buses, instead of cooperation with Hungary in producing the Ikarus buses, or the purchases (under pressure from various groups) of foreign licences, often inappropriate and badly evaluated by the Polish specialists and scientists.

At the same time small-scale industries which, especially in the countryside, were generally quite efficient, were restricted or even completely eliminated in an administrative fashion.

The distorted industrial structure, in consequence, led to stagnation in supplying agriculture—there was a marked deficiency of adequate storage facilities and of land improvement programs. The delay in increasing the prices of agricultural purchases [by the government] undermined the profitability of agricultural production. The decline of rural self-government contributed to the bureaucratization of a large segment of agricultural services, and, thus, aggravated even further the negative phenomena. Insufficient profitability of production restricted the prospect of development for agriculture and, combined with the socio-economic conditions in the villages, led to an excessive exodus of young people to the cities, which, in turn, aggravated the lodging and social problems there.

The attempts to increase agricultural production, and especially breeding, through costly import investments and considerable outlays into the so-called specialized farms, did not produce the anticipated results (partly because those investments and outlays were not always rationally utilized). Attempts were made to compensate for the population's increased purchasing power, and its pressure upon the market, by increasing the consumption of imports, and especially of grain and fodder, which—second only to the investments policy—led to a substantial increase of indebtedness to the capitalist countries.

The indebtedness—resulting from the investments on credit, the growing imports to cover the current consumer needs (especially after 1975), and to supply industry with raw materials and resources—led to such a heavy burden in the balance of payments that in 1976-1978 credit payments (capital and interest) amounted to half of the profits from exports, and in 1979-1980 to the total of them.

At the turn of 1975-1976 economic tensions appeared that were critical in their dimensions. In response the so-called economic manœuvre was undertaken aimed at reducing the growth and at restructuring investments, channelling production more into the consumer industries, accelerating exports and arresting foreign indebtedness. But the pressures from the various industrial branches which had undertaken ambitious investment programmes of their own successfully countered this manœuvre. Above all, the state-economy leadership followed a policy of postponing the crisis through obtaining additional credits, which only deepened and aggravated its future consequences.

An analysis of the economic contradictions in that decade—which the policy of that time not only failed to solve, but in fact intensified—is contained in the government report of June 1981 which was subsequently submitted to the parliament and the public. It was also reviewed by the IX Congress of the party. This Commission, thus, needs not repeat the detailed findings and conclusions of that report.

In the 1970s the price and wage policies (and the determination of the incomes of the population) were incompatible, resulting on both sides in social dissatisfaction. They were also incompatible with considerations of economic efficiency.

The prices policy ignored the proper relationship between their level and the actual costs of production. It was also inconsistent, and was treated in a one-sided fashion as an instrument of political influence. Despite the freezing of prices of basic foodstuffs, there was a general and accelerated increase in prices. There were also adverse changes in price structures, caused by the above-mentioned freezing of some prices, along with an increased demand for food caused by the increased incomes of the population. This was not helped by the partial price increases (for instance, the adoption of the so-called commercial prices) which were not a part of a general reform, arrived at after authentic consultation with the society. In these circumstances the increase in commercial prices in July 1980 became the proverbial spark which ignited the explosion of social dissatisfaction.

The determination of wages and incomes of the population was also not sufficiently consistent. Generally speaking, it was divorced from the effectiveness of the national economy. In essence it was characterized by a faster distribution of national income than the growth of the economy permitted (in 1971-1975 the corresponding figures were 12 per cent and 10 per cent respectively). This to a large extent meant consumption on credit. Together with the slowing down of economic growth after the mid-1970s this sharpened the imbalance between the growth of production and the growth of wages.

There also appeared inconsistencies in the increase of incomes and wages among various professional groups and among various classes and social strata. The discrepancy between the lowest and the highest incomes widened (in the 1970s it increased by two and a half times); and, furthermore, it was accompanied by an expansion of privileges (which were usually secret and not socially acceptable) contributing to the augmentation of some incomes, especially among segments of the leading economic and administrative cadres.

Against this background the shortcomings to the health services and cultural facilities were particularly painfully felt by the society. For example, in the second half of the 1970s the number of books published drastically declined.

During that decade, despite unprecedented progress in housing construction, a discrepancy arose between the expectations for private apartments, induced by the government propaganda, and the existing conditions. The number of persons per room declined from 1.37 in 1970 to 1.10 in 1981, yet a large number of new marriages resulted in a situation where the proportion of apartments shared by more than one family actually remained stable (in 1978 amounting to almost 30 per cent). The costs and the effects of constructing private lodgings were also adversely affected by the one-sided emphasis on the "factory-houses" which consumed a lot of capital, while at the same time the traditional construction materials were ignored, and the small-scale production of building components was altogether eliminated.

Deeply harmful to the entire social and political life were the deformations in the internal life of the party, incompatible with Leninist principles. The mechanisms of internal criticism and control, both in the central and the local party and state cadres, were effectively blocked. The lack of a proper turnover of personnel in the structures of authority (in the party as well as the state), was conducive to conceit, mechanical performance of activities and cutting off the flow of genuine information.

Simultaneously the collegiality of the leadership gradually became purely formal. In reality the decisions were made by narrow, informal groups (a process accelerated by the combining of various functions), and particularly by the First Secretary. The election of the party executives, in reality, amounted to the acceptance of pre-determined lists. The party leadership did not respond to criticism, most of the time ignoring it completely; in some cases the activists who indulged in it were deprived of their influence.

The role of the Council of Ministers was reduced. It was replaced by its Presidium and, above all, by the premier and a few of his closest collaborators. There were also ambiguities and improprieties in the sphere of legal regulations, especially in those governing the relationship between the government and the parliament. The role of the parliament was not sufficiently respected; the subordination of the Supreme Chamber of Control to the Premier prepresented a good example of these tendencies.

In the mid-1970s the system of national councils and local administration was reformed and the structure of the territorial division of the country was radically changed (increasing the number of provinces from 17 to 49, and eliminating the districts and creating communes). These changes, which were not properly prepared and preceded by social discussions, produced various perturbations. In particular, at the very time when the country was faced with an increasing crisis, the long-established, customary structures of the organization and activity of the social actiff were destroyed.

The deformations and faults spreading in the country adversely affected the position of the social organizations which were supposed to be the main instruments of socialist democracy. The growth of bureaucratic centralism hampered the genuine social initiative and activity which should have provided the society with a feeling of authentic participation in public life and the decisions taken there. Particularly harmful was the restricting of the role of the national councils. The trade unions became bureaucratized and lost some of their statutory functions. The institutions which were supposed to provide channels for the working class activities, such as the Committees of the Workers' Self-government, in reality were not self-governing and lost their dynamism.

At the same time several new social measures were introduced, such as equalizing of holidays for all employees, offering free medical services to private farmers, introducing 60 days benefits for mothers of sick children, and creating an alimony fund. But expanding the social services without linking them to increased labour efficiency, with the economy ridden by increasing tensions and indebtedness, could not but adversely influence its state. Some of the new regulations in the Labour Law, moreover, weakened the work discipline.

Exceptionally negative effects in the social consciousness were produced by divorcing wages and social services from work efficiency, which led to the treatment of the state as an institution from which only benefits could be expected. The direct reason for the spread of this attitude was voluntarism in the decisions, which made the people believe that everything depended on the government's will and not on the objective processes and possibilities. This led to a tendency towards ever-increasing demands. It became apparent, moreover that those social groups, branches or regions which knew how to fight for their interests, and which had better connections, could actually receive more. The tendencies to make demands were further aroused by the propaganda which stressed consumption, and did not sufficiently emphasize the need for increased output and work efficiency.

Against the background of a real strenghtening of the ideals of socialism among the working people (and especially the ideals of social ownership of the means of production, and equality and social justice), departing from these principles, particularly when there was an obvious discrepancy btween the existing practices and the continually proclaimed and socially accepted slogans was badly received. The political and ideological damage flowing from this gradually acquired more and more drastic dimensions. The youth viewed this situation as especially threatening to its prospects in life. At the same time the young people could not find answers to their anxieties in the youth movement which often carried out only ritualistic activities and, moreover, was undergoing a difficult period of formal reorganization.

Particularly harmful was the insufficiency and serious neglect of ideological work in the party and in the society, including superficiality in analysis and ritualism in action, reluctance to admit the existing ideological contradictions, adherence to shallow optimism which, for example, was expressed in the erroneous thesis about reaching the state of moral and political unity of the nation, and the avoidance of a sharp struggle against the opponents of socialism.

All of the above-described objectives and subjective processes culminated in the second half of the 1970s.

It was against this background that the need to change the situation was more and more universally felt by the working people; although this was complicated by the generally low level of social knowledge about the economic laws and mechanisms, and by the intensified activities of the groups, external as well as internal, hostile to socialism. Gradually the danger of an especially acute conflict became real.

The sharp conflict which erupted in mid-1980 was preceded by alarming signals appearing in 1976 and subsequent years.

At the turn of 1975-1976 most of the symptoms of the sickness in the economy were already visible. In 1976 the economic imbalance, particularly in supplying the market with food, markedly worsened. The steady increases in wages, along with the postponing from year to year of increases in prices of the basic foodstuffs, intensified the market pressure upon food, and especially upon meat, beyond control (and this was aggravated for several years by poor harvests). And the increasing since 1973 of the prices of other goods and services had led to even greater, absolutely irrational, price disproportions.

After many discussions among the party state leaders, ultimately also with the participation of the provincial representatives, it was decided to go ahead with the increases in food prices. Mainly as a result of pressure from the premier, P. Jaroszewicz, the solution selected was to make one, great increase, which was to restore the profitability of all, or almost all, basic food products, with the increase in the price of meat amounting to 69 per cent.

The society, which had become convinced by the entire economic policy that the relationship between prices and wages is not determined by the objective economic forces, but by the government's will, was startled by the size and the scale of the increases. Furthermore, the system of compensation which-although decreasing with higher incomes, was nevertheless in absolute terms higher for the higher and lower for the lower earning persons—violated society's sense of justice. Thus, the announcement about the price increases on June 26-27, 1976—which was made by premier P. Jaroszewicz in the parliament on June 24, and was supported, in the name of the deputies from all the parties, by E. Babiuch—after only one day of parliamentary debate and quite superficial consultations with the representatives of the enterprises, institutions and the communes (the new price lists having already been distributed), aroused social opposition.

On June 25 in the enterprises there was agitation and spontaneous disbelief in the efficacy of consultations as well as a conviction that the government would only respond to massive pressure. In 10 provinces there were strikes and meetings in the enterprises. In Radom, Ursus, and, on a smaller scale, in Plock, there were street demonstrations.

In Radom, before 8 a.m. there was a strike in the General Walter Mechanical Enterprise, and then 1,000 workers marched into the streets calling upon the workers from the other enterprises to abandon work and join the demonstration. At 10 a.m. a crowd of 2,000 gathered in front of the Provincial Committee building, while in the atmosphere of great agitation small incidents took place in the city and the enterprises. The demonstrators, being addressed at 12:30 m. by the provincial first secretary, Janusz Prokopiak, requested him to convey to the central authorities their demand for the withdrawal of the food price increases. J. Prokopiak accordingly telegraphed the secretary of the Central Committee, J. Szydlak, and promised the demonstrators to have a reply for them by 2 p.m. In the crowd in the street, emotions prevailed, the hooligan and brawling elements joined in, and shops were devastated and looted. A group of demonstrators broke into the Provincial Committee buidling and was devastating it. There were attempts to attack the Provincial Office, the Provincial Command of the Citizens' Militia and the prison. At 2:30 p.m. an action to disperse the crowd was undertaken by units of the Citizens' Militia, equipped with hand gas throwers, batons and water cannons. In accordance with an order from the central authorities the militiamen fought in closed formations and had no firearms. The crowd attacked the militiamen with stones, spread gasoline on the streets and started fires, erected barricades and set the Provincial Committee building on fire. Two drunk persons, who tried to start a truck loaded with concrete slabs to turn it against the forces of order, were run over by it and died as a result of injuries.

On the same day in the Mechanical Enterprise "Ursus" near Warsaw, 90 per cent of the labourers interrupted work demanding the withdrawal of the price increases. About 400 people took to the streets. At 9:30 a.m. about 2,000 people gathered at the nearby railway line. The crowd stopped both the commuters' and the long-distance trains, and there were instances of devastating and burning the carriages. At 5 p.m. the demonstrators tore up the rails and cut them with acetylene torches, and started to erect a barricade with a derailed locomotive. At 7:20 p.m. the forces of order of the Citizens' Militia went into action using tear gas and petards. At 11 p.m. order was restored and technicians from the Polish State Railroads started to repair the damage. During these events 15 militiamen and 1 person from the crowd were hurt.

In Plock at 10 a.m. there was a meeting in the Masovian Petro-Refining Enterprise in which 300 people participated. At 4:20 p.m. a part of the demonstrators (some 200 persons) moved into the city and marched on the Provincial Committee building. At 5:10 p.m. the procession, which had grown to 400 persons, reached the Provincial Committee, where its first secretary, Franciszek Teklinski, spoke to the crowds. Some of the demonstrators tried unsuccessfuly to enter the Harvest Machine Factory to interrupt its work. At 8:40 p.m;

some demonstrators threw stones at the Provincial Committee building, breaking its windows. At 9:10 p.m. the forces of order of the Citizens' Militia entered into action and within an hour restored calm before the Provincial Committee building and in the entire city. There were no casualties.

On the same day, the party leadership, determined to avoid the use of force, to defuse the situation and to prevent the strikes from spreading, decided to withdraw the price increases. At 8 p.m. the chairman of the Council of Ministers announced on television that the bill to change prices would be withdrawn from parliament, and the existing retail food prices would be maintained. Within a few days there were no more strikes or demonstrations in the entire country.

Next day the decision was reached to launch a great propaganda campaign which, in the words of E. Babiuch, was "to transform yesterday's events into support for the First Secretary, the Central Committee, the government and the chairman of the Council of Ministers". In all the provinces massive meetings were held under the slogan: "We are with you comrade Gierek", condemning the events in Radom and Ursus as caused by troublemakers. An intense propaganda campaign was also undertaken by the mass media.

With regard to the participants in the disturbances, judicial-administrative and disciplinary steps were taken. Nine hundred and thirty-one persons in Radom and 180 in Ursus were immediately released. But in the cases of 162 (mostly in Radom) this decision was soon reversed.

Neither the Central Committee or the Politbureau ever undertook a political-social analysis of the June events. Instead attempts were made to obscure the matter. This was achieved partly by quickly abandoning the repressive measures. Even by the end of July 1976 the State Council had issued a directive requiring lenient treatment for those prosecuted persons who before June 25 held a steady job, had a good reputation in their community and had no previous criminal record. In February 1977 a State Council resolution conditionally suspended the sentences of the remaining participants in the June 1976 events; while on July 19 the State Council's decree on amnesty, and its resolution on clemency, in the legal sense closed the matter. The people who were released from employment found work in other enterprises and some returned to their former posts.

The lack of a clear ruling on how long the price increases were to be postponed caused panic at the market and purchases of all goods which could be stored. This compelled the government to introduce sugar rationing. At the same time increases in the prices paid [by the government] for agricultural products, and an accompanying increase in prices of the goods used in agricultural production, led to further distortion of the relationship between the food prices and the prices of purchasing [by the government] of agricultural produce. As a result, production of food by the farmers for their own consumption, and, especially at the small farms, even for their own breeding stock, ceased to be profitable.

So once more retreat from the absolutely necessary price increases and a public discussion of the entire price and compensation issue, and the government's subsequent fear to raise the matter publicly, led to the demoralizing conviction—in the society and the working class—that there was no relationship between the prices and wages and the effects of one's own, and the enterprise's work. This strengthened the tendencies to press for concessions from the government.

The fact that no conclusions were drawn from the June events—either in the economic sphere (the failure of the economic manoeuvre), or in the system of government and the internal party life—and that, in effect, an attitude of muddling through was adopted, marked a decisive step towards a profound crisis.

The weaknesses and the inconsistencies of the government, its divorce from the working class, and the worst possible form of dialogue with the masses involving propagandistic whitewash, opened up opportunities for the anti-socialist opposition. They in turn, were encouraged by the growing momentum of a reactionary and confrontationist political course by the United States and its allies.

In 1976 the apparent conflict between the workers and the government offered an opportunity for the small cosmopolitan-intelligentsia opposition groups—which had been active in Poland for several years and were more and more actively supported from outside—to assume the formal role of "the defenders of the working class". In September 1976 the so-called Committee for the Defence of the Workers was established, and in September 1977 it was transformed into the Committee of Social Self-Defence—KOR. The major role there was assumed by people known for years for their revisionist activities, including those from 1968, and some of them at first resorted to socialist phraseology. The main thrust of the ideological attack by KOR was an attempt to undermine in the consciousness of the workers and the intelligentsia, and especially the younger generation, the confidence in the ability of People's Poland to satisfy the needs of the people, including a charge that the existing system is not amenable to reform. Their second thrust was to question the leading role of the party and its ability to guide the society; while the third was to undermine

Poland's alliance with the Soviet Union and the international socialist system, by finding pretexts in history and falsifying contemporary events in a way which aroused one-sided pro-western sentiments, particularly among the vulnerable intelligentsia milieux.

The deepening of the crisis symptoms, the reluctance of the government to admit the growing social contradictions, and its feeble attempts to oppose the anti-socialist actions, contributed to the intensifying of the illegal groups' activities and their conviction that they could carry on with impunity. This was strengthened by their belief in a possible blackmail by the western countries, should the administration resort to repressive measures [against the opposition], through the threat of withdrawing credits. The improved organizational-propagandistic efficiency of the illegal groups—assisted by western instructions, propaganda and financial support—their expanding of training and indoctrination, especially among the youth, their issuing of clandestine publications, and their spreading of emissaries into especially volatile places, proved to be particularly dangerous at the time of the explosion in mid-1980.

At that time, side by side with the Social Self-Defence Committee—KOR, which meanwhile had developed political aspirations, the Confederation of Independent Poland—an illegal organization committed to extreme nationalist, anti-socialist and anti-Soviet slogans—was formed on September 1, 1979 followed by the illegal Founding Committee of the Independent Trade Unions on the Coast, and the Movement of Young Poland.

In the ideology of the opposition groups a foremost place was given to the anarcho-syndicalist conception, which perversely counterposed the idea of the self-governing socialist state and the personal or group interests of the workers to the general interests of the working class. Yet anarcho-syndicalism, as Marx and Lenin have already proved, can be only a stage, since it is a petit-bourgeois and reactionary ideology, leading to a counter-revolution.

The ideas, the activities and the direct penetration by the opposition groups decisively influenced the deformations among the workers, and the dangerous evolution of the Independent and Self-Governing Trade Union "Solidarity", which came into existence in mid-1980.

Towards the end of the 1970s the developments in state-Church relationships had greatly significant influence on the social atmosphere. An important contribution to the social consciousness was made by the election in October 1978 of the Polish cardinal, Karol Wojtyla, as pope, and his visit to Poland in June 1979.

The visit of John Paul II demonstrated that the Church in Poland can undertake the initiative in promoting the popular slogans, which, even though they are shared by socialist humanism, in the 1970s were not appreciated in the ideological work. These include, among others, the moral value of the individual as manifested in one's attitude towards other people and the entire society, and the dignity of human work. The failure to draw the proper conclusions from this experience, especially with regard to the younger generation, represented one more, serious error on the part of the political leadership of that time.

Attempts were made, especially by E. Gierek during his meetings with Cardinal S. Wyszynski, his visit to Pope Paul VI, and his speech in Mielec, to constructively develop a policy of normalization in state-Church relations—based on recognition of the socialist changes, respect for Poland's international alliances and adherence to the legal order—and to transform it into cooperation in the moral-educational sphere.

The inability of the political leadership to draw the conclusions from the intensifying signals of an approaching crisis, came to the surface particularly strongly during the electoral campaign conducted in the entire party before its VIII Congress in February 1980.

In the course of the pre-Congress discussions, and especially at the meetings of the basic cells, the workers' as well as the intelligentsia and the peasants' actiff presented sharp criticism of the visibly deteriorating situation at the market and the threats to the standard of living, and, in this context, the basic discrepancy btween the official reports and the truth about the economic situation and its social perception. Above all, however, the actiff of many basic cells postulated and demanded profound changes in the system of governing and the management of the economy. Over those issues the leading cadres were sharply criticized.

There was also criticism of the poor state of the internal party life—cultivating illusions and continuing the propaganda of success, striving for an increase in the party membership in a purely formalistic fashion (on the opening day of the VIII Congress the party numbered 3,100,000 members and candidates), violating intra-party democracy, and overlooking critical opinions while rewarding opportunism, servility and careerism.

The tide of the workers' criticisms was accompanied by manifestations of their will to try to improve the situation and to participate in the difficult—in view of the intensifying atmosphere of dissatisfaction in the entire society—tasks ahead, and the hope that the VIII Congress would undertake an honest analysis of the situation, reveal the truth, and show the way out of it.

This opportunity for the party, to assume the initiative in finding and implementing a programme of renewal, was not utilized by the VIII Congress. The leading group did not appreciate the gravity of the situation, and it did not reveal its true nature. A special disillusionment among the party actiff was produced by the avoidance of an analysis of the catastrophic economic perils rising since the VII Congress, in favour of concealing them by presenting only the averages for the entire decade, visibly manipulating discussions at the congress, and rigging the elections to the new Central Committee. E. Gierek and his collaborators attempted to improve the situation by a change in the post of the premier, yet without any criticism of P. Jaroszewicz and his cabinet.

A few months later there took place the explosion of worker protest on a scale unprecedented in the history of People's Poland. Only these events could finally mobilize the party leadership towards a reassessment and change. At the V Plenum (August 30, 1980) the Central Committee received and approved the reports of the Government Commissions which conducted negotiations with the workers' representatives over their postulates in Gdansk and Szczecin. On August 30 an agreement was signed in Szczecin, and on August 31 in Gdansk. At the IV Plenum (on August 24, 1980) and the first session of the VI Plenum (in the night of September 5-6, 1980) there were changes in the leading posts in the party and the government—E. Gierek and his closest collaborators were removed.

After the second session of the VI Plenum (October 4-6, 1980) there began—under conditions of a sharp class struggle and in an unusually difficult political situation—the process of profound political change and moral renovation known as the process of socialist renewal.

The party, while undergoing a profound crisis and transforming itself internally, at the same time constructed and undertook the realization of the programme which was fully developed by the historic Extraordinary IX Congress of the PUWP on July 14-20, 1981.

*   *   *

The crisis of 1980 was greater than any of these preceding it. This was so because, among other things, in 1980 there appeared a phenomenon which may be described as the accumulation of crises. The previous waves of crisis had been stopped (in 1956 because of the personal appeal of W. Gomulka, and in 1970 because of the popularity of the programme of economic growth and the changes and reforms announced by E. Gierek). In contrast, in 1980—in the conditions of visible growth of the crisis symptoms in the economy, which had been going on for several years, and the increasing negative political and ideological-moral phenomena—there was no possibility of the party's arresting the crisis, for the party still had no programme for overcoming the difficulties and improving the situation.

Owing to the process of industrial-economic modernization, the development of education and dynamic cultural policy, the Polish society had quickly modernized its structure and changed its sociopolitical consciousness, although the shortcomings in ideological-educational work often were not conducive to the appropriate direction of these changes. In the social, and above all in the workers' consciousness, various processes were taking place: once the main ideals of socialism were firmly implanted (unfortunately, more with regard to the rights, and less with regard to the duties of the working people), there grew natural aspirations towards real participation and influence over the country's fate, and opposition against the incompatibility between the government's postulates and activities. Growing contradictions between the proclaimed programmes and the actual achievements, intensified by the exaggerated opinions about them, were particularly badly received by the young people, who are especially sensitive to their prospects in life. As a whole these trends contributed to the subjective feeling of disillusionment and criticism which became entrenched in the social consciousness; while the special contradiction between the workers' aspirations and the government's activities released the crisis phenomena.

Against this background there emerged a universal conviction of the necessity of changing the past economic and political practices. At the same time, drawing conclusions from the way the past crises were overcome, the working class demanded institutional guarantees of the changes. Hence, for instance, sprang up the support for the revival of the trade unions' movement, and, then, especially in the initial phase of its development, for the Independent and Self-Governing Trade Union—"Solidarity".

APPENDIX II

POLAND IN 1984
REFLECTIONS UPON FORTY YEARS OF DEVELOPMENT

by Jan Szczepanski[*]

Theoretical concepts of development

The term social development or development of the society is being used in social sciences, and in popular and political writings, in several different ways. Generally speaking it implies the changes which enrich the relationships among various elements in any system. Thus, if in a certain society changes are occurring which enrich its composition, structure and functions, we refer to it as a developing society. Different social sciences focus upon specific features of development. In sociology it is defined as the changes which broaden and differentiate the micro- and macro-structures of the existing institutions, the value systems as well as social relationships. In social and economic policy, development is conceived as a process that creates new elements in the system through economic activity aimed at improving the standard of living, satisfying the various needs at a higher level, expanding social services, etc. In popular writings these two concepts of social development are merged into a single whole which is used more as a political goal than an analytical tool. In everyday usage the term development is identified with progress; while in sociology the two concepts differ. In sociology progress is not an empirical, but a normative concept which implies bringing the society closer to some clearly defined ideal vision. Not all development, then, is progressive.

In the history of People's Poland since 1944, and especially after the war against Germany and, then, the civil war, changes in the society have been taking place simultaneously at several different levels.

In the first place there were the spontaneous phenomena of everyday life occurring among the people, within families, in the work places, institutions and social organizations—all aimed at satisfying the ordinary needs. These were natural changes serving the continuity

---

[*]Professor Jan Szczepanski at one time was President of the International Sociological Association, Director of the Institute of Philosophy and Sociology in the Polish Academy of Sciences and, then, the Academy's Vice President. Subsequently he was a non-party member of the State Council, and in 1981 chairman of the special parliamentary commission to negotiate with the workers. In March 1984, at the time when he wrote his essay, he was Chairman of the Economic and Social Council. Selection by A.B.

of life through the observing of traditional customs and habits and the preserving of the old ways of life and values. After the end of the war, returning home or settling in a new place, millions of Poles longed for a return to "normal life". They simply wanted to do their work and have a family—in other words they strove to achieve the conditions of which they had dreamed during the occupation. These spontaneous processes were at the root of all the other social changes.

The second level of changes consisted of a deliberate social restructuring through the liquidation of the former propertied classes (the landlords and the bourgeoisie), the transformation of political institutions, the creation of a new economic system through nationalization, the implementation of agricultural reform, the replacement of the market economy with a planned one, etc. The development of at first a people's democracy, and, then, socialism, was a complex task. It took place in many different spheres because—in accordance with the ideal vision of the new system—it concerned not only all aspects of public life, but, and at times quite profoundly, some aspects of the private life as well. The reconstruction of the state administration and the judiciary, of the system of education and cultural institutions, all involved complicated amalgams of interrelated social phenomena.

The third plane included the planned changes in social policies, the improvement in professional training, the expansion of employment (including the employment of women), and the determination of wages and social benefits linked to the anticipated economic growth. A rapid industrialization—which was launched during the Three Year Plan and continued during the Six Year Plan—led to the massive flow of the population from the countryside and the growth of the cities, and in this way released powerful mechanisms of both vertical and horizontal movement. It soon became apparent, however, that these processes cannot be fully controlled, and, indeed, that at times they produce results altogether different from those which are anticipated.

The fourth amalgam in the processes of change was brought about by an unforeseen, and, often, a rather undesirable, overlapping of the planned and the spontaneous phenomena. The preservation of the old consciousness and habits among the people led to a clash between the traditional value system and the new ideals (above all, between religion and Marxism-Leninism). The gap between the time-honoured customs and the new patterns of behaviour resulted in a discrepancy between the education offered in the school and that offered in the family, and between the widely differing attitudes towards property inherited from the past and those expected under socialism.

The elements determining the changes

The above four processes were all interrelated and they interacted upon each other. In each, moreover, were present some elements which pre-determined the limits of change. These were as follows:

i) In the first place there were the war-time human losses which amounted to about one fifth of the pre-war Polish population. Almost every family lost some members. It is natural that the shock of such a bloodbath had to adversely affect the psychological balance of the nation, particularly since—as in every war—those who perished included the most worthy, able and idealistic people.

ii) The second element which destabilized the society was the shift of the country's territory which resulted in the migration of millions of people into the new lands, as well as the destruction of many cities and towns which brought about additional resettlement of the population. These produced a situation where a very considerable proportion of the Poles found themselves in a new geographical environment and in new communities with no traditional social bonds—which had negative effects upon their behaviour.

iii) The immediate post-war years in particular, but the entire last four decades in general, have been characterized by a high population growth, resulting in the rejuvenescence of the entire society. In the environment created by the above mentioned destabilizing phenomena and the revolutionary changes in education and in the work places, the process of both conscious and spontaneous socialization of the youth was distorted. The adaptation of the young people, moreover, was disturbed by periodic crises which put into question the accomplishments of the existing system. Thus, both the education and the socialization of the younger generation took a different course than that anticipated in the ideal vision of the new order.

iv) The rapid industrialization, leading to the establishment and expansion of big industrial enterprises, many of which were located outside the traditional industrial centres, resulted in the migration of rural population into new cities and towns, without established social bonds and accustomed patterns of behaviour, Thus tendencies towards anti-social, and even pathological, behaviour—especially concerning labour ethics—were aggravated. These phenomena adversely affected the entire social development, particularly at the time of acute social crises.

v) The failures in managing the socialized economy, the errors in planning and implementing economic policies, led to conflicts between the management and the workers, which contributed to poor performance and created barriers to economic progress. Even more importantly, they had negative effects upon the behaviour of the people, the functioning of the state institutions and enterprises, and, last but not least, upon relations between the administration and the people.

vi) The ideal vision of the new system presented by the ideologues and the politicians was daily compared by the people with the actual functioning of the work places, of the transportation system, of performance in the various offices and the patterns of life in various families. Such a confrontation between ideals and their realization, of course, is present everywhere; yet, in Poland it had particularly devastating effects.

The above described processes were not the only ones which adversely affected the developmental process, but they were particularly significant. The single most important element was the industrialization which—in accordance with Marxist theory—should create new productive forces: additional tools and methods of production as well as a skilled worker class and highly qualified cadres of engineers and managers. This, in turn, should lead to changes in their consciousness and improvements in the standard of living. Hence, the term "economic policy" was replaced by "socio-economic policy", for its social effects were judged to be even more important than the economic ones.

The forces of development

Research into the process of industrialization in Poland, its methods and scope as well as the results and consequences, enables one to try to sum up its overall achievements in the last forty years.

Objectively speaking, the basic aims of the development have been accomplished. Relatively strong industry with a high productive capacity has been built. An educational system with a wide network of professional schools and universities has been created. In one year now there are more graduates than in a pre-war decade. It has produced more than 200,000 engineers, several tens of thousands of economists and many specialists and managers. Apart from the various research institutes at the universities and the Academy of Sciences, thousands of specialized research institutes and laboratories have been set up. It was assumed that the central planning and management of the economy would be facilitated by concentrating the available means into some areas critical to socio-economic progress, thus assisting them to achieve quickly the desired results, after which they could be turned to other tasks. In this way a strongly centralized economic administration was established and gradually became a major part of the state apparatus.

The actual results, however, have been different from those which were anticipated. First of all this type of economy has not been immune to failures and crises stemming both from outside influences and from its own built-in errors and inefficiencies. Even during the Six Year Plan the Korean War and necessity of arms production resulted in the system's breakdown; while the imposition of heavy burdens upon the working class led to the Poznan strike and culminated in a major political crisis.

The economy, it seems, has been burdened by excessive political expectations. The planned economy was introduced by the Communist party which came to power after overcoming the "London camp" at the end of the war and defeating the forces of opposition in a civil war. The socialized economy, thus, was to become the main instrument in consolidating the existing political system. The nationalized enterprise became an integral part of the new political framework and its political goals were judged to be no less important than the economic ones. It was not only supposed to contribute to the development of the technical-material base of the system, but it was also conceived as the basic unit for organizing the political activities of the working class: it assumed the functions of training and educating the labourers and looking after their social and cultural needs. I believe that it was precisely the lack of appreciation by the political leadership of the burdens imposed upon individual enterprises which has been responsible for the periodic shortcomings in economic growth.

After the Six Year Plan in the 1960s it appeared that the Polish economy would enter into a phase of "self-generating growth". In analysing the process of industrialization in Poland, I, for one, expected that after the basic industrialization—which developed the basic means of production—was accomplished, harmonious development in the 1970s would follow. Why did it not happen and why did the next decade, despite continued intensive industrial investments, end in a tragic failure and culminate in a new crisis, even more acute than all the previous ones?

A comparison of the Szydlak and Kubiak Commissions' reports is instructive here. For they clearly reveal the political reason—or, to be precise, the fact that the economy has been managed in a fashion which has led to repeated inefficiencies. Examining the attempts at economic reforms—from the one undertaken by the Economic Council to the establishment of the "big economic organizations"—reveals the presence of powerful forces of inertia in the system of running the economy which are resistant to any innovations.

And here we touch upon the central problem. On the one hand there were the phenomena, mechanisms and processes which tended to destabilize the society and made the consolidation of the new system difficult; on the other hand were those elements of the new system which managed to become consolidated, and, in order to preserve stability, tended towards inertia and resistance to any changes. This leads to a simple conclusion. Precisely because the general conditions of the society were unstable, in the political cadres there was a feeling of insecurity, which made them protect at all costs those stable elements of the system which seemed to guarantee its continuity. It was for those reasons that the socialized economy, the socialized enterprises and their centralized planning and management were regarded as crucial to the management of the entire system. This was even more so, because in the economy there survived an important segment of private agriculture which was viewed as a potential threat to the system. And in the sphere of social consciousness there was the strong Catholic Church. Yet, the events of 1980-1981 demonstrated that neither the individual farmers nor the Church posed major dangers to the system.

One might then conclude, that in following the Marxist theory of development the political leaders exaggerated the role of changes in economic and social macro-structures, assuming that changes in social consciousness and micro-structures would automatically follow. Yet, in the modern world, due to the role of communications and the public media, the free flow of cultural values is greatly facilitated. The cinema, radio, television, magazines, sport, music, travel, participation in international organizations, etc., all influence social consciousness. As early as 1964 I observed that a social-economic structure whose members act in a fashion incompatible with its values cannot be maintained.

It should also be remembered that the several million Poles who live abroad in a way participate in the national life. Their letters, parcels and visits have affected the private lives of many individuals and families in Poland, widening the gap between the macro- and the micro-social consciousness.... The progress of mass culture and tourism, and contacts with the families abroad have prompted comparisons between the reality of life in this country and an idealized picture of the mass consumption civilization in the capitalist West.

Since the very beginning of the cold war in the 1940s, moreover, Poland has found itself at the crossroads between the two opposed political blocs. It was in the interest of the western powers to support those forces in the country which were opposed to the development of a socialist society and its integration with the other socialist countries. In other words their objectives were to expand Poland's independence from the USSR and to produce the greatest possible difficulties for the Soviet Union. [To that end they used primarily] economic policies and radio propaganda. This international struggle has had a strong impact upon the process of social changes. . . . It is well known, of course, that people do not act in accordance with what the existing reality is, but rather in accordance with how they perceive it. The divorce between the actual situation and the way the people tended to see it, from the outset represented an important element in the changes taking place in Poland.

The conflicting developmental forces

The changes in the Polish society over the last forty years, thus, were an amalgam between those advanced by the system and those advanced by its opponents. . . . The social conflicts among various groups and communities as well as among those of various sociopolitical positions and aspirations, were in fact sharpened and perpetuated by the fluctuations and the zig-zags in party policy: at first introducing some policies, then abandoning them, and even branding them as errors and deviations. The changes in the party's course, which were periodically repeated, disoriented the people and undermined their confidence in the government. This way they weakened the process of systematic restructuring of the society. At the same time they intensified the role of the spontaneous changes inherent in the natural mechanisms of collective life as well as the conscious activities of the forces opposing the system.

The spontaneous elements contributing to the complex system of development are difficult to analyze on their own. There is no doubt, however, that the destabilizing forces which were present in Poland after 1939 greatly complicated both the consolidation of the system and the emergence of patterns of behaviour centred around everyday professional work and regular social interaction within families and local communities. In particular, the instability of the local communities, which play a crucial role in determining human behaviour (and especially that of the young people), led to non-conformism and the refusal to accept an orderly way of life. In Western Europe the great migration from the countryside to the cities took place gradually and without breaking radically the bonds between the rural and urban communities. In Poland the massive and rapid population shift undermined the stability of the local communities in both the villages and the towns.

After forty years of changes, then, the Polish society still remains fluid. The basic elements of the new system, and, above all, the socialized enterprises, still do not represent sufficiently stabilizing social forces, while constant changes in the existing institutions do not help to improve this situation. The attempts to create new patterns of behaviour have come out differently than planned. Socializing the youth has been adversely affected by the fluctuating educational policies and there has been no effective synchronization of the activities in this realm among the families, schools, work places, mass media and the cultural institutions. The family and the Church represent separate elements, different from the schools, and promote their own values and patterns of behaviour. . . .

The contradictory influences came abruptly to the surface in 1980-1981. The basic political and economic institutions which should secure the effective functioning of the socialist system are still not stabilized. They are rendered ineffective by continuing internal conflicts, contributing to new tensions. . . . In the economy the available means and the readiness to work both have been reduced, and, yet, it is essential to raise both production and consumption. . . . The institutions of educating and socializing the youth are in no better shape.

The viability of the system has, above all, been demonstrated by the gradual overcoming of the economic, political and social crisis. New demands are now being directed at the institutions of economic planning and management which will test their efficiency. The masses employed in the national economy will also have to demonstrate whether they are capable of orderly and efficient work effort. As we know from history, nations undertake great efforts either at times of crisis, when they strive towards some collective goal, or in conditions of stability, when hard work provides them with opportunities to attain attractive individual goals. The present crisis offers neither a great national goal, nor the personal opportunities inherent in stability. Hence is its overcoming so difficult.

The present state of the society

A comparison of the present state of the Polish society with that in 1939 or 1945 reveals great changes, but it is not a particularly fruitful exercise. The society of 1939 was completely transformed during the war and the occupation. The propertied and educated classes were destroyed and the economy was ruined. Millions of people were expelled from the territories incorporated into the German *Reich* or were deported for forced labour. After the war there emerged a new Polish society situated within different borders, ethnically homogeneous (while before the war 36 per cent of the population belonged to national minorities), adhering to a single religion (over 95 per cent of the post-war population were Catholics), and with one third of its people living in the newly-acquired territories. In 1945 it was a society arising anew in a different geographical and political environment, with a new *Weltanschauung* and with interrupted social structures and institutions.

It is natural that such a society strove spontaneously and persistently to restore its own identity and the system of values which had enabled it to survive in the past ten centuries. In this sense the destruction of traditional structures did not facilitate revolutionary changes; on the contrary, it made them more difficult. Opponents of the revolution not only appealed to the forces which consciously and intentionally opposed the new system, but also to those people who subconsciously desired to bring the changes to an end and to restore stability based on the traditional values.

Forty years after the revolutionary Manifesto of July 1944, the Polish society is still in a state of intense ferment—where the discordant and conflicting elements dominate over those of stability and harmonious development. The level of achievement in the economy, culture and politics has been less than was anticipated. Still, industry has been developed, many new cities have been built, highways have been constructed, a strong educational system has been established and cadres of specialists have been trained. There are numerous research and development institutes. In the last four decades many cultural institutions have been founded; there are excellent orchestras, theatres and galleries; in the arts many outstanding literary, plastic and musical works have been created. Then why are all of those achievements so denigrated by public opinion?

Perhaps this is so because the present situation is not being compared with that in 1939 or in 1945, but rather with some ideal vision, occasionally sketched by propaganda and at times articulated by day-dreams, that creates an imaginary picture of "what could have been". Neglecting one's achievements, however, is also an element in social conflict. The Polish society thus enters the future with aroused aspirations, unclear images of how its hopes could be realized, conflicts among various social groups and classes and a deep sense of injury in the hearts of the citizens.

To the question "what next?" the answers vary a good deal. Some point to the confused and tense international situation. Others stress the internal conflicts—the divergences which prevent the evolution of a common programme and exacerbate the difficulties in mobilizing the society to pursue some common goal or to undertake some work which would give meaning to its life. Yet, some historians would argue that this has been so for centuries, and that this is almost the normal state of affairs in Poland. They would also stress that the Polish society must not be compared with that of the Germans or the Czechs for it is governed by its own rules—even though the Poles are not always content with them.

APPENDIX III

POLAND'S FUTURE*

The sources of conflict

The source of Communist power is Moscow's will. Of decisive significance is the fact, sealed at the Conferences in Yalta and Pottsdam, that at the end of World War II we found ourselves in the Soviet sphere of influence. The Communists, who received power in Poland from Stalin, have ever since remained faithful to their assigned role: that of an instrument of Soviet domination of our country. At no time have they obtained a legitimization of their authority from the nation. They have not even tried.

The outside origin of the Communist government and the role which it has performed for Moscow are more than sufficient reasons for it to be in conflict with the nation. The people are aware that it is an alien authority whose first loyalty is to its powerful protector, above that to its own nation. Indeed, during the entire post-war period Polish dignity and national pride have been systematically insulted, although since 1956 this has been done in a somewhat less obtrusive manner. But the problem is not merely one of emotions; it also concerns vital national interests.

An important, though solitary gain for Poland stemming from its subordination to the USSR was the shift of its western boundary to the Oder-Neisse rivers. This gain, of course, was not a gracious gift to Poland by the USSR; Poland first had to lose half of its pre-war territory to the USSR, and it marked the shift to the west of the Soviet sphere of influence. At that time the future of Germany was still unknown. And as the years have gone by, fewer and fewer Poles have continued to believe that the maintenance of this border is inseparably linked to the maintenance of the Yalta system and Poland's continued subordination to the USSR.

---

*Excerpts from *Polityka polska*, No. 1, Autumn 1982. As reprinted in *Mysl Polska* (London), November 1, 1983 and in *Trybuna* (London), No. 46/102, 1984. Selection and subtitles by A. B.

Stalin was not satisfied with merely imposing upon Poland a pro-Russian government to act as a guarantor of the USSR's imperial interests. After the revolution in 1917 Russia was not just a state like any other. It was an ideological state—the centre of the world Communist movement. This was also one of the main reasons for the new Russian power. The Central-European countries which became subordinated to the USSR were supposed to become like "the first socialist state". They had to adopt the new system.

This naturally applied to Poland too. It implied submitting the Polish society to the same transformation—although carried out in a less drastic fashion—that the Soviet society had undergone. For Communism is a complete totalitarian system. Politics, ideology, culture, economics are all parts of it. When it is on the offensive—as it was in Poland until 1956—it aims to embrace all of social and individual life.

The great majority of the Poles were not ready to accept the straightjacket imposed upon them. What Communism stood for in ideology, culture, political institutions and practice, was incompatible with the traditional view of the Polish nation. To agree to the new system would have meant abandoning the Christian-European civilization and the Polish national traditions. And though at least the system seemed to offer the people economic progress and material comforts, in fact it only brought with it backwardness and poverty. It wasted the nation's hard work.

Except for the early post-war years, ending at the latest with the elections in 1947, the objective of the Polish people has not been to win back political power from the Communists. The attempts by the authentic representatives of the people to participate in the government stopped when it became obvious that the referendum, the elections, and the toleration of an official opposition were merely for the sake of appearances, and would not in the least affect the question of who would rule the country. This had already been decided by the international constellation of power and by the naked and systematic repression inside the country. The fate of Poland had been settled on the battlefields of World War II and at the Big Three Conferences.

In those circumstances it would have been utopian to put forward a programme for regaining national sovereignty and independence. There were more urgent tasks for the Poles. Their first objectives had to be to protect their national identity, to preserve their spiritual freedom and unity, and to maintain their personal freedom and rights, insofar as those were possible in the country of "real socialism".

This was not minimalism; just the opposite—in the circumstances of the late 1940s and the early 1950s, it was romantic maximalism. The struggle was conducted for the preservation of private property in agriculture, for the independence of the Catholic Church, for an authentic character of the Polish culture, and for respectt of the basic human rights.

Primate Wyszynski's programme

In the Polish national struggle a historic role was played by the Catholic Church, led by Stefan Cardinal Wyszynski. In a system which destroyed all independent authorities, ruined all political life, and eradicated the ideological and political elites, the only remaining authority was the Church and its Primate. The Church, of course, also found itself under attack—especially in the early 1950s, and, then, again in the 1960s—but it came out of these confrontations stronger than ever.

The Church, thus, became the repository of the national identity and as such it had to assume the responsibility for representing the national interests, for speaking on behalf of the nation, for formulating a national programme, and for nurturing various social initiatives which had nowhere else to turn. Fortunately, during the hour of such great trial the Church was led by a great man who was able to rise to this challenge.

The national programme of Primate Wyszynski was inseparably linked to the religious one. In fact, they complemented each other. The strengthening of the faith and the spreading of Christian ethics were aimed at bringing about a moral revival of the society, which would arrest the disintegrative tendenceies brought about by Communism. The Primate's programme was addressed to every individual living in Poland as much as to the nation as a whole. In his teaching he stressed the close links between Catholicism and Polishdom and the intimate links between the Polish and western values and traditions.

The Primate assumed that as long as the Yalta system remained in force it was not feasible to try to replace the existing political system with one in which the people would exert a decisive role. This could be accomplished neither by a one-time decisive struggle, nor by a piecemeal taking over of the government bit by bit. It was necessary, then, to accept the fact that for the time being Poland could not be "ours", that it could not restore its sovereignty and that all attempts to try to do so would end in defeat.

What was feasible, although extremely difficult, was to develop the internal, spiritual sovereignty of the nation. If this could be accomplished the Polish national identity would be saved. The programme of Primate Wyszynski, thus, was set in a broad, historical perspective, designed on a scale of generations, and it accepted the fact that the national objectives cannot be realized all at once. Its goal was to so prepare the Poles, that when the opportunity would once again rise, they could resume the struggle for their national rights.

Yet, Primate Wyszynski's programme was not exclusively directed at the future. In fact, the Primate initiated and supported all sorts of social pressures upon the government aimed at expanding the scope of personal right. and freedoms "here and now". The totalitarian system was compelled gradually to retreat.

The retreat of Communism

Over the decades Communism in Poland has evolved and retreated. It may appear that its basic elements: dependence upon the USSR, the monopoly of power by the Communist party, and the dogmas of Communist ideology, over time have stayed the same. Yet, it would be a great mistake to believe that nothing has changed. For the Poles it has been by no means unimportant whether the Church is independent or subordinate to the state, whether agriculture is private or collectivized, whether there are a few individuals or tens of thousands of political prisoners, and whether they have a genuine Polish or a sovietized culture. There can be no doubt that between 1945 and 1975 the quality of life in Poland decisively improved. Over those years we also won greater freedom than most of the other nations in the Soviet sphere of influence.

Various developments contributed to such an outcome: these included changes in world politics, and an evolution in the Communist camp, especially after the death of Stalin, but an essential, and even a crucial role was played by the pressure from the Polish society itself. This was illustrated by the events in 1956, 1968, 1970 and 1976. These were its flashpoints, but the pressure was persistent.

The Communist party retreated before the society, and it even to some extent changed itself. With the growth in its membership it became "polonized". The open struggle against the national traditions and values was replaced by appeals to a "surrogate" nationalism, where the national heroes were both Kosciuszko and Traugutt as well as Dzierzynski and Nowotko. A false image of history was created, where the People's Poland was presented as the crowning achievement.

The open struggle against the Church was supplanted by tactics intended to dull its vigilance and even to win it to the government side. Stalinist terror was replaced by relatively lenient repressions under Gomulka and Gierek. The militant Marxism was moderated, and while during the Gierek years it still remained the official ideology, in practice it became moribund. The revolutionary ascetism practiced during the Stalinist period, and to a degree still under Gomulka, was abandoned during the Gierek rule in favour of an openly bourgeois slogan: *enrichissez vous.*

The party under Gierek was not frightening. It was no longer regarded just as a group of renegades serving a foreign power. The society compelled the party to abandon some of the gains it had made before 1956. But this process was not all one-sided. The party also influenced the society and "softened" it. Although the great majority of the nation still remained in silent opposition, nevertheless at no other time in the history of the People's Poland (except for a period of mistaken trust in Gomulka in 1956) were so many people indifferent, or even trying to look for positive aspects in the Communist regime, as in the midst of the Gierek era.

Certainly the situation was influenced by relative economic prosperity, which rested upon western credits. But it was also at this very time that the first phenomena which contributed to the radical change in 1980 appeared.

The upheaval of 1980-81

What were the factors—spiritual, ideological and political—which contributed to the Polish August? Or, to put it in a more roundabout way, what were the elements without which it would not have happened? There were five of them:

i) The Polish nation, despite the several decades of Communist rule, had managed to retain its own identity. The Poles refused to be sovietized, they overcame the barrier of fear, and, when they sensed an opportunity to do so, they came forward to reclaim their rights. The national consciousness and the desire for greater freedom was especially strongly manifested by the very social stratum which the Communist ideology expected would be the foundation of the new system, namely, the workers in large scale industry.

ii) There had come of age a new and numerous generation which did not remember the war or the Stalinist period, and, therefore, was free from the bitter memories of the defeats and helplessness under a totalitiarian system.

iii) There was the election of Karol Wojtyla to the Throne of Saint
Peter and his visit to Poland in 1979. These events had two
consequences: first, the teaching of John Paul II deepened the
religiosity of the Poles and at the same time made them more
aware of human dignity and personal rights; and, second, it
consolidated the Poles' national consciousness and solidarity.
In June, 1979 during the meetings with the Pope we saw ourselves coming together, and we experienced the unity of our
thoughts and emotions.

iv) The standard of living declined tangibly, heralding a growing
economic crisis in People's Poland.

v) Opposition groups of all kinds sprang up. They played a great
role in arousing the society even before August 1980; then they
had a decisive impact upon the August strikes' acquiring a political character; and, finally, they influenced the establishment
and the course of "Solidarity".

The need for a detached analysis

We cannot arrive at a programme for the future without examining
the events which have taken place in Poland in the past several years.
It is easy to determine the end of the upheaval: it happened, of
course, on the night of 12 to 13 December, 1981. But it is more difficult to establish its beginning. For it did not start with a single
event, but with a whole series of events, going back to the mid-1970s.
Yet, it is clear that, regardless of its epilogue, this was a period of exceptional significance in the national history. Thus, it has to be seen
in a broad historical perspective.

It was a time of national awakening—the activization of at first
small political groups and moral elites, and, then, of the broad masses
of millions of people who participated during the Polish August in
the concept and the movement that was "Solidarity". It was a time
of greatness.

In the consciousness of many Poles the pehnomena of the pre-
August democratic opposition, and, especially, of the Polish August
and "Solidarity", have become myths and even national relics. This is
not helpful to evaluating them objectively, for relics are to be revered,
not re-examined. Hence the danger of their idolization and an apologetic defence. This is even more natural because they are being denounced by the regime's propaganda in its attempts to create an "anti-
legend", where the villains are the "anti-socialist forces" and the
"Solidarity extremists". But, still, a detached analysis is needed.

This is not just for the sake of searching out objective historical truth, although this is important too. It is even more urgent for the sake of the future. The greatness and accomplishments of the recent past were accompanied by errors of weakness and small-mindedness. These played a not inconsiderable part in the defeat which we suffered on December 13, 1981. Some of them are still evident today. In trying to shape the future, and in order to avoid committing them again it is necessary to recognize these past errors which we did not have to make, and to be aware of those weaknesses and limitations which, at least in the near future, we shall not be able to overcome.

The events of December, 1981, were not the inevitable outcome of the Polish August. We did not fully utilize the great opportunity which arose with August, 1980, and the founding of "Solidarity". To a large extent this was our own fault. Both the society and its leaders were responsible.

The view is not popular. There are many people who subscribe to the fatalistic-deterministic theory, asserting that "it had to be this way"—"it had to end like this". According to them the Communist system could never accept the existence of an independent movement which, moreover, enjoyed the support of the majority of the society. The clash, then, was inevitable, and its outcome was predetermined; the only unknowns being the date and the extent of the casualties. The proponents of this theory, however, are divided among those who believe, despite everything, that the appearance of "Solidarity" was worthwhile; and those who merely invoke it to emphasize the futility of all resistance, and use it to justify their own neutral, or even collaborationist positions.

Among those who have adopted the stance of active resistance against martial law, the view prevails that the events of December 13 were merely a lost battle, but the war continues and can be won by the nation. But during war one must fight and not worry over dissecting the past, which only leads to a search for scapegoats and undermines the morale in your own ranks.

It is not a question of finding scapegoats. It is also not true that December 13, 1981 finally determined the outcome of the struggle between the Communist government and the nation. Furthermore, it did not erase the accomplishments of the Polish August from the nation's memory. Yet, December 13, 1981, was not just an incident. It closed an important chatper in the history of Poland, and opened up an entirely new one. It transformed what had been just a confrontation onto a plane of dramatic conflict. Every day the nation pays a high price for it, and the cost may continue to go up in the future.

Precisely because the struggle goes on we must search for the errors which we have committed so far. It would be a mistake to content ourselves by claiming that right was on our side, while our adversary was demonstrated to be—even though this is true—perfidious and treacherous.

We are committed to the idea of an independent and democratic Poland, but let us have no illusions that this can be accomplished today or tomorrow. For Polish maximalist goals to be achieved in the future, there must first be outside changes over which we have no influence, as well as the accomplishment of some internal goals. And the latter, fortunately, is entirely up to us.

The outside determinants

The starting point in formulating the political programme for today and tomorrow must be a realistic assessment of Poland's position in the international sphere.

The basic fact which affects our position is the post-Yalta division of Europe. Although there have been some recent attempts—generally restricted to rhetoric—to question this division, it is binding and still determines the political reality of Europe. It is because of this fact that Poland remains in the Soviet sphere of influence. Our country, because of its geographical position, and its demographic and economic potential, is particularly important to the USSR. It is located at the very heart of its system of satellite states.

The USSR is not an ordinary imperialist power, a simple continuation of Tsarist Russia. It is an ideological power—the main centre of the world Communist movement. The Communist ideology legitimizes the very existence of the state and its political system. It also sanctions the Soviet domination in our part of Europe. It is the glue which holds the Soviet bloc together.

The USSR is also one of the two world superpowers. It is faced with internal challenges with which it will have to cope. They are: the nationalities problem, the erosion of ideology, inefficiency in the political-economic system, the inability to resolve the complex issues of an industrial society and satisfy its needs and, in the long-run, keeping up in the East-West rivalry. These problems may force the Soviet state to adopt far-reaching systemic changes, or drastically to reduce its power. Yet, unless there is a war catastrophe, it is unlikely that these reforms will take place in the near future. On the contrary, it appears, we are faced here with changes which will take years, if not decades.

The USSR is opposed by the western bloc which is itself torn apart by internal differences, and where both neo-Munich appeasement trends and Communist subversion are present. The outcome of the East-West confrontation, then, is by no means pre-determined.

Sympathy and assistance from the western societies are helpful to us, but they have certain very definite limits. They are determined by the notion of western security, as well as by the fact that we have already been abandoned at Yalta as a legitimate part of the Soviet bloc. None of the leading Western politicians takes the policy of liberation seriously. This even includes the statesmen who are most sympathetic towards us. They do conceal their views. They are, of course, first of all concerned to uphold their own national interest, and they will not prejudice it for Poland. We should not lament over this, but we just should be aware of this situation. And at the same time we should realize that the possibility of a "spirit of Munich" must not be ruled out. Even worse, someone may try to exploit Poland as an instrument in the East-West rivalry, natually at our expense.

It would also be a mistake to go on looking for support for those states which, like ourselves, are at the mercy of the USSR. Even if they sympathize with our cause, they cannot render us any effecttive assistance. The support of the opposition groups in those countries is reduced to mere moral suasion. It must not be ignored, but it will be of no help to us in facing naked power.

In the past several years the political climate in Europe and in the world has systematically deteriorated. It has been a long time since the danger of a conflict between the two superpowers has been so acute. This does not mean that we anticipate a world catastrophe. But we do have to note that, in the present international situation, the consolidation of the satellites bloc is of crucial significance to the USSR.

What cannot be attained?

Before trying to answer what is possible and realistic, in our present position, we ought to state what is unattainable and unrealistic.

It is not realistic to hope for a resolution of the Polish problem through an agreement between the authentic representatives of the Polish nation and the USSR, while excluding the Polish Communists. This is ruled out by the ideological nature of the Soviet state. By accepting the "Finlandization" of Poland, the USSR would start the process of disintegration of the very foundations upon which its power and domination in our part of Europe rest. This is, therefore, just an illusion.

It is also not realistic to try to confront the USSR with a *fait accompli* by removing the Communist party from power and transforming the party state into a national state. This cannot be accomplished by a national upheaval—whether in the form of a general strike or an uprising, or a repeat of the post-August rapid evolution towards changing the nature of the system and the character of the state.

The USSR would not permit the Polish Communist government to surrender to such a "counter-revolution". This would not only establish a dangerous precedent in the bloc as a whole, but it would discredit the Soviet system itself. It must be accepted as axiomatic that the USSR would be willing to pay a very high price to avoid such consequences. In the extreme it would be ready to intervene militarily in Poland. And for us that would be a tragedy.

Neither is it possible to carry out another sort of *fait accompli*, namely, to reach an agreement between the Polish society and the Communist government which would basically alter the existing political system. Apart from the fact that it is absurd to believe that the party and the state authorities would be inclined towards such a solution, it should be remembered that the Communist government in Poland is not sovereign, but remains primarily a tool of a foreign power. Its freedom of manoeuvre, therefore, is severely restricted.

The conclusion from all of these considerations must be that for the time being trying to wrestle political power from the Communist party would be a futile endeavour. It could even result in potentially grave consequences for the Polish nation. This does not mean, however, that we should abandon our vision of eventual independence. But it should be seen in a proper persepctive, so that when such an attempt is made the conditions will be ripe for its realization.

A sovereign society

What, then, should be the political programme for the millions of the Poles for today and tomorrow? What is the programme which does not expose the nation to mortal danger and at the same time brings it closer to our cherished goal of independence?

Such a programme is the building of the internal sovereignty of the nation. It is not a new programme; it has already been elaborated by Primate Wyszynski. Its essence is the defence and the development of the national community in the context of a non-sovereign, alien state. The nation which is internally sovereign is conscious of its goals, and is consciously shaping its fate. It is a nation of free people, in the deepest Christian understanding of freedom. It is a nation faithful to its heritage, cultivating and ready to uphold its own identity, but at the same time free from chauvinism and megalomania and open to the values developed by the others.

It is a nation consciously striving for independence and able to advance not only through great upheavals, but also through patient, systematic efforts; a nation ready to take advantage of any opportunities in the future. It is a fully developed nation having its own hierarchy of moral, ideological, political, cultural and economic elites. Such a nation, even though deprived of its sovereign state, could be an independent political subject exerting not inconsiderable influence in our continent.

Is this a realistic programme? Is it possible to attain internal sovereignty for the nation against the state which commands powerful means to undermine national authority and social unity? Certainly this is not an easy task. Yet, it is within the realm of our possibilities.

For we also have significant means at our disposal. Our strength lies in the strong bonds of the Polish national community and its accomplishments—above all in the sphere of social consciousness and the patterns of behaviour which were born during August, 1980, and in the "Solidarity" period. It should be noted that forty years of destructive activity have failed to undermine and to eradicate the great Polish traditions and the heritage from the generations of the past.

In advancing its internal sovereignty the nation can also count on the continued support of the Catholic Church. The Church, which guides the people in the spiritual sphere, also conducts a realistic national policy and educates the society in its attachment to freedom. It authority is strengthened by the fact that the Throne of Saint Peter is occupied by a Pole.

In the chain of natural communities the family is the essential unit. It develops the basic spiritual and community values. The demographic factor is of great significance in determining our place in Europe and our changes of regaining independence. It is important to create for the Polish family healthy social conditions which would contribute to its harmonious development.

These last years—the active period of democratic opposition, the open existence of "Solidarity", and martial law—have witnessed a positive development of various lay authorities: the moral, social and political elites. They are indispensable for the society in providing patterns of behaviour and ethical models, for elevating the level of political culture, and finally for formulating and submitting for general discussion new ideas and programmes.

In all responsibility, we counterpose the vision of a sovereign society to the concept—so particularly strongly advocated after December 13, 1981—of an "underground society". There are times when clandestine activities are indispensable to retaining the society's dignity, honour and will to resist. Yet, in the long-run an underground society is unreal, and even a dangerous illusion. By its very nature a clandestine movement is a temporary and compulsory device, and as such also unnatural. It is impossible to take an entire society underground. What should be done clandestinely, then, is only what cannot be done openly. These activities are restricted to *samizdat* publishing and self-education.

At the same time the development of an open, authentic culture and education should not be neglected. It is very important that worthwhile books should appear and that "readable" papers should be available. And the schools and the universities should produce graduates who are not only wise and competent, but also honest.

A significant role in shaping public opinion is played by the Polish emigrés. The emigrés have often occupied a special place in Polish history. During the "Solidarity" and martial law period another wave of emigrés has left the country. Yet, in the final analysis, the fate of Poland and the Poles will be determined at home. This all the more so now, when, after the recent experiences, not only individuals and small groups, but the society as a whole has regained its independent consciousness.

In the struggle for the restoration of national rights it is no longer just small elites, but the broad masses, that are involved. After the experiences of August, 1980, and "Solidarity", millions of people are aware of their duties toward their country, they share common ideals and are, if necessary, ready to make sacrifices for the sake of their goals. These millions are over the Vistula and will stay here. They will choose and shape their own future.

Pressure upon the government

Concentrating upon the development of internal sovereignty does not imply abandoning the attempts to influence the government. One of the most important tasks ahead for the society is to apply pressure upon the state and, in this way, to compel it to retreat and evolve. We have to tolerate the Communist state—at present we have no other choice. But we should not just passively accept it. We can influence it through persistent pressure, so it will hinder as little as possible the progress of the nation.

There are spheres of national life where no compromises whatso-
ever with the Communist government are possible. These include the
spiritual foundations of our life, the nation's identity and the development of its internal sovereignty. Yet, we do not exclude *a priori*
the possibilities of limited compromises with the Communist authorities.

One such sphere is the relationship between the government and
the society. In exchange for the abandonment of the attempts on
the part of the society to transform People's Poland into a state of
the nation, the Communists might accept the autonomy of national
life, and, above all the existence of institutions and social organizations independent of the government. Such a compromise could be
a realistic programme for a "new August", whenever suitable circumstances for its repetition arise. At present this is not feasible, and
such an attempt would end in a defeat. But the times change.

Yet, just a "new August" is not the ultimate aim of Polish politics.
Its final goal is an independent statehood. It is impossible today to
anticipate the time needed to realize this aspiration. But let us not
forget that what may appear unrealistic today and even tomorrow,
may prove to be attainable the day after tomorrow.

INDEX

EAST EUROPEAN MONOGRAPHS

The *East European Monographs* comprise scholarly books on the history and civilization of Eastern Europe. They are published under the editorship of Stephen Fischer-Galati, in the belief that these studies contribute substantially to the knowledge of the area and serve to stimulate scholarship and research.

1. *Political Ideas and the Enlightenment in the Romanian Principalities, 1750–1831.* By Vlad Georgescu. 1971.
2. *America, Italy and the Birth of Yugoslavia, 1917-1919.* By Dragan R. Zivjinovic. 1972.
3. *Jewish Nobles and Geniuses in Modern Hungary.* By William O. McCagg, Jr. 1972.
4. *Mixail Soloxov in Yugoslavia: Reception and Literary Impact.* By Robert F. Price. 1973.
5. *The Historical and Nationalist Thought of Nicolae Iorga.* By William O. Oldson. 1973.
6. *Guide to Polish Libraries and Archives.* By Richard C. Lewanski. 1974.
7. *Vienna Broadcasts to Slovakia, 1938-1939: A Case Study in Subversion.* By Henry Delfiner. 1974.
8. *The 1917 Revolution in Latvia.* By Andrew Ezergailis. 1974.
9. *The Ukraine in the United Nations Organization: A Study in Soviet Foreign Policy. 1944-1950.* By Konstantin Sawczuk. 1975.
10. *The Bosnian Church: A New Interpretation.* By John V. A. Fine, Jr., 1975.
11. *Intellectual and Social Developments in the Habsburg Empire from Maria Theresa to World War I.* Edited by Stanley B. Winters and Joseph Held. 1975.
12. *Ljudevit Gaj and the Illyrian Movement.* By Elinor Murray Despalatovic. 1975.
13. *Tolerance and Movements of Religious Dissent in Eastern Europe,* Edited by Bela K. Kiraly. 1975.
14. *The Parish Republic: Hlinka's Slovak People's Party, 1939-1945.* By Yeshayahu Jelinek. 1976.
15. *The Russian Annexation of Bessarabia, 1774-1828.* By George F. Jewsbury. 1976.
16. *Modern Hungarian Historiography.* By Steven Bela Vardy. 1976.
17. *Values and Community in Multi-National Yugoslavia.* By Gary K. Bertsch. 1976.
18. *The Greek Socialist Movement and the First World War: the Road to Unity.* By George B. Leon. 1976.
19. *The Radical Left in the Hungarian Revolution of 1848.* By Laszlo Deme. 1976.
20. *Hungary between Wilson and Lenin: The Hungarian Revolution of 1918-1919 and the Big Three.* By Peter Pastor. 1976.

21. *The Crises of France's East-Central European Diplomacy, 1933–1938.* By Anthony J. Komjathy. 1976.

22. *Polish Politics and National Reform, 1775–1788.* By Daniel Stone. 1976.

23. *The Habsburg Empire in World War I.* Edited by Robert A. Kann, Bela K. Kiraly, and Paula S. Fichtner. 1977.

24. *The Slovenes and Yugoslavism, 1890–1914.* By Carole Rogel. 1977.

25. *German-Hungarian Relations and the Swabian Problem.* By Thomas Spira. 1977.

26. *The Metamorphosis of a Social Class in Hungary During the Reign of Young Franz Joseph.* By Peter I. Hidas. 1977.

27. *Tax Reform in Eighteenth Century Lombardy.* By Daniel M. Klang. 1977.

28. *Tradition versus Revolution: Russia and the Balkans in 1917.* By Robert H. Johnston. 1977.

29. *Winter into Spring: The Czechoslovak Press and the Reform Movement 1963–1968.* By Frank L. Kaplan. 1977.

30. *The Catholic Church and the Soviet Government, 1939–1949.* By Dennis J. Dunn. 1977.

31. *The Hungarian Labor Service System, 1939–1945.* By Randolph L. Braham. 1977.

32. *Consciousness and History: Nationalist Critics of Greek Society 1897–1914.* By Gerasimos Augustinos. 1977.

33. *Emigration in Polish Social and Political Thought, 1870–1914.* By Benjamin P. Murdzek. 1977.

34. *Serbian Poetry and Milutin Bojic.* By Mihailo Dordevic. 1977.

35. *The Baranya Dispute: Diplomacy in the Vortex of Ideologies, 1918–1921.* By Leslie C. Tihany. 1978.

36. *The United States in Prague, 1945–1948.* By Walter Ullmann. 1978.

37. *Rush to the Alps: The Evolution of Vacationing in Switzerland.* By Paul P. Bernard. 1978.

38. *Transportation in Eastern Europe: Empirical Findings.* By Bogdan Mieczkowski. 1978.

39. *The Polish Underground State: A Guide to the Underground, 1939–1945.* By Stefan Korbonski. 1978.

40. *The Hungarian Revolution of 1956 in Retrospect.* Edited by Bela K. Kiraly and Paul Jonas. 1978.

41. *Boleslaw Limanowski (1935–1935): A Study in Socialism and Nationalism.* By Kazimiera Janina Cottam. 1978.

42. *The Lingering Shadow of Nazism: The Austrian Independent Party Movement Since 1945.* By Max E. Riedlsperger. 1978.

43. *The Catholic Church, Dissent and Nationality in Soviet Lithuania.* By V. Stanley Vardys. 1978.

44. *The Development of Parliamentary Government in Serbia.* By Alex N. Dragnich. 1978.

45. *Divide and Conquer: German Efforts to Conclude a Separate Peace, 1914–1918.* By L. L. Farrar, Jr. 1978.

46. *The Prague Slav Congress of 1848.* By Lawrence D. Orton. 1978.

47. *The Nobility and the Making of the Hussite Revolution.* By John M. Klassen. 1978.

48. *The Cultural Limits of Revolutionary Politics: Change and Continuity in Socialist Czechoslovakia.* By David W. Paul. 1979.

49. *On the Border of War and Peace: Polish Intelligence and Diplomacy in 1937–1939 and the Origins of the Ultra Secret.* By Richard A. Woytak. 1979.

50. *Bear and Foxes: The International Relations of the East European States 1965–1969.* By Ronald Haly Linden. 1979.

51. *Czechoslovakia: The Heritage of Ages Past.* Edited by Ivan Volgyes and Hans Brisch. 1979.

52. *Prime Minister Gyula Andrassy's Influence on Habsburg Foreign Policy.* By Janos Decsy. 1979.

53. *Citizens for the Fatherland: Education, Educators, and Pedagogical Ideals in Eighteenth Century Russia.* By J. L. Black. 1979.

54. *A History of the "Proletariat": The Emergence of Marxism in the Kingdom of Poland, 1870-1887.* By Norman M. Naimark. 1979.

55. *The Slovak Autonomy Movement, 1935-1939: A Study in Unrelenting Nationalism.* By Dorothea H. El Mallakh. 1979.

56. *Diplomat in Exile: Francis Pulszky's Political Activities in England, 1849-1860.* By Thomas Kabdebo. 1979.

57. *The German Struggle Against the Yugoslav Guerrillas in World War II: German Counter-Insurgency in Yugoslavia, 1941-1943.* By Paul N. Hehn. 1979.

58. *The Emergence of the Romanian National State.* By Gerald J. Bobango. 1979.

59. *Stewards of the Land: The American Farm School and Modern Greece.* By Brenda L. Marder. 1979.

60. *Roman Dmowski: Party, Tactics, Ideology, 1895-1907.* By Alvin M. Fountain, II. 1980.

61. *International and Domestic Politics in Greece During the Crimean War.* By Jon V. Kofas. 1980.

62. *Fires on the Mountain: The Macedonian Revolutionary Movement and the Kidnapping of Ellen Stone.* By Laura Beth Sherman. 1980.

63. *The Modernization of Agriculture: Rural Transformation in Hungary, 1848-1975.* Edited by Joseph Held. 1980.

64. *Britain and the War for Yugoslavia, 1940-1943.* By Mark C. Wheeler. 1980.

65. *The Turn to the Right: The Ideological Origins and Development of Ukrainian Nationalism, 1919-1929.* By Alexander J. Motyl. 1980.

66. *The Maple Leaf and the White Eagle: Canadian-Polish Relations, 1918-1978.* By Aloysius Balawyder. 1980.

67. *Antecedents of Revolution: Alexander I and the Polish Congress Kingdom, 1815-1825.* By Frank W. Thackeray. 1980.

68. *Blood Libel at Tiszaeszlar.* By Andrew Handler. 1980.

69. *Democratic Centralism in Romania: A Study of Local Communist Politics.* By Daniel N. Nelson. 1980.

70. *The Challenge of Communist Education: A Look at the German Democratic Republic.* By Margrete Siebert Klein. 1980.

71. *The Fortifications and Defense of Constantinople.* By Byron C. P. Tsangadas. 1980.

72. *Balkan Cultural Studies.* By Stavro Skendi. 1980.

73. *Studies in Ethnicity: The East European Experience in America.* Edited by Charles A. Ward, Philip Shashko, and Donald E. Pienkos. 1980.

74. *The Logic of "Normalization:" The Soviet Intervention in Czechoslovakia and the Czechoslovak Response.* By Fred Eidlin. 1980.

75. *Red Cross, Black Eagle: A Biography of Albania's American Schol.* By Joan Fultz Kontos. 1981.

76. *Nationalism in Contemporary Europe.* By Franjo Tudjman. 1981.

77. *Great Power Rivalry at the Turkish Straits: The Montreux Conference and Convention of 1936.* By Anthony R. DeLuca. 1981.

78. *Islam Under the Double Eagle: The Muslims of Bosnia and Hercegovina, 1878-1914.* By Robert J. Donia. 1981.

79. *Five Eleventh Century Hungarian Kings: Their Policies and Their Relations with Rome.* By Z. J. Kosztolnyik. 1981.
80. *Prelude to Appeasement: East European Central Diplomacy in the Early 1930's.* By Lisanne Radice. 1981.
81. *The Soviet Regime in Czechoslovakia.* By Zdenek Krystufek. 1981.
82. *School Strikes in Prussian Poland, 1901-1907: The Struggle Over Bilingual Education.* By John J. Kulczychi. 1981.
83. *Romantic Nationalism and Liberalism: Joachim Lelewel and the Polish National Idea.* By Joan S. Skurnowicz. 1981.
84. *The "Thaw" In Bulgarian Literature.* By Atanas Slavov. 1981.
85. *The Political Thought of Thomas G. Masaryk.* By Roman Szporluk. 1981.
86. *Prussian Poland in the German Empire, 1871-1900.* By Richard Blanke. 1981.
87. *The Mazepists: Ukrainian Separatism in the Early Eighteenth Century.* By Orest Subtelny. 1981.
88. *The Battle for the Marchlands: The Russo-Polish Campaign of 1920.* By Adam Zamoyski. 1981.
89. *Milovan Djilas: A Revolutionary as a Writer.* By Dennis Reinhartz. 1981.
90. *The Second Republic: The Disintegration of Post-Munich Czechoslovakia, October 1938-March 1939.* By Theodore Prochazka, Sr. 1981.
91. *Financial Relations of Greece and the Great Powers, 1832-1862.* By Jon V. Kofas. 1981.
92. *Religion and Politics: Bishop Valerian Trifa and His Times.* By Gerald J. Bobango. 1981.
93. *The Politics of Ethnicity in Eastern Europe.* Edited by George Klein and Milan J. Reban. 1981.
94. *Czech Writers and Politics.* By Alfred French. 1981.
95. *Nation and Ideology: Essays in Honor of Wayne S. Vucinich.* Edited by Ivo Banac, John G. Ackerman, and Roman Szporluk. 1981.
96. *For God and Peter the Great: The Works of Thomas Consett, 1723-1729.* Edited by James Cracraft. 1982.
97. *The Geopolitics of Leninism.* By Stanley W. Page. 1982
98. *Karel Havlicek (1821-1856): A National Liberation Leader of the Czech Renascence.* By Barbara K. Reinfeld. 1982.
99. *Were-Wolf and Vampire in Romania.* By Harry A. Senn. 1982.
100. *Ferdinand I of Austria: The Politics of Dynasticism in the Age of Reformation.* By Paula Sutter Fichtner. 1982
101. *France in Greece During World War I: A Study in the Politics of Power.* By Alexander S. Mitrakos. 1982.
102. *Authoritarian Politics in a Transitional State: Istvan Bethlen and the Unified Party in Hungary, 1919-1926.* By William M. Batkay. 1982.
103. *Romania Between East and West: Historical Essays in Memory of Constantin C. Giurescu.* Edited by Stephen Fischer-Galati, Radu R. Florescu and George R. Ursul. 1982.
104. *War and Society in East Central Europe: From Hunyadi to Rakoczi— War and Society in Late Medieval and Early Modern Hungary.* Edited by János Bak and Béla K. Király. 1982.
105. *Total War and Peace Making: A Case Study on Trianon.* Edited by Béla K. Király, Peter Pastor, and Ivan Sanders. 1982
106. *Army, Aristocracy, and Monarchy: Essays on War, Society, and Government in Austria, 1618-1780.* Edited by Wayne S. Vucinich. 1982.
107. *The First Serbian Uprising, 1804-1813.* Edited by Wayne S. Vucinich. 1982.